INFERTILITY: NURSING AND CARING

Edited by

LIZ MEERABEAU BSc(Hons), PhD, RGN, RHV, RNT, RHVT, MBA
Liaison Officer, Research and Development Division, Department of Health

and

JANE DENTON RGN, RM
Nursing Director, Multiple Births Foundation, Queen Charlotte's and Chelsea Hospital

with 16 Contributors

SCUTARI PRESS
London

Scutari Press is a division of RCN Publishing Company Ltd

First published 1995

British Library Cataloguing in Publication Data

Meerabeau, Liz
   Infertility: Nursing and Caring
   I. Title II. Denton, Jane
   610.736

   ISBN 1-873853-27-0

Typeset by Words & Graphics Ltd, Anstey, Leicester

Printed in Great Britain by Antony Rowe Ltd, Chippenham, Wiltshire

Contents

Contributors

Stephen Bennett MB BS, MRCOG, Senior Registrar, Leicester General Hospital.

Peter Braude BSc, MA, PhD, FRCOG, Professor and Chairman, Division of Obstetrics and Gynaecology, UMDS, Guy's and St Thomas' Hospital Trust, London.

Elizabeth M Bryan MD, FRCP, DCH, Honorary Consultant Paediatrician at Queen Charlotte's and Chelsea Hospital, London, Senior Lecturer, Royal Postgraduate Medical School and Medical Director of the Multiple Births Foundation.

Alan Burnell, Director, Post-Adoption Centre, London.

Sandra M Cant RGN, RM, Infertility Sister, Aberdeen Maternity Hospital.

Jennifer Clifford BA (Hons) Lond., Psychotherapist, Member of IPC (WPF), and Independent Counsellor, Assisted Conception Unit, University College Hospital, London.

Liz Corrigan BA (Hons), SRN, Business Manager and Nursing Director, Reproductive Medicine Group, St. Michael's Hospital, Bristol.

Jane Denton RGN, RM, Nursing Director, Multiple Births Foundation, Queen Charlotte's and Chelsea Hospital, London.

John Dickson, Executive Director, ISSUE (The National Fertility Association) Ltd., Birmingham.

Veronica English BA (Hons), Communications Manager, Human Fertilisation and Embryology Authority.

Margaret Inglis SRN, SCM, MTD, Dip. Counselling, Counsellor, Department of Women's and Children's Health, Royal Free Hospital Trust, London.

Deborah Kiddy BA, RGN, Clinical Nurse Specialist, Reproductive Medicine, St. Mary's NHS Trust, London.

Liz Latarche SRN, Dip. Counselling, Sister Coordinator, Ovum Donation Programme, Lister Hospital, London.

Liz Meerabeau * BSc (Hons), PhD, MBA, RGN, RHV, RNT, RHVT, Liaison Officer, Research and Development, Department of Health.

Richard Rowson, Lecturer in Moral Philosophy, University of Glamorgan and Honorary Tutor in Medical Ethics, St Mary's Hospital Medical School.

Anwar A Soubra MD, Visiting Registrar, Reproductive Medicine, Guy's and St Thomas' Hospital Trust, London.

Alison Taylor MB BS, MRCOG, Senior Registrar, Assisted Conception Unit, Guy's and St Thomas' Hospital Trust, London.

Allan Templeton MD, FRCOG, Regius Professor and Head of Obstetrics and Gynaecology, Aberdeen Royal Hospital.

* *writing in a personal capacity*

Acknowledgement

Scutari Press is grateful to Organon Laboratories for assisting in the publication of this book.

Introduction

Fertility treatment has hit the headlines many times in the last 15 years, since the birth of Louise Brown, the first 'test tube' baby; it has been particularly controversial and has given rise to huge moral and ethical dilemmas. Multiple births have led to tragically early deaths, and there have been debates in the press on whether particular women should have been treated. Infertility is an important topic, since it raises many issues in the fields of health policy and ethics. It may be regarded as a very private affair, only for the individual or couple concerned and the team treating them, whereas others see fertility treatment as undermining the fabric of society. Most fertility problems are symptom-free, or give rise to painless symptoms. But they have a great effect on the lives of the people concerned, particularly if they have no living children. It can be easy to dismiss infertility as not life threatening and, therefore, not a priority for treatment.

Fertility treatment is a growth area and a field in which nurses are developing their role. The number of specialist nurses is increasing in many fields, and this may be a trend in fertility nursing. There are many medical books, self-help books that give a good overview of tests and treatments and specialist journals, but no books specifically written for nurses. This book is designed to fill that gap.

WHO SHOULD READ THIS BOOK?

We have written this book with many groups of nurses in mind. The prime target group is nurses involved in some way with fertility treatment, either in a specialist unit, in a district general hospital or as practice nurses. Many of these nurses will be working in small teams in which there may be only one other nurse, or they may be the only nurse; there are, therefore, important issues about the risk of professional isolation that will need addressing. We have aimed to produce a book that can be used as a text on courses in fertility nursing, but it will also be of value to other nurses in gynaecology, to midwives and to Project 2000 students. We are particularly keen to reach the latter group, since issues about family formation, and sociological and social policy issues related to the family, are an important part of the Common Foundation Programme.

We also feel that nurses, as informed citizens, should have an understanding of the issues raised by fertility treatment. Two further groups we would like to reach are nurses involved in purchasing care and senior nurses among the providers of care. It has become apparent to one of the editors (Jane Denton) that there is little understanding of what fertility nursing entails among other nurses not involved in the specialty. We hope both to increase people's knowledge and, in some instances, change their attitudes.

The aims of the book are:

- to give nurses a thorough grounding in practice issues relating to treatment and the organisation of services, plus an understanding of patients' perspectives and a grasp of ethical and policy issues;
- to be practical, readable and accessible, but also, whenever possible, firmly grounded in research;
- to disseminate good practice in a field in which there are many different approaches;
- to indicate the range of practice, so that nurses can talk through with colleagues how their role can be developed;
- to help nurses involved in fertility nursing to develop their ability to deal with moral and ethical issues and to reflect on their role in what may sometimes be a controversial area of practice.

We are a nurse sociologist who undertook her doctoral research in this area (Liz Meerabeau) and a nurse who is well known in this particular field and has extensive practice-based knowledge of the specialty (Jane Denton).

The philosophy of the book is, firstly, that nursing practice should be research based when research is available. In many areas of nursing, however, there is no detailed body of research; we also think it important that we value good and innovative practice, which may not necessarily have a strong research base, and that this is shared with other practitioners. Nurses should also be reflective practitioners, so chapter authors will be encouraged to reflect upon their experience and, where possible, generalise from it.

Secondly, we believe that it is important to listen to clients' views. The first chapter, by Liz Meerabeau, will be based on people's own accounts; Margaret Inglis and Jennifer Clifford's chapter on counselling will also draw on patients' perceptions of their needs.

Thirdly, we believe in the value of interprofessional team working, the holistic care needed in fertility treatment being a prime example of the importance of a team approach. The authors are from a range of disciplines, although the nursing view will provide the overall focus. Chapters are written from different viewpoints and in different styles: some in the formal prose of scientific discourse, others in a more discursive way, which suits their more exploratory subject matter.

Sociological aspects of infertility treatment

This chapter will consider the social setting in which people experience infertility and infertility treatment. It will examine the difficulty of being different and the subtle pressures that this can bring as friends and relatives establish their own families. Secondly, it will discuss the problem of uncertainty, which can put strain on the relationship and makes it difficult for people to decide when to cease treatment; many years can elapse, during which they may be reluctant to change to other life goals.

Policy issues in infertility

Fertility treatment is an important example of the debate about choice, consumerism and priority setting. There are links to the chapter on ethical issues, for example, to the question of whether or not treatment should be provided for particular groups of people. Nurses working in this area should be well informed on these debates.

The epidemiology of infertility

This chapter will discuss the difficulty of establishing the prevalence of fertility problems in the UK and what their causes may be. Little is known about causation, and there is much debate; for example, there has been considerable recent discussion on whether the average sperm count is falling and whether or not this is causing male fertility problems.

Investigation and treatment

This chapter will include an outline of the investigation and treatment of fertility problems. Much of the chapter will be devoted to the more established treatments, but new treatments will also be outlined. The risks and side-effects of treatments will also be included.

The development of the nurse's role

One of the features of nursing practice in this specialty is the diversity of experience and roles. The RCN Fertility Nurses Group survey revealed that the majority of involved nurses are RGNs, and approximately half are midwives. Most have had some postbasic training, but they feel insufficiently prepared to care for fertility patients. Many nurses work within the private sector. There is a great variation in clinical practice, nurses in some units doing little more than chaperone doctors, while others are performing such procedures as insemination and embryo transfer, preparing semen samples and using ultrasound scanning to monitor follicular growth.

In order to develop the role fully, nurses must have a broad knowledge of all areas of fertility, to enable them to function as members of the multidisciplinary team, which is essential for the provision of high-quality treatment. There is also a need to give a clearer focus to the nursing role and establish some standardisation. This will help to establish the specialty within the nursing profession and enhance its value within the nursing career structure.

The nurse's role in specific treatments

This chapter will outline the nurse's role in three main areas of treatment: ovulation induction, in vitro fertilisation (IVF) and associated techiques, and donor insemination (DI). It will also include the problems usually experienced by patients undergoing these treatments and the implications that these may have for nursing care.

Ovulation induction is an area of nursing practice that illustrates the expanded role of the nurse. IVF is a particularly time-consuming and stressful treatment, since hopes can be built up, only to be dashed when egg retrieval cannot take place or when implantation fails.

DI does not, of course, remedy the male partner's fertility problem, and the couple will be offered counselling to explore their feelings about this. Some women seeking DI will be lesbians or heterosexual women who do not wish to have a sexual relationship in order to conceive.

Ethical dilemmas

Fertility treatment has clear ethical dimensions, in that it involves the creation of another life. This chapter examines the various ways in which judgements can be made, for example the various views on the moral status of the embryo, looks at appeals to what is 'natural', 'fair' or a 'moral right', and examines, in particular, the difficult decisions to be made in relation to multiple births.

The role of the Human Fertilisation and Embryology Authority

The previous chapter leads very naturally into this one. The Human Fertilisation and Embryology Authority (HFEA) was set up by legislation following the recommendations of the Warnock Report and regulates treatments involving donor gametes and the creation of embryos, and research using gametes and embryos. The HFEA also collects data from the licensed centres and produces an annual report.

Counselling

Clinics licensed by the HFEA must offer counselling; there is a debate about the extent to which nurses should be involved in counselling, since some writers maintain that they may be too close to the physical aspects of treatment and that they may have trouble differentiating their professional boundaries as a nurse from those as a counsellor. We also need to know more about what couples want from counselling, as opposed to what we think they need.

Support groups

This chapter will include a practically based account for nurses on the issues to be considered in setting up a local support group.

Infertility and adoption today

We felt that it was important to include a chapter on this subject, since we suspected that many nurses caring for infertile couples may not be totally *au fait* with the current position on adoption. Many of the issues raised are complementary to those raised by the writers of the two previous chapters.

We also recognise, however, that there are topics to which we do not do justice within this book, such as egg donation and surrogacy.

WHAT'S IN A NAME?

Our first practical problem was what to call this book. The working title was Fertility Nursing, and the specialist group in the RCN is, of course, called the Fertility Nurses Group. It has a positive ring to it and some patients prefer it, but we thought that non-specialists might either interpret the term as applying to both the promotion and the prevention of fertility (i.e. family planning) or think that the book had little to offer the generalist; we hope we have demonstrated that the latter is not true.

Like many other authors, we have used 'she' for the nurse. As far as we know, there are no male infertility nurses, although no doubt if there are, they will write and tell us.

Subfertility or infertility? We are not consistent. One of our contributors, Alison Taylor, felt strongly that 'subfertility' captures the uncertainty of the situation: few people are absolutely unable to conceive or father children. One of the editors (Liz Meerabeau) has used the term 'subfertility' in previous writing for this very reason but, on this occasion, deferred to the other editor (Jane Denton), who feels that when it comes to conveying the essence of the experience, 'infertility' has more meaning. Rather than insist that our contributors conformed, we felt that we should respect their wishes and reflect the variety of opinions.

Patients, clients or couples? 'Client' does not seem very applicable when someone is on her back having an internal examination! Much of the time we use 'couple', while recognising that single women also undergo treatment. This has caused embarrassment to one of the editors, who is not sure whether couple is a singular or plural noun, but the problem is not only grammatical. It is recognised as good practice to treat the couple as a unit, but are they singular (a unit) or plural (two individuals with potentially differing needs and viewpoints)? We expect that there are places in the book where readers will disagree with us; we hope this will lead to a productive exchange of views.

Liz Meerabeau
Jane Denton

1

Sociological aspects of fertility treatment

Liz Meerabeau

INTRODUCTION

Sociology can add to our understanding of the problem of infertility in several ways. The family is, of course, one of the important sociological 'institutions', along with law and education, and has the important function of socialising new members into society (or not, as the current 'moral panic' in the UK about the adequacy of single parenthood indicates). An important aspect of the debate about fertility treatments is, therefore, the extent to which assisted conception changes our understanding of what constitutes a family (Strathern, 1992). The working of institutions can be illuminated by studying people who do not, for some reason, fit the usual norms; the study of deviance is, therefore, an important sociological topic (Freidson, 1972) and can help us to understand the experience of being different. A further important sociological topic that can help us understand the experience of infertility is that of modernity, which originated with the work of Elias in the 1930s and has subsequently become a central debate (Elias, 1985). Although, in his later work, Elias is specifically discussing the process of dying, he makes several relevant points, such as the relative certainty of Western life compared with that of the Third World and our own historical past, so that planning becomes possible, the faith that science will resolve what residual uncertainties are left and the emphasis in our societies on competent performance. Berger et al (1974), in their discussion of modernity, emphasise the greater perceived freedom of choice, and potential insecurity, that we may feel. They discuss the decline of religion as an institution that can give meaning in Western society; it has to a

1

certain extent, been replaced by medicine, although the latter does not give satisfactory explanations for coping with misfortune in the way in which religion can.

Another relevant branch of sociology is the sociology of health and healing, from which concepts such as the patient career and stigma can be used to help us to understand the experience of fertility treatment. Linked areas of sociology that overlap with these are the sociology of the body and the sociology of emotions. An important topic from the latter is the management of emotions (Hochschild, 1983), which can help us to explore the subjects of 'obsession', 'desperation' and how the infertile present themselves as competent adults. Sociology rarely gives clearcut answers but can help us by broadening our understanding of the context in which our practice takes place. In this chapter, I have drawn on my own study and have confined myself mainly to British, American and a small amount of Australian literature, but it is important to bear in mind that the meaning of infertility to a couple or an individual will be affected by the meaning of parenthood in a particular society (e.g. McGilvray, 1982; Baluch et al, 1993).

PARENTHOOD AND NON-PARENTHOOD

Several writers (e.g. Peck and Senderowitz, 1974) have claimed that both the USA and the UK are pronatalist. Much of this literature dates from the early or mid-1970s feminist movement. These authors argue that there is a considerable pressure on women to become mothers; a pressure that is far greater than that on men to become fathers. It is, however, very difficult to pin down how this pressure manifests itself. Women's magazines are said to be one source; another is said to be prospective grandparents, although much of the literature indicates that, at least in Britain, they are reluctant to seem interfering (Cunningham-Burley, 1984).

Parenthood is generally held to be a central status for adults, particularly women. The sociological concept of status passage was developed by Glaser and Strauss (1971), drawing on earlier anthropological work on rites of passage, by which, in some societies, young men make the transition to adulthood by means of various trials and tribulations. Berger and Luckmann (1967) consider that the rite of passage is an important way for us to impose a sense of order on an uncertain world and that developmental psychology has a similar function, in reassuring us that we are 'living correctly'. Not all statuses are of equal weight to the individual's sense of self. It is when our most important statuses, in which we have most emotional investment, such as that of parent, are at risk that our sense of identity is threatened. Infertile people may be said to be suffering from a blocked status passage, as they cope with the uncertainty of whether or not treatment will succeed. Despite the variety of lifestyles available in the UK and the USA, most young adults expect to become parents. Even the phrase 'family planning' implies that conception is straightforward and can be fitted into a well-ordered life plan, despite the well-known statistic of the high number of couples who will experience difficulty in conceiving (although Franklin [1992] considers that pregnancy may now be less taken for granted).

Campbell (1985) states that marriage is a series of stages informed by a cultural timetable and that the early, exclusive stage of being a couple is not expected to last. It may not be easy to develop alternatives to parenting, and the individualism of our culture may create several problems for the infertile. The relative privacy of the nuclear family reduces the opportunity for the childless to care for other people's children, whereas Lessor (1993), in her small study of ovum donation by sisters, observes that, in some other cultures, there is no distinction made between one's own children and those of a sibling. Modernity may also reduce the opportunity for emotional expression. Elias (1985) claims that in modern societies, we do not easily express emotion, except to pets and young children, hence perhaps one of the popular stereotypes of the childless as pet owners.

Although parenthood is an important status, there is, in our society, a diversity of lifestyles, and the childless may be seen as simply wanting to be like everyone else if they pursue fertility treatment (Franklin, 1990). Humphrey (1969) remarked on the fact that the childless in Britain did not develop other interests and attributed it to lack of resilience, although he also recognised that many wives were constrained by the primacy of their husband's career. Veevers (1976) states that the freedom of childlessness may be a fantasy and may be seldom used. Several feminist critiques of fertility treatment claim that it emphasises parenthood as the only successful outcome to treatment, rather than helping couples (particularly women) to develop other life goals (Strickler, 1992).

Voluntary childlessness

Veevers, a Canadian, has written extensively on the subject of voluntary childlessness (e.g. Veevers, 1979), using deviance as an organising concept. Whereas the involuntarily childless have a physical blemish, the voluntarily childless have a character blemish, since they do not wish to undertake the duties and joys of parenthood (perhaps because they have what Veevers calls a Hobbesian view of children as 'nasty, brutish and short'). Subsequent British studies of the voluntarily childless (e.g. Porter, 1980) have questioned the usefulness of deviance as a concept, since the childless are generally very 'ordinary' and have often simply developed a routine of unproblematic contraception and never made the decision to become parents. Childlessness can also help to resolve the tension that Askham

(1976) identified in the modern marriage, between developing personal identity and maintaining marital stability.

Children can be a mixed blessing, and the literature on why people have them indicates that it is very difficult to put into words. Many studies are large-scale, international surveys, concerned with the number of children couples decide to have (e.g. Miller and Newman, 1978) and whether this can be modified in the light of concerns about overpopulation. More detailed in-depth studies of smaller numbers of people (e.g. Busfield and Paddon, 1977; Payne, 1978) have identified issues such as the 'naturalness' of parenthood, the contribution of children to family life and the enjoyment of children. Busfield and Paddon conclude that it is not surprising that most people have children, since, in their eyes, not to do so would be to deny satisfaction and a valued social identity and to put the marriage at risk.

GENDER DIFFERENCES

Most of the literature on parenting (e.g. Lewis and O'Brien, 1987) indicates that, despite the advent of the so-called 'New Man', the onus falls most heavily on the mother, and it involves greater life changes for her. Most modern sociologists would not go so far as the functionalists of the 1940s and 1950s (e.g. Parsons and Bales, 1985), who stated that men play instrumental, and women expressive, roles in the family, and the essentialist argument that women differ innately from men is hotly contested (Sayers, 1982). However, several studies have found that men have difficulty expressing emotion (James, 1989; Duncombe and Marsden, 1993). Motherhood is also biologically dramatic in a way that fatherhood is not, as indicated by our very different use of the verbs 'to mother' and 'to father'. It is, therefore, not surprising that women are generally found to be more isolated by infertility than are men (e.g. Greil et al, 1988), although men with a fertility problem may find it harder to share their distress and may also feel that they must keep a 'stiff upper lip' to support their partner (Mason, 1993).

THE EXPERIENCE OF INFERTILITY

There have been many studies of the experience of infertility from a psychological perspective (e.g. Humphrey, 1975; Allison, 1979; Cooper, 1979; Feuer, 1983) and several self-help books by people who have themselves undergone treatment (Houghton and Houghton, 1977; Pfeffer and Woollett, 1983). There have also been several sociological studies, most recently that by Monach (1993). Owens' (1986) study of 30 Welsh, working class couples explores issues such as conformity and the pressure to parent and couples' view of themselves not as childless but as prospective parents. Recent American studies include Olshansky's (1987) work with 15 couples, which examines the process of taking on an infertile identity. Sandelowski and Pollock (1986) identify three themes: the experience of uncertainty and ambiguity, the awareness of time passing and feelings of being different.

One problem with most studies is that they are taken from a sample of those who have sought treatment, and we have little information on those who do not. Demographic data from the US National Survey of Family Growth indicate that there are differences between users and non-users of services (Hirsch and Mosher, 1987). Several of the US studies are particularly skewed, since they are recruited from Resolve, the US self-help group, whose membership is estimated to represent only 1 in 8000 of infertile people. This may be one reason why the people in these studies, unlike those in the British studies to date, tend to be very active and well informed 'consumers' of health care.

My own study (Meerabeau, 1989) was carried out in 1983/4 and involved observation in three NHS clinics plus in-depth taped interviews, usually of 2–3 hours, with 41 couples and 9 women at various stages of treatment (mean length of treatment 29 months; range 2 weeks to 10 years) who were recruited via the clinics. Nineteen had had experience of other clinics before their current referral. The mean ages were 30 for the women and 32 for the men; all lived in the Home Counties or London, and middle class occupations were over-represented. At least one person in each couple was British, and none had a live child of their marriage or was caring for a young child from a previous marriage. One-third of the women had been pregnant. In 17 couples, the woman had a fertility problem, in 5, the man, in 14, both, and in 14, neither had a problem diagnosed. They were, with three exceptions, interviewed in their own home, and in all but the first three interviews involving a couple, the partners were interviewed together. There are disadvantages to this approach, since there may be a tendency to present a united front, but the advantage is that it can give some insight into the dynamics between the couple (Allan, 1980). However, Duncombe and Marsden (1993) caution that the interviewer should be careful not to further weaken an already weak relationship.

All three clinics observed were either part of a teaching hospital or linked to one, and all three had specialist staff, although most combined fertility work with gynaecology or urology. None had a fully coordinated service and all had to refer men for specialist help, although one senior registrar undertook DI herself. IVF was offered within one of the hospitals, although by a different consultant. The range of tests and treatment offered was mainly for ovulatory problems and cervical mucus problems. The nursing role in all three clinics was fairly minimal, being confined to chaperoning, organising records and explaining tests to new patients.

SEEKING HELP

There are several sociological studies on how people interpret bodily changes and decide what treatment they need (e.g. Zola, 1973; Hannay, 1979; Locker, 1981); whether they consult a medical practitioner will depend on the problem, the strength of their social networks and their culture. There are generally few triggers with fertility problems, since many people are symptom-free and their only 'symptom' is a lack of change, i.e. the lack of conception. In my study, as in Owens' (1986, see above), the main trigger was time elapsing, and most were aware that 1 year of 'unprotected' intercourse was the usual medical criterion for referral. Few (8 women, no men) had discussed it with anyone else whereas in Owens' study women in particular were rather more likely to discuss with their family whether or not to visit the GP. The visit to the GP was regarded as an 'errand', a necessary prelude to referral to a specialist; only a minority of men (7) went with their wives. Little was expected of the GP, and the only criticism was of the 5 GPs who said to go away and keep trying. The outcome was that 18 women were referred immediately, 9 had an internal examination, 9 were given temperature charts and 12 GPs requested the husband to give a sperm sample. Unfortunately, the latter did not however save any time, except where the GP used the same laboratory as the clinic to which he or she referred the couple, since as in Monach's (1993) study, laboratories seem not to believe others' results. Another important clinical issue was that 2 women did not have their rubella status assessed by their GP, with the result that they then had to contracept while they were immunised.

MEN'S PARTICIPATION IN TREATMENT

Greil et al (1988), in their US study, claim that there is a 'his and hers' experience of infertility: that women generally become far more involved in treatment and that this can put further strain on the relationship. Although in many UK clinics emphasis is put on treating the couple, men, in practice, easily feel peripheral (Meerabeau, 1991; Mason, 1993; Monach, 1993), as they do in childbirth (Richman, 1982); they are not used to taking on a rather diffuse, supportive role. In my study, all but two men had attended at least one clinic appointment, and most were pleased just to be invited to the consultation; those who had greater expectations were disappointed. Several of the general hospital clinics that men had attended with their partners before their current referral did not even allow them in the consulting room:

> They didn't want me to go in with her. I mean, we were married and they refused point blank. I felt they didn't want me in the waiting room.

Even though 19 men had a low sperm count, 9 did not see it as a problem and were not receiving any treatment; they did not see themselves as patients. The 10 men who were treated for their fertility problem presented a picture similar to that of the men interviewed by Mason (1993) and described with wry humour a general lack of coordination of treatment.

Generally, the people I interviewed did not expect the doctor to spend much time in discussion; they were described approvingly as 'nice but brisk' or 'business-like', and simple conversational niceties, such as enquiring about Christmas or the summer holiday, were regarded as sufficient. Baruch (1982), in his study of paediatric clinics, also found that parents expected clinical detachment in their consultations, rather than any exploration of feelings. The format of the clinic, the crowded consulting room, obviously in one hospital meant to accommodate only one patient, and, in particular, the restricted time available for discussion did not encourage an unhurried exploration of couples' feelings about their problems. Several authors (e.g. Richman and Goldthorpe, 1977; Murcott, 1981; Meredith, 1993) have emphasised the time pressure in medicine. The latter considers that surgeons have problems switching from their clinical style of discourse and that this is an argument for greater nurse involvement. Lessor (1993) also considers that it is difficult to discuss intimate matters as a triad and that one member of the threesome tends to get left out. Because of this, potential conflict between the couple could not be explored (Pfeffer and Woollett, 1983).

EMOTIONAL NEUTRALITY

The structure of the clinics also resulted in emotional neutrality, which was also found by Strong (1979) in his study of Scottish paediatric clinics and called by him the 'bureaucratic format'. The medical literature on infertility, like that on childhood handicap, refers to guilt and distress, but this was not discussed as a topic in the clinics, and when patients did become upset, they tried hard to regain their composure and saved their tears until they were outside the consulting room. The doctor would pause while they recovered, but sorrow did not then become a topic of conversation. The failure to explore emotions could be a source of underlying tension in the clinic, as Strong found, since modern medicine is expected to be successful, and failure may be seen as failure of the individual doctor. If no remedy for painful feelings is offered other than the resolution of the medical problem that has caused them, this puts a greater onus on the doctor to succeed.

SEXUALITY AND EMBARRASSMENT

Although many of the medical texts suggest that poor sexual technique is a potential cause of failure to conceive, and should therefore be enquired about in the consultation, this was not investigated in the clinics I observed. One consultant confined his enquiries to a jocular, 'How often do you have sex? Once a week, once a month, or once a year?' Several studies have explored the embarrassment that both doctors and patients may experience in discussing sexual matters. Henslin and Biggs (1971) and Emerson (1970a, b) have studied the gynaecological examination, in which the doctor, particularly if of the opposite sex, must maintain a balance between 'the insult of sexual familiarity' and 'the insult of unacknowledged identity' (Emerson, 1970b: p. 85), and the patient must be neither too coy nor immodest. Staff work at maintaining a matter-of-fact stance, whereby the pelvic area is viewed as being like any other part of the body, but our primary socialisation into our culture has taught us that it is not. Weijts et al (1993) reviewed the Dutch literature, which indicates that at least 40% of GPs and gynaecologists have difficulty discussing sexual matters; their conversational analysis of gynaecological consultations found that both doctor and patient tend to delay mentioning sexual matters, use hesitations and pauses and avoid precise terminology. In their study, doctors generally gave the impression that they did not wish to discuss such matters, although there is some evidence that female gynaecologists may be more comfortable with the topic. For the male patient, the problem may be worse, since male sexuality is inextricably linked to performance, and even the routine male test involves a sexual act – masturbation. Paul, one of my interviewees, felt that male doctors may identify too closely with their patients:

> I think there's a bit of smoking behind the boys' lav sort of mentality about it, it's all a bit of a laugh, yeah, I think there's a flippant approach. I mean half of it is nervous, isn't it, there for the grace sort of thing.

SELF-HELP

As indicated above, the people interviewed did not expect much discussion at their clinic appointments, but a surprising finding was that most also did not wish to find out more about their treatment, and their knowledge was quite tentative. Apart from trying to lead a reasonably healthy life, they were not sure what else they could do. Psychosocial influences on health are frequently invoked by middle class respondents (Blaxter, 1990); 34 out of the 91 people interviewed in my study thought that stress and trying too hard could prevent conception and that if they became too involved with their treatment, this would be exacerbated:

> If you're relaxed, you're more likely to fall pregnant. It could be with Elaine there's nothing wrong with her and the only reason she's not falling is because she's so fraught about it.

> It's a vicious circle if you start to worry about your periods. I think sometimes I wish I didn't have to watch myself so closely, taking my temperature.

Where people gave reasons for fertility problems, they were very tentative; for example, Tony's wife thought that his weight might have something to do with his low sperm count, but he retorted that men twice his size had families. Generally, causation is not well established in fertility problems, and it was rarely discussed in the clinics. In some medical conditions, such as migraine, sufferers learn from painful trial and error what precipitates an episode and what can be done to relieve it, but many infertile people are symptom-free, with no way of knowing, for example, whether bathing the testicles in cold water is having much effect or not. Replies to my questions about remedies showed a heavy reliance on medical expertise and a tendency to caricature alternative medicine with references to old wives' tales, such as 'dancing round the giant oak tree at midnight':

> I think it was the doctor who said Alex should wear loose-fitting underpants, but I mean that's based on scientific fact anyway, so I wouldn't call it a folk thing. Not in the way that you swing the cat in the air three times or something!

> My mum read an article in a magazine; 'You know what your trouble is, you're wearing tight trousers, and hot baths and things.' I'm on the phone saying, 'Yeah mum.'

> I think his mum, since she's been at home, she's got nothing better to do than to watch TV.

The couples I interviewed, while grumbling good-humouredly about the NHS, were not active consumers and did not feel it was their place to suggest treatment to the doctor; for example, the five couples having or contemplating DI had not suggested it themselves. Nineteen out of the 50 couples had previously attended a local clinic and had then requested referral, but the treatment they were being offered in the new clinic did not differ substantially from that in the first, and they did not request specific treatments or tests. This unwillingness to explore other avenues of treatment was unexpected, since studies of health care in Britain (Broome and Wallace, 1984) generally indicate that people want more information. American studies (e.g. Sandelowski et al, 1989) confirm this, and the literature on health behaviour would have predicted that the people interviewed in this study would be well-informed 'consumers'. Many were middle class and would, therefore, be expected to have a greater knowledge of health matters (Townsend and Davidson, 1982) and a notion of the body as 'something to be maintained and monitored' (Radley and Green, 1987: p. 201). Women are also expected to take greater responsibility for health care and health knowledge (Graham, 1984; Martin, 1987). Several had read a general health encyclopaedia, read articles in women's magazines or browsed through a fertility book in a bookseller's but it went no further than that, and they were concerned that greater knowledge would make them 'paranoid' or 'hypochondriac' or destroy what should be a natural, spontaneous process. As Patrick said quite vehemently:

> That's what your consultant gets paid for, not for you to read books and become self taught about it; in other words, what's the point of going to him in the first place. That's how I look at it ... I have got better things to do with my time than sit down and read articles. I don't have time to read a book to have a child ... the whole concept of analysing it, going into it, to my mind is not part of the spontaneity and spontaneous nature, what I understand marriage and the production of children to be about.

For many couples, the strategy with most chance of success was to attend the clinic, take any prescribed drugs and otherwise try to banish the problem from their day-to-day concerns. This strategy also underlay their feelings about self-help organisations: only 6 out of the 50 couples had either joined one or thought that they might. They did not generally see self-help groups as having any other role than discussion, and, as indicated above, they did not wish to dwell on the subject; 'just a group of people talking', 'alright if you want that kind of thing, if you're desperate', 'if the hospital can't help us, no-one can'. Since the couples in this study, like those in Owens' (1986), did not see themselves as infertile but as 'parents in waiting', they had no great wish to associate with other infertile couples, unlike the women studied by Sandelowski et al (1989), who actively sought out other women with fertility problems.

PARENTS IN WAITING

In my study, the majority had taken it for granted that they would become parents and compared themselves to others in their social group:

> Chris' sister has just become pregnant – the worst thing on her mind was

trying to tell me and Chris. Circumstances being what they are, the oldest one in the family usually has the baby first. All of Chris' life, Chris has always done everything first. I know it sounds a bit childish, but we got the first of everything.

The idea of a family was simply a progression: people met at a certain age, they got married, had children, it was that sort of thing.

Their recollections of their courtship and early married life indicated a broad consensus of what constitutes a 'normal' middle class life plan, in which couples contracept for several years until secure housing and basic household equipment are obtained and the couple feel they know each other (Mansfield, 1982; May, 1982; Jackson, 1983). They also felt that they should be 'mature' enough to cope with children, yet young enough to enjoy them:

When you get to 30, you're getting on a bit. If you're too old, you lose patience.

Under 21, you're still learning and finding things out. You've got to be able to look after yourselves before you can look after someone else.

I wouldn't go over 40. I don't know why. Forty always sounds a lot older than 39. When he's 20, I'd be 60. Do I want all the problems a 20 year old fetches up when I'm 60? At 60, you'd be thinking of your retirement.

Twenty people, both men and women, referred to their own or others' experience as the child of older parents, who were generally seen as less active, less able to empathise and rather an embarrassment at the school gates. Although Jackson (1983: p. 38) claims that 'men's vista of fertility is endless', the men in my study were almost as age conscious as were their wives, since they wanted to be active with their children; when asked about their view of fatherhood, football in the park figured highly. Lee, a plumber, who had, as a young teenager, cared for the children of his much older brothers, was the most explicit of the men in expressing his enjoyment of children:

There's just so much you can share with a kid. I suppose it's just going back to your childhood again, you can be a child with them. I love to cuddle little babies. When they're just born, they're so nice, and when they get a little bit older, you can be a little kid, and when they go to school you can help them, play football with them, then they grow up and you can go down the pub with them, they're friends. I'd give up anything to have a kid.

Many people, however, were revising their view of what constituted the 'ideal' age for parenthood, as time elapsed:

> For all I know I could still be trying for a baby at 40, but I wouldn't let that stop me, because my life wouldn't be complete without children.

The determination to persevere with fertility treatment can curtail other options; although age limits on adoption have recently been relaxed in the UK, they were, at the time of this study, quite strict, and it was not unusual for couples to emerge from fertility treatment to find that they were now too old to be considered. In this study, two couples were actively involved in pursuing adoption and 16 women and 17 men thought they might consider it. The main criterion in their decision was whether or not they attached importance to blood ties (Strathern, 1992), as this conversation between Mark and Fran illustrates:

> Who's gonna say you're going to love it when it's older, cos it's not yours?

> But things grow up like.

> You're just saying that. They always say don't he take after his mother, don't he take after his dad. That baby, his dad could be a mass murderer.

UNCERTAINTY

The lack of symptoms or clear-cut results to tests left many feeling in a state of limbo and ambivalent as to whether or not they would rather have a definite problem diagnosed:

> I'd investigate [adoption]. That's as far as I would go, because the optimist in me would still say hang on for a second. But because of the length of the procedure, I'd have to consider it ... Circumstances would be a lot easier if there was a definite, incurable problem.

> It wouldn't be so bad if there was something radically wrong with you liked blocked tubes or something of that nature. Something physical. You could get to grips with it and perhaps circumvent it by test tube babies or whatever. But when there's nothing physically wrong with you, it's just a little bit of hormone imbalance, and it's a hit and miss affair, that's what's so terribly frustrating.

Trouble is, cos he's told me there's nothing really wrong, I'm looking on the bright side again. We're back at square one now there's a chance. Sometimes I think it's kinder if they turn round – I don't think I'd even believe that though. I can't believe that either.

I think that if I had been told 2 years ago that I definitely wouldn't have any, there's no way that I would have been jumping on the test tube bandwagon. I'd have just got on, carved myself a career. I feel that since we got here, I have literally pottered from month to month, never wanting to get terribly tied down to anything, just in case something happens.

Melanie, quoted above, was a nurse but was not currently using her nursing skills. Like many of the other women, she was acutely aware of the stalemate in her job situation; only four of the women interviewed anticipated going out to work when (if) they had their baby, so their sense of marking time was greater than that of their partner.

Most of the couples in this study coped by avoiding thinking too much about the future; as in Woollett's (1985) study, the focus changed from having a child to the finite time span of ovulation and menstruation. Most did not even consider the possibility that they might not succeed, and it felt tactless even to ask them this question.

THE MARITAL RELATIONSHIP

Much of the literature produced by the two self-help groups ISSUE and Child refers to the considerable interpersonal tension generated by treatment: the word 'treadmill' is often used. Studies of marital relationships have generally been rather variable in quality (Duncombe and Marsden, 1993), and the concept of marital satisfaction is difficult to operationalise; this may be why the psychological studies on childlessness produce rather confusing results (Callan, 1987). It is also important not to fall into the trap of seeing other marriages as unproblematic; common sense tells us that they are not (Mansfield and Collard, 1988), and marital satisfaction generally *decreases* with the arrival of children (Thornes and Collard, 1979). There is also no link between the incidence of childlessness and divorce if controlled for wife's age at marriage and the length of marriage (Gibson, 1980). Nevertheless, Berger (1980), Connolly et al (1987) and Feuer (1983) state that the sexual relationship is particularly disrupted when the man has a fertility problem and is 'firing blanks', to quote an often-used metaphor. Humphrey (1969), Owens (1982) and Monach (1993) also think that the man is more stigmatised by having a fertility problem than is the woman and that male infertility is unconsciously equated with impotence.

Many couples in my study who had been in treatment for more than a year presented themselves as competent adults who recognised that marriage does not always go smoothly. They reported that they had become closer, but this was often at some cost:

> It might sound funny like, a lot of people say to have a good marriage you've got to have problems to bring you together. That's marriage, isn't it, cos you're partners.

Tests and treatment could add to the stress and reduce sexual intercourse to something mechanical. As Becker and Nachtigall (1992: p. 463) state, 'health concerns contaminate the intimate aspects of daily life':

> I don't care who you are, I cannot just, 'my temperature's gone up' go up there and perform, and I will not do that just because of a chart; we've done all that before, and we've had more rows than anything. I'd rather say right, I'll not have a kid, than do things like that. Because to me that should be natural, not bloody set out.

TALKING TO OTHERS

Some of the stress that couples in the study experienced could perhaps have been reduced by obtaining emotional support from other family members and friends. Forty out of the 50 couples had told their parents that they were attending a clinic, mainly so that they would know why they had not yet become grandparents (Meerabeau, 1989). Generally, however, they did not discuss their attendance with them. Marriage and parenthood problems in the UK are usually regarded as best coped with by the couple themselves (Pearlin and Schooler, 1978; Woollett, 1985), and Brannen and Collard (1982: p. 107) consider that the social pressures and taboos constraining people from disclosing problems related to sex are immense, particularly for men. Parents were also said to be reluctant to 'pry'. For a minority of couples, their parents had no other grandchildren and had their own grief and disappointment (Shapiro, 1982). As Helen said:

> My father, I think he's taken it badly, and he doesn't talk about it to my mum. I seem to be able to talk to him better over the phone about it than actually speaking face to face, because I do get a bit emotional about it ... I do feel guilty. I did say well there's a bit of hope, but I don't want to say too much because I don't want their hopes to rise.

DI is a particularly sensitive issue. Four couples in this study were involved in it and one was contemplating it; two had told one set of parents and three had told neither, confirming findings by Monach (1993) and larger studies by Snowden and Snowden (1984) and Humphrey (1983). In the former study, 50% kept DI entirely secret, and few had told the whole family. They were particularly wary of the generation gap, since attitudes to DI in their parents' generation were considerably more disapproving than are those today, as discussed in Chapter 2.

BEING DIFFERENT

The word 'stigma' is often used in connection with infertility. The term was popularised in social science by Goffman (1963); it derives from the mark applied to Greek slaves, and was later used to refer to the marks of Christ on the Cross, but is now used metaphorically to refer to a trait that differentiates and discredits the individual. Some traits may not, however, be obvious: infertility is one example, another being epilepsy. In these instances, the individual is discreditable rather than discredited. The literature on deviance has also been drawn upon, especially by Veevers (1979); Lemert (1951) differentiated between primary deviance, in which the individual differs from the norm in some way, and secondary deviance, in which, because of that difference, the individual has now embarked on a deviant 'career'. This is closely linked to labelling theory, in which the primary deviance is detected and defined by an agency, which then labels the individual. These concepts have obvious usefulness, for example in looking at how people become labelled as mentally ill, but the 'ordinariness' of infertile people may not make this approach as applicable in this context.

In Meerabeau (1989), only a minority (12 women and 6 men) said that they felt in some way odd or incomplete, or a failure:

Unfortunately, women are still brought up, however feminist you are, as what one is brought into the world for. I think we're still very conditioned to it. So I think one still feels a sense of failure.

A more pervasive feeling was that of being different; couples were gradually left behind by their friends as the latter went on to have second and third children and their time and attention were consumed by parenthood.

I work hard at not being left out. I don't exclude myself from conversations about children. I talk in a way that I appear very interested – I hope. But I'm more and more excluded from that world.

None described situations of crude teasing such as that in Miall's (1985) Canadian study, and the infrequent comments of the 'I'll come and show

you how to do it' variety were good-naturedly rebuffed. Two-thirds of the
women and eight of the men, however, experienced feelings of unease in
conversations with others, particularly around the topic of pregnancy, as
Paul and Geraldine indicate:

> It's a terrible rift. I can only listen so long to the talk. All right, maybe
> they don't go on about it as much as women – a chauvinist comment,
> but I think it's true. Women can go on at great length about Mothercare
> and that sort of thing. But I mean, you know that they are into it quietly.
> And they know they haven't got much in common, so they'll keep
> schtum about it, and I know it's very artificial ... it does create this
> artificiality, and it's very painful to me, cos many of my friends are in
> this position. It makes it worse when all they can talk is baby talk.

> I felt terrible when I heard about the baby. She [sister] said I've got some
> great news, I'm pregnant. I just couldn't say anything. In the end I just
> started sobbing and put the phone down. I don't begrudge her having
> the baby, it's just that I'm envious of her having the baby. It took about
> 6 weeks before I could speak to her without being silly, getting emotional
> and crying.

Generally, the announcement of a wanted pregnancy should be greeted
with pleasure by all hearers, especially women. If it is known that the person
who is about to hear the news has been trying unsuccessfully for a child,
however, it can seem tactless for the announcer to be too cheerful. The
announcer can carry on as usual, although this may be hurtful, or avoid the
situation, which can be even more hurtful, because special consideration can
be subtly degrading (Baruch, 1982; Locker, 1983). Many childless women
also feel uneasy when asked by casual acquaintances if they have children. It is
usually asked in a spirit of polite enquiry, expecting the answer 'yes', and 'no'
leaves a hole in the conversational fabric that requires repair work. The
questioner is not, however, expecting to hear of some personal problem and
may feel that he or she has committed a *faux pas*:

> I say I've had an ectopic, but then people think 'Oh my God, what did I
> ask?'

One way of handling this situation is to be matter of fact:

> People are usually shocked at my answers because I'm so cool and
> collected about it. I'm not breaking down in tears, and people's
> immediate reaction is they don't think you really want children.

CONCLUSION

The studies of infertile couples in the UK have all been fairly small scale, and we cannot claim that they are necessarily representative. However, they portray a similar picture, of couples who feel rather isolated from their friends, are not active consumers of health care and stoically try to put their problem to the back of their minds and get on with their lives. Whether or not that is the best way of coping with fertility problems will be discussed in further chapters.

References

Allan G A (1980) A note on interviewing spouses together. *Journal of Marriage and the Family*, **42**: 205–10.

Allison J R (1979) Role and role conflict of women in infertile couples. *Psychology of Women Quarterly*, **4**(1): 97–113.

Askham J (1976) Identity and stability within the marriage relationship. *Journal of Marriage and the Family*, **38**(3): 535–47.

Baluch B, Manyande A and Aghssa M A (1993) Failure to Conceive with in Vitro Fertilisation: the Middle Eastern Experience. Unpublished paper, University of Luton.

Baruch G (1982) Moral Tales: Interviewing Parents of Congenitally Ill Children. Unpublished PhD thesis, University of London.

Becker G and Nachtigall R (1992) Eager for medicalisation: the social production of infertility as a disease. *Sociology of Health and Illness*, 14(4): 456–71.

Berger D (1980) Impotence following the discovery of azoospermia. *Fertility and Sterility*, **34**: 154–6.

Berger P and Luckmann T (1967) *The Social Construction of Reality.* Harmondsworth: Penguin.

Berger P, Berger B and Kellner H (1974) *The Homeless Mind.* Harmondsworth: Penguin.

Blaxter M (1990) *Health and Lifestyles.* London: Routledge.

Brannen J and Collard J (1982) *Marriages in Trouble.* London: Tavistock.

Broome A and Wallace L (1984) *Psychology and Gynaecological Problems.* London: Tavistock.

Busfield J and Paddon M (1977) *Thinking about Children.* London: Cambridge University Press.

Callan V (1987) The personal and marital adjustment of mothers and of voluntarily and involuntarily childless wives. *Journal of Marriage and the Family*, **49**: 847–56.

Campbell E (1985) *The Childless Marriage.* London: Tavistock.

Connolly K, Edelmann R and Cooke I (1987) Distress and marital problems associated with infertility. *Journal of Reproductive and Infant Psychology*, **5**: 49–57.

Cooper S (1979) Female Infertility: Its Effect on Self Esteem, Body Image, Locus of Control, and Behavior. Unpublished PhD thesis, Boston University.

Cunningham-Burley S (1984) On telling the news: grandparenthood as an announceable event. *International Journal of Sociology and Social Policy*, **4**(4): 52–69.

Duncombe J and Marsden D (1993) Love and intimacy: the gender division of emotion and 'emotion work'. *Sociology*, **27**(2): 221–41.

Elias N (1985) *The Loneliness of the Dying*. Oxford: Basil Blackwell.

Emerson J (1970a) Nothing unusual is happening. In: Shibutani T (ed.) *Human Nature and Collective Behavior*, pp. 208–22. Englewood Cliffs, NJ: Prentice Hall.

Emerson J (1970b) Behavior in private places: sustaining definitions of reality in gynecological examinations. In: Dreitzel H (ed.) *Recent Sociology*, pp. 74–97. New York: Macmillan.

Feuer G (1983) The Psychological Impact of Infertility on the Lives of Men. Unpublished PhD thesis, University of Pennsylvania.

Franklin S (1990) Deconstructing 'desperateness': the social construction of infertility in popular representations of new reproductive technologies. In: McNeil M, Varcoe I and Yearley S (eds) *The New Reproductive Technologies*, pp. 200–29. London: Macmillan.

Franklin S (1992) Making sense of missed conceptions: anthropological perspectives on unexplained infertility. In: Stacey M (ed.) *Changing Human Reproduction*, pp. 75–91. London: Sage.

Freidson E (1972) Disability as social deviance. In: Boydell C, Grindstaff C and Whitehead P (eds) *Deviant Behavior and Social Reaction*, pp. 4–23. Toronto: Holt, Rinehart and Winston.

Gibson C (1980) Childlessness and marital instability: a re-examination of the evidence. *Journal of Biosocial Science*, **12**: 121–32.

Glaser B and Strauss A (1971) *Status Passage*. London: Routledge and Kegan Paul.

Goffman E (1963) *Stigma: Notes on the Management of a Spoiled Identity*. New Jersey: Prentice Hall.

Graham H (1984) *Women, Health and the Family*. Brighton: Wheatsheaf.

Greil A, Leitko T and Porter K (1988) Infertility: his and hers. *Gender and Society*, **2**(2): 172–99.

Hannay D (1979) *The Symptom Iceberg: A Study of Community Health*. London: Routledge and Kegan Paul.

Henslin J and Biggs M (1971) Dramaturgical desexualisation: the sociology of the vaginal examination. In: Henslin J (ed.) *Studies in the Sociology of Sex*. New York: Appleton–Century–Crofts.

Hirsch M and Mosher W (1987) Characteristics of infertile women in the United States and their use of fertility services. *Fertility and Sterility*, **47**(4): 618–25.

Hochschild A (1983) *The Managed Heart: The Commercialization of Human Feeling*. Berkeley: University of California Press.

Houghton P and Houghton D (1977) *Unfocussed Grief*. Birmingham: Birmingham Settlement.

Humphrey M (1969) *The Hostage Seekers*. London: Longman.

Humphrey M (1975) The effect of children upon the marriage relationship. *British Journal of Medical Psychology*, **48**: 273–9.

Humphrey M (1983) Paper given at NAC meeting, Isleworth.

Jackson B (1983) *Fatherhood*. London: George Allan and Unwin.

James N (1989) Emotional labour: skill and work in the regulation of feeling. *Sociological Review*, **37**(1): 15–42.

Lemert E (1951) *Social Pathology*. New York: McGraw-Hill.

Lessor R (1993) All in the family: social processes in ovarian egg donation between sisters. *Sociology of Health and Illness*, **15**(3): 393–413.

Lewis C and O'Brien M (1987) *Reassessing Fatherhood: New Observations on Fathers and the Modern Family*. London: Sage.

Locker D (1981) *Symptoms and Illness: The Cognitive Organisation of Disorder*. London: Tavistock.

Locker D (1983) *Disability and Disadvantage: The Consequences of Chronic Illness*. London: Tavistock.

McGilvray D (1982) Sexual power and fertility in Sri Lanka. In: McCormack C, (ed.) *Ethnography of Fertility and Birth*. London: Academic Press.

Mansfield P (1982) Getting ready for parenthood: attitudes to and expectations of having children of a group of newly weds. *International Journal of Social Policy*, **2**: 28–9.

Mansfield P and Collard, J (1988) *The Beginning of the Rest of Your Life?* London: Macmillan.

Martin E (1987) *The Woman in the Body: A Cultural Analysis of Reproduction*. New York: Beacon Press.

Mason M–C (1993) *Male Infertility: Men Talking*. London: Routledge.

May K (1982) Factors contributing to first time fathers' readiness for fatherhood. *Family Relations*, **31**: 353–62.

Meerabeau E (1989) Parents in Waiting: The Experience of Subfertile Couples. Unpublished PhD thesis, University of London.

Meerabeau E (1991) Husbands' participation in fertility treatment: they also serve who only stand and wait. *Sociology of Health and Illness*, **13**(3): 396–410.

Meredith P (1993) Patient participation in decision-making and consent to treatment. *Sociology of Health and Illness*, **15**(3): 315–36.

Miall C (1985) Perceptions of informal sanctioning and the stigma of involuntary childlessness. *Deviant Behaviour*, **6**: 383–403.

Miller W and Newman L (1978) *The First Child and Family Formation*. Chapel Hill: University of North Carolina.

Monach J (1993) *Childless, No Choice*. London: Routledge.

Murcott A (1981) On the typification of 'bad patients'. In: Atkinson P and Heath C (eds). *Medical Work: Realities and Routines,* Aldershot: Gower.

Olshansky E (1987) Identity of self as infertile: an example of theory generating research. *Advances in Nursing Science,* **9**(2): 54–63.

Owens D (1982) The desire to father: reproductive ideologies and involuntarily childless men. In: McKee L and O'Brien M (eds) *The Father Figure,* pp. 72–86. London: Tavistock.

Owens D (1986) The Desire for Children: A Sociological Study of Involuntary Childlessness. Unpublished PhD thesis, University College, Cardiff.

Parsons T and Bales, R. (1985) *Family Socialization and the Interaction Process.* Glencoe, IL: Free Press.

Payne J (1978) Talking about children: an examination of accounts about reproduction and family life. *Journal of Biosocial Science,* **10**: 367–74.

Pearlin L and Schooler C (1978) The structure of coping. *Journal of Health and Social Behaviour,* **19**: 2–21.

Peck E and Senderowitz J (1974) *Pronatalism: The Myth of Mom and Apple Pie.* New York: Thomas Y Crowell.

Pfeffer N and Woollett A (1983) *The Experience of Infertility.* London: Virago.

Pfeffer N (1987) Artificial Insemination, in vitro fertilisation and the stigma of infertility. In: Stanworth M (ed.) *Reproductive Technologies: Gender Motherhood and Medicine,* pp. 81–97. Oxford: Basil Blackwell/Polity Press.

Porter M (1980) Willing Deviants? A Study of Childlessness. Unpublished PhD thesis, University of Aberdeen.

Radley A and Green R (1987) Illness as adjustment: a methodology and conceptual framework. *Sociology of Health and Illness,* **9**(2): 179–207.

Richman J (1982) Men's experience of pregnancy and childbirth. In: McKee L and O'Brien M (eds) *The Father Figure,* pp. 89–103. London: Tavistock.

Richman J and Goldthorpe W (1977) When was your last period: temporal aspects of gynaecological diagnosis. In: Dingwall R (ed.) *Health Care and Health Knowledge,* pp. 160–82. London: Croom Helm.

Sandelowski M and Pollock C (1986) Women's experience of infertility. *Image: Journal of Nursing Scholarship,* **18**(4): 140–4.

Sandelowski M, Harris B and Holditch-Davis D (1989) Mazing: infertile couples and the quest for a child. *Image: Journal of Nursing Scholarship,* **21**(4): 220–6.

Sayers J (1982) *Biological Politics.* London: Tavistock.

Shapiro C (1982) The impact of infertility on the marital relationship. *Social Casework,* **63**(7): 387–93.

Snowden R and Snowden E (1984) *The Gift of a Child.* London: George Allan and Unwin.

Strathern M (1992) The meaning of assisted kinship. In: Stacey M (ed.) *Changing Human Reproduction*, pp. 148–69. London: Sage.

Strickler J (1992) Reproductive technology: problem or solution? *Sociology of Health and Illness*, **14**(1): 111–32.

Strong P (1979) *The Ceremonial Order of the Clinic: Parents, Doctors and Medical Bureaucracies*. London: Routledge and Kegan Paul.

Thornes B and Collard J (1979) *Who Divorces?* London: Routledge and Kegan Paul.

Townsend P and Davidson N (1982) *Inequalities in Health*. Harmondsworth: Penguin.

Veevers J (1976) The lifestyle of voluntary childless couples. In: Larson L (ed.) *The Canadian Family in Comparative Perspective*, pp. 395–411. Scarborough, Ontario: Prentice Hall.

Veevers J (1979) Voluntary childlessness: a review of issues and evidence. *Marriage and Family Review*, **2**(2): 1–26.

Weijts W, Houtkoop H and Mullen P (1993) Talking delicacy: speaking about sexuality during gynaecological consultations. *Sociology of Health and Illness*, **15**(3): 295–314.

Woollett A (1985) Childlessness: strategies for coping with infertility. *International Journal of Behavioural Development*, **8**: 473–82.

Zola I (1973) Pathways to the doctor: from person to patient. *Social Science and Medicine*, **7**: 677–89.

2

Policy issues in infertility

Liz Meerabeau

INTRODUCTION

The birth in July 1978 of Louise Brown, the first 'test tube baby', heralded 15 years of debate about reproductive technologies. Since that time, fertility treatment has frequently hit the headlines, and terms such as 'in vitro fertilisation' and 'egg donation' have become commonplace. At the time of writing, the debate has moved rapidly, within the space of a few weeks, from the 'unnaturalness' of giving birth at the age of 59 (and subsequent reports that the French government is contemplating making egg donation to postmenopausal women illegal) to accusations that doctors are 'playing God' by implanting the eggs of a white woman in a black woman and anxieties about the use of ova from aborted fetuses. In 1993, the debates were about gender selection and (following the birth of sextuplets to an unmarried couple) the 'vetting' of potential parents. Such issues will be returned to in Chapter 7 on ethics; in this chapter, they will be addressed from a social policy perspective, by examining the literature on how fertility treatment is changing our understanding of the family. The feminist literature critiquing fertility treatment will also be addressed. In the second part of the chapter, the provision of fertility treatment in the UK will be discussed and will be set in the context of some of the broader debates about prioritising, 'health gain' and consumerism.

Many people hold contradictory views about biotechnology (Yoxen and Hyde, 1987). Nelkin (1984) states that there has been a declining trust in science generally and increasing calls for greater scientific accountability and more public participation in policy making. The new reproductive technologies offer hope to infertile couples and can be seen as technological progress. On the other hand, there are concerns about unforeseen risks and about unforeseen effects on the social structure. For example, there is little systematic research on what the social effects of trade in embryos and ova would be (Stacey, 1992). Like other biotechnologies, assisted reproduction is seen as 'unnatural', although this objection could be extended to most if not all medical interventions. It also forces either doctors, or society through the legal system, to make decisions in situations in which there were once simple biological 'givens', such as the menopause, as the French legislation mentioned above illustrates. Social relations were previously rooted in natural facts, which were seen as immutable; the more legal certainty is given to social parenthood, however, the fewer assumptions we can make about biological relationships, as the German term 'split motherhood' indicates.

KINSHIP AND THE 'NORMAL' FAMILY

Although fewer than 1 in 4 households now conforms to the traditional image of a married or cohabiting couple with children (Office of Population Censuses and Surveys, 1992), the image is still a powerful one, and, as discussed in the previous chapter, those of us who do not conform to it may feel stigmatised. Strathern (1992) considers that the concept of kinship in 'Euro-America' is becoming more complex with the advent of assisted reproduction and other social changes. Kinship connects the domain of society and the domain of nature; the social arrangements provide a cultural context for the natural processes, and the family is a financial unit as well as a biological one. Blood ties are important in determining family obligations (Finch, 1989); an unambiguous kinsperson is one who is related by blood and whose social relationship is acknowledged. In assisted reproduction, the biological parent may not be the social parent. Although 'social parenthood often outranks biological parenthood' (Glover et al, 1989: p. 35), the emphasis on individuality and blood ties as the source of individual identity in our society means that it is now argued that a person has the right to know his or her origins; this may create problems for the biological parent (such as a sperm donor), and the parent has no corresponding right to seek out his or her child. The child has rights as an individual, and the state can, if necessary, intervene; this has been highlighted in a dramatic way by the series of cases in both the UK and the USA in which a child has asked through the courts to be removed from his or her parents.

Under Section 27 of the Human Fertilisation and Embryology Act, the woman who carries the child is legally the mother, whether or not the child is genetically hers. Section 28 of the Act provides for the husband or partner of a woman who has conceived through donation to be treated in law as the father of the child, as long as he consented to the treatment. Haimes (1992) has a table of the multiplicity of family relationships created through third-party conceptions; this is even more complicated when the

donor parent is a blood relative of the nurturing parent. Haimes examines
the debate on who should be told what in the case of DI and distinguishes
three phases of changing attitude: up to the early 1980s, the early to mid-
1980s and 1984 onwards. Up to the early 1980s, there was little public
awareness of DI, and secrecy was assumed, although questioned by
Snowden and Snowden (1984), who felt that secrecy would erode the fabric
of society. The Warnock Committee recommended that children should be
told how they were conceived but not the donor's identity. Since then, both
these positions have been argued, but others argue that, as in adoption, the
child should have access at the age of 18 to information about the donor's
identity. The Human Fertilisation and Embryology Act allows those
conceived by DI, egg donation or IVF to apply at the age of 18 to the
HFEA for information on whether they were born as the consequence of
treatment; they may also apply before the age of 18 if they wish to know
whether or not they are related to an intended spouse. Exactly what other
information the HFEA will be able to disclose to individuals about 'their'
egg or sperm donor will depend on what is set out in regulations, yet to be
made, under the Act. Under Section 31(5) of the 1990 Act, the regulations
will not be retrospective. Therefore, no-one who donates eggs or sperm up
to the date the regulations are made, on the basis that they will remain
anonymous, will have their identity passed on to their genetic offspring.

In Sweden, the 1983 legislation gives the child the right to identifying
information; in Australia, the Waller Report (1983) recommended that
non-identifying information should be given and full identifying information should be held on a register. The Glover Report (Glover, 1989)
recommended that EC member states should adopt the Swedish model, but
they have not as yet done so. Opinion is generally divided between the
clinical and social work professions, the latter arguing for the removal of
donor anonymity (Walby and Symons, 1990). This is based on experience
with adoption, since there are few data on people conceived by DI. The
two sides of the debate put different weight on the importance of genetic
ties and on how they prioritise the needs of one family member over those
of others, including the donor's family. Haimes reminds us that, in most
Western societies, interest in origins and families is a cultural norm and is
used to place ourselves and others socially. For example, Bruce (1990) cites
Articles 7 and 8 of the 1989 United Nations Convention on the Rights of
the Child, which state that the child has the right to a name, a nationality
and knowledge of his or her parents and the right to preserve his or her
identity. Children conceived by DI are thus being treated exceptionally in
not being given this information, and DI families are seen as 'different'.

In an earlier paper, Haimes (1990) reviewed the arguments for
anonymity of the donor – that donors would not want to incur parental
responsibility and would be embarrassed by the possible reaction of others.
The first issue could be easily resolved, Haimes claims, by clearly defining
the legal relations between child, parent and donor. It is also argued that

the child will feel stigmatised by knowing the name of his or her donor parent, but Haimes argues that this is more likely to result from gamete donation itself than from knowing the donor's name. Legal difficulties are, therefore, resolvable; emotional difficulties are often cited but not often explored. Haimes also discusses policy statements, such as those in the Warnock Report (Warnock, 1985), and the different notions of the family that are used in such reports. Haimes states that, in the Warnock Report, 'families by donation' are 'problematic but allowable', but the single person who wishes treatment is distinctly problematic since she does not conform to the ideal family type of two parents of differing sexes plus children. References to ordinary families and ordinary methods of creating a family are frequently invoked in the context of assisted reproduction; for example, in the debate about whether or not assisted conception should be allowed for postmenopausal women, some commentators have argued that this is discriminatory, because elderly men are not prevented from fathering a child by the usual means.

Strathern has recently led a team looking at 'the representation of kinship in the context of the new reproductive technologies' (Edwards et al, 1993). Price, a member of the team, has found that doctors are also concerned about where the lines should be drawn, for example whether a daughter should be able to donate eggs to her mother. Edwards and Hirsch, other members of the team, have found that lay people have a sophisticated understanding of the new technologies and their possibilities. They were sympathetic to infertile people and felt that they should be helped in whatever way possible, but they also felt that some forms of assistance were inappropriate and that limits should be placed on the actions of scientists. Franklin examined how kinship was portrayed in the parliamentary debates during the passage of the Human Fertilisation and Embryology Act 1990. The greatest controversy centred around the status and rights of the embryo and what is seen as the commodification of reproduction. In the end, the belief in technological progress prevailed, and embryo research was allowed under licence. There have also been several recent books (Mason, 1990; Douglas, 1991; Sutherland and McCall Smith, 1991) exploring legal aspects of the family with respect to assisted reproduction.

THE FEMINIST CRITIQUE

Interestingly, many feminists are wary of techniques of assisted reproduction, and shifting alliances have been made between women opposed to the new technologies and religious and other groups whose views on the family are very different from those of feminists. The feminist campaigns of the 1970s were more concerned with abortion than with assisted reproduction; in 1971, Firestone enthusiastically advocated assisted reproduction as a way in which women could escape from being defined by their biology. Since then, much of the literature has been critical. There are two underlying arguments: firstly, that much obstetric and gynaecological practice is misogynist and, secondly, that much 'malestream' science is not objective but is imbued with a particular (oppressive) view of women. Much of the literature argues that the new technologies were created in the interests of patriarchy and remove what control women have over reproduction. For example, Crowe (1985) argues that women do not have a real choice about whether or not to accept treatment, since the social pressure to have children is so great; whether or not this argument is accepted depends on whether we see ourselves as free agents or as heavily socialised by the society in which we live.

Other feminist writers (e.g. Rose, 1987) argue that doctors have too much control over deciding who is suitable for treatment. Thomas and Heberton (1991), from a social work background, have an argument similar to that of Rose; they criticise Section 13(5) of the Human Fertilisation and Embryology Act 1990, which states that 'a woman shall not be provided with treatment services unless account has been taken of the welfare of any child who may be born as a result of the treatment', which may include enquiry into any possible criminal record. Thomas and Heberton draw on a decision made before the passing of the Act, upheld by judicial review, in which treatment was withdrawn from a woman who had a conviction for prostitution and allowing premises to be used as a brothel. They query the relevance of this to her competence as a mother, and argue that doctors will increasingly decide who is 'suitable' to become a parent. The evidence that doctors are in fact acting as gatekeepers to the new technologies is not strong. Price (1993) found that the three NHS IVF units have age restrictions but that the clinicians she interviewed were reluctant to deny treatment on other grounds; they thought that 'unstable' patients would not persist with treatment. The Warnock Report (1984: para. 2.5) did not restrict treatment to married couples, although an amendment to that effect was narrowly defeated in the House of Lords during the passage of the Human Fertilisation and Embryology Act. The controversy in the UK in 1991 over virgin births did not result in treatment being withdrawn from this group of women, although the HFEA guidelines stated that they should have counselling. A US study by Leiblum and Williams (1993) reviews the argument for screening, that of safeguarding the potential child, versus the argument that full-scale screening is costly and superfluous, since most people in fertility treatment are highly motivated. Their survey of the Psychology Special Interest Group of the American Fertility Society found that the majority of respondents did not have an explicit policy but had informal criteria. The four main ones were substance abuse, physical abuse, severe marital strife and coercion by one spouse; criteria were generally more stringent the more invasive the treatment. In the UK, Humphrey et al (1991) also argue that most couples can be screened rather than undergoing intensive investigation.

There are, therefore, a variety of debates, not always well founded on fact, about whether doctors act as gatekeepers or, alternatively, persuade women to accept unwanted treatment. Both Stanworth and her contributors (1987) and Eichler (1987) point out that there are a variety of reproductive technologies and that feminists should not dismiss them out of hand, but learn as much as possible about them in order to further women's aims. They argue that medical advances have offered women more control over their reproductive lives, although they have, on the other hand, increased the potential for others to take control over them, which can only be countered by knowledge. Stanworth (1987) and Eichler (1987) also argue that women have varying needs, depending on their culture and prior experience, and that it is important to see reproductive technologies as just one element of the politics and organisation of health care in general.

THE HISTORY OF FERTILITY TREATMENT

Pfeffer (1987) argues that the development of techniques to treat infertility has been generated by doctors eager to develop an expertise and to distance themselves from the 'sordid' routine treatments, rather than in response to the requests and needs of patients. Pfeffer (1987, 1993) discusses the history of fertility treatment in the UK in the context of various concerns about the birth rate and 'racial degeneration', the latter prompted by a venereal disease epidemic before and during World War I. Concern about the birth rate during World War II, exacerbated by lack of information (there was no 1941 census), led to the 1943 Royal Commission on Population, which reported 5 years later. Its recommendation that fertility and family planning services should be part of the NHS was not acted upon; postwar social reforms 'reinstated the belief that a married woman's reproductive capacity was her husband's affair' (Pfeffer, 1993: p. 109). Although some GPs were keen to take on fertility work in the early days of the NHS, they mostly found it too demanding. The Family Planning Association had a role after 1945, especially outside London; by 1960, 246 of its 311 clinics offered fertility advice, although this was mainly the temperature chart and advice on technique. This source of advice dwindled after family planning clinics were taken into the NHS in 1974.

Both Warnock (1985) and Pfeffer (1987) outline the ethical controversies that surrounded treatment for infertility by the use of DI. This has been used for a considerable period of time but was publicised only in 1945; not only was it regarded as a threat to the inviolability of the marital relationship, but also DI in the interwar period was tainted by its association with eugenics, and by 1945 it was linked to anxieties about scientific 'progress' fuelled by the atom bomb and by the use of artificial insemination for breeding cattle. The 1948 Commission appointed by the Archbishop of Canterbury recommended that DI should be a criminal offence, and it was strongly discouraged by the 1960 Feversham Report. During the 1960s, the climate became more liberal, and DI gradually became more acceptable. Nevertheless, a BMA survey in 1971 found that only 10 out of 513 gynaecologists provided it, although another 91 said they would arrange it. The Peel Committee (Panel of Human Artificial Insemination Report, 1973) recommended that DI should be available on the NHS, but in 1977, the Royal College of Obstetrics and Gynaecology (RCOG) found that there were only 22 DI centres in the UK, the greatest problem being lack of finance. As recently as 1988, the Social Attitudes Survey found that only 50% of the general public questioned thought that DI should be legal (Harding, 1988). This may have changed as the debate has moved on to yet more controversial forms of treatment and the advent of AIDS has led to more widespread discussion of male sexuality.

After the war, the basal body temperature chart became the routine test, but treatment of failure to ovulate was *ad hoc* and not very successful. The major technical innovation of hormonal stimulation was introduced in the 1960s and aroused concern about its safety in the wake of the thalidomide scandal and about its appropriateness as awareness of world over-population grew. Multiple births hit the headlines and have continued to do so, most notably with the Walton sextuplets in the mid 1980s.

The third major innovation in fertility treatment was in vitro fertilisation, which was again controversial; the two pioneers, Steptoe and Edwards, were unable to obtain funding for much of their work (Edwards and Steptoe, 1980). Edwards' original work in genetics was on mice, whereas Steptoe developed the laparoscopic technique. Their first unsuccessful IVF attempt was in 1971; Lesley Brown became the first woman to bear a child through IVF in 1978. Use of the technique then increased quite rapidly, and in 1983 there were 579 women treated, resulting in 192 conceptions (Warnock Report, 1984).

THE ADVENT OF LEGISLATION

The Committee of Enquiry into Human Fertilisation and Embryology (the Warnock Committee) was set up in 1982; its terms of reference were 'To consider recent and potential developments in medicine and science related to human fertilisation and embryology; to consider what policies and safeguards should be applied, including consideration of the social, ethical and legal implications of these developments; and to make recommenda-tions' (Warnock, 1985: p. 4). The committee included a philosopher (the chair, Mary Warnock) and representatives from law, medicine, theology, natural science and psychology. The work was divided into two sections, one reviewing infertility and current services, the other discussing 'the pursuit of knowledge', primarily embryo research. The main treatments discussed were artificial insemination, IVF, egg donation, surrogacy and freezing eggs. There was particular controversy over the point at which research on the embryo should be permitted, leading to a minority report (as there was on surrogacy). Organisations such as the Society for the Protection of Unborn Children and LIFE opposed it at any stage. The majority of the committee felt that the early embryo was so different from a full human being that it might 'legitimately be used as a means to an end that was good for other humans' (Warnock, 1985: p. xv). There ensued a debate on the definition of what a 'very early' embryo was. The RCOG (1983) suggested that the criterion should relate to neural development, thought to take place around day 17; the Medical Research Council (MRC) (1985) suggested day 14, the end of the implantation stage and the formation of the 'primitive streak' or the beginning of differentiation into embryo and placenta, and this was eventually adopted.

While Warnock was reporting, surrogacy hit the headlines, with the birth of Baby Cotton. This prompted a Conservative backbencher, Anna McCurley, to introduce a Private Member's Bill to outlaw surrogacy, but it did not receive government support since Warnock was imminently expected, and had a brief career (commercial surrogacy was eventually prohibited by the Surrogacy Arrangements Act 1985). The Conservative MP Enoch Powell was more successful; in early 1985, having read the Warnock Report, he placed a Private Member's Bill, the Unborn Children (Protection) Bill, before the House of Commons, thus pre-empting Government legislation. If passed, it would have prohibited embryo research altogether, on the grounds that a fertilised egg should have full legal protection. It would also have made in vitro fertilisation very bureaucratic, since it required the express written consent of a Minister to enable a named woman to 'bear a child by embryo insertion'; the punishment for contravention would have been up to 2 years' imprisonment. Adroit use of parliamentary procedure, and considerable lobbying by religious communities, kept the bill afloat from January to March, when it got through its committee stage; the government, including the Health Minister, Kenneth Clarke, remained studiedly neutral. On May 5th it was talked out, amid scenes of uproar, in which Dafydd Wigley, who was passionately opposed to the Bill on the grounds that it would prevent research into genetic disease, damaged the Speaker's chair. On May 9th, its last chance seemed to disappear when Janet Fookes, Conservative MP for Plymouth, whose kerb crawling Bill preceded the Powell Bill in the Parliamentary business, refused to give way. However, the Bill was resurrected yet again on May 23rd by Andrew Bowden, the Conservative MP for Brighton Kemp Town and again on June 7th, when a group led by Dennis Skinner, the Labour MP for Bolsover, talked it out. The Bill returned in January 1986, brought forward by another MP, Kenneth Hargreaves, but it was ultimately defeated, partly, Crowe (1990) claims, through the lobbying of PROGRESS, a coalition of clinicians, geneticists and developmental physiologists backed by the British Medical Association (BMA), the Family Planning Association, MIND, Mencap and the National Association for the Childless.

It was thought by commentators that the strength of support that the Powell Bill had attracted in its early stages would constrain the eventual government legislation, although this proved not to be the case. The Voluntary Licensing Authority was set up in 1985, to be followed by the Interim Licensing Authority; the HFEA (1991) began licensing in September 1991. In 1987, a DHSS White Paper sought views on whether there should be control by a licensing authority, whether couples requesting ovum or sperm donation should be vetted as in adoption and whether a child resulting from egg or embryo donation should have the same legal status as one from DI. (Clause 27 of the Family Law Reform Bill of 1986 made provision for the child of DI to be legitimate if the social father had consented to his wife's insemination.) Views were also sought on whether egg donation should be prohibited, whether there should be a register with donor information and whether the child should be told the donor's name on reaching maturity. The arguments for embryo experimentation were also laid out. The Human Fertilisation and Embryology Bill was introduced in November 1989; there were concerns that the Bill would be used as a vehicle for MPs opposed to abortion to lower the gestational age limit, but its passage was relatively smooth and it was enacted in November 1990. The Human Fertilisation and Embryology Act and work of the HFEA are discussed in Chapter 8.

RECENT DEVELOPMENTS

The most recent controversies, both of which have required deliberation by the HFEA, have been the treatment of postmenopausal women, and the use of fetal ova, leading to debates about the 'naturalness' of interventions and phrases such as 'designer children'. 'The lid on Pandora's box is open', said Stuart Horner, chair of the BMA ethics committee (Jones, 1994a). Many writers (e.g. Jones, 1994a; Neuberger, 1994) have pointed out that, by definition, medical interventions are unnatural. Robert Winston (1993) expressed worries that hardening of public opinion against the activities of the Italian, Dr Antinori, in treating older women would bring 'a highly valuable and vulnerable technology into public disrepute', since doctors and scientists were suspected of 'tampering with the very elements of human life'.

In the current controversy around the use of fetal ovarian tissue, two frequent arguments are that a resulting child would find it difficult to come to terms with the fact that his or her mother had never really lived and the risk of fetuses being conceived solely for the purpose of producing ovarian tissue. Roger Gosden, the Edinburgh scientist working on animal fetuses, is reported to have had letters addressed to him as 'Dr Frankenstein', again an illustration of the imagery that this technology evokes.

The technology has emerged since the legislation was framed; at the time of writing, the HFEA has banned the use of fetal and cadaveric eggs for treatment (although they may be used for research), following a 6-month consultation period on the discussion paper, 'Donated Ovarian Tissue in Embryo Research and Assisted Conception' (see Chapter 8). The Royal College of Midwives (RCM), Royal College of Nursing (RCN) and BMA consider that if there is a shortage of eggs, this may be best addressed by increasing the number of live donors (Dillner, 1994). Prior to this, in April 1994, Dame Jill Knight successfully tabled an amendment to the Criminal Justice and Public Order Bill, prohibiting the use of cells from embryos or fetuses for the purpose of providing fertility services.

A poll for the *Observer* (Jones, 1994b) showed that over one-third of those questioned thought it could be right to use aborted fetuses for fertility treatment; 57% were against. However, only 33% believed that the law should be tightened and 62% thought doctors and or patients should decide. Fifty-two per cent believed that fertility treatment should be widely available on the NHS and 55% that society places too much emphasis on having children. Seventy-seven per cent agreed that it was easy for those who had not experienced infertility to moralise about couples with difficulties. In the same issue of the *Observer*, attention was drawn to the lack of follow-up studies on IVF children (McKie, 1994), although two recent studies (Golombok et al, 1993; Weaver et al, 1993) show positive outcomes for the parent–child relationship.

Plommer et al (1994) review the differing approaches to regulating fertility treatment. Germany and Sweden have imposed restrictive legal codes, and France may soon join them. Both ban the implantation of a donated egg, and thus the debate on postmenopausal motherhood cannot arise; the maximum penalty in Germany, where there are understandable sensitivities about eugenics, is 3 years' imprisonment. Italy and the USA have little regulation and leave it up to doctors and patients; left-wing members of the parliamentary Bioethics Committee have called for legislation in Italy, but there is little indication that this will happen in the USA. The UK is in the middle of the spectrum and is in the vanguard in having a regulatory authority. There is no correlation between restrictiveness or otherwise and whether treatment is private or state provided, since in Germany treatment is free and in France four cycles of IVF are free (Kon, 1993).

PROVISION OF FERTILITY SERVICES

Although the sanctity of human life provides the dominant motif in the debates, a subtheme is the use of resources within the NHS. The infertile are at a disadvantage here, since the problem cannot be construed as life threatening. Attempts to equate the mental pain of infertility with other, more physical, types of pain (Lilford, quoted by Kon, 1993) may be counterproductive, since it can seem as if the pain of, for example, cancer and arthritis of the hip are being minimised. A recent US study, however, (Domar et al, 1993), which uses a symptom checklist, claims that the scores of infertile people were similar to those of people with cancer and hypertension, although lower than those with chronic pain and HIV. The Warnock Committee (Warnock, 1985: pp. 9–10) countered the argument that infertility is not life threatening by claiming that the health service deals with many non-lifethreatening malfunctions and that the inability to have children should be treated, like any other malfunction. Dr Frank Atherton, Bradford's Director of Public Health, argues that infertility is an illness requiring treatment in the same way as varicose veins or ischaemic heart disease (Kon, 1993). Doctor Antinori, currently very much in the news for his treatment of postmenopausal women, speaks of 'the inalienable civil right to have a child' (Bonazzi, 1993). Blyth (1990) quotes the United States Supreme Court assertion that women have a 'fundamental right to bear or beget children'. Liu (1991) examines whether or not there can be a right to reproduce, by analysing Article 12 of the European Convention on Human Rights and discussing whether such a right entails only unaided biological parenthood or also the right to be helped to achieve parenthood.

Several surveys of fertility services in the UK have been undertaken. Owens and Read (1979) surveyed 303 members and prospective members of the National Association for the Childless (NAC, now ISSUE). More than half found the GP and hospital doctors to be helpful; only one-quarter found the GP, and one-fifth for the hospital doctor, not helpful. Seventy-two per cent saw a specialist within 6 months of first seeing the GP; 10%, however, were neither referred on nor successfully treated. Forty per cent felt that everything possible had been done. The best aspects of treatment were sympathetic attitudes from staff (29% of wives, 22% of husbands) and good, up-to-date treatment (19% and 10% respectively). The worst were delay (29% and 22% respectively), lack of sympathy (16% of each) and lack of information (9% and 10% respectively). The major improvements suggested were more prompt treatment, a more sympathetic attitude and more information. Eighteen per cent had tried the private sector first, and 22% had transferred from the NHS to the private sector, but private medicine was no more likely to be successful; its main advantage was speed.

The Warnock Report (Warnock, 1985) found that there were few data on the provision of services and recommended a large-scale survey; a comprehensive survey was commissioned by Frank Dobson, Shadow Minister of Health (Mathieson, 1986), in consultation with Robert

Winston of Hammersmith Hospital, involving a postal survey of the 200 district health authorities (DHAs) of England and Wales. Many districts did not know their success rates or average length of attendance. The modal length of waiting lists was 10–20 weeks. Of the 170 DHAs that responded, only 71 had separate fertility clinics. Forty-eight Districts provided literature or counselling, and 40 provided the three basic tests deemed necessary (ultrasonography, rapid radioimmune assay of hormones and tubal surgery with a microscope). The overall picture was of a patchy service, facilities being concentrated in the south of England. Patients trailed from one clinic to another, with long waits in between appointments, providing 'much time for reflection, but little information to reflect on'.

At the time, there was one NHS-funded IVF clinic, in Manchester, which had a 4-year waiting list. There were only 53 DI clinics nationally, 25 of which were private. Mathieson also gave some data on the cost of private treatment, which ranged from £45 for DI to £2000 for one cycle of IVF.

A similar impression is given by Pfeffer and Quick's London survey (1988), which recommends a coordinated service, with GPs taking on more of the preliminary investigations, using clear protocols, and regional tertiary or specialist centres. They recommended that there should be more data collected on outcomes, including length of time in treatment, a key worker should have responsibility for giving information, clinic visits should be reduced by coordinating tests and the hours for tests should be more flexible. In particular, the quality of semen testing needed to be reviewed, a point also made by the Congress of the United States Office of Technology Assessment (1988) and, more recently, by Byrd (1992). Pfeffer and Quick found that some services, such as rapid radioimmune assay, were not used, even though the service was provided free as a condition of the drug company's product licence. They commented that Warnock's recommendations had not been implemented; a similar picture of services in Scotland was gained by a survey by NAC (now ISSUE), outlined (in October 1989) in *Conceive*.

An update of the Mathieson survey, by Harriet Harman, at that time (1990) Shadow Minister of Health, commented on the lack of centrally held information on fertility services. Based on a survey of DHAs, the report commented that women living in the Oxford or West Midlands region had a better chance of referral to a designated fertility clinic than did women in the North Western region. In the former, there were 18.8 clinics per one million women aged 15–44; in the latter, 1.2. Districts reported that little literature was available either to GPs or to patients and that most health authorities relied on GPs' knowledge of the networks.

The College of Health was commissioned by ISSUE, the national fertility association, to undertake a survey of fertility services in the whole UK for National Fertility Week in May 1993. A postal questionnaire was sent to all purchasing authorities, with an 84.5% response rate. Only 21%

of respondents had a formal policy for purchasing fertility services; 41% used a block contract, and 22% were unable to give details of the fertility services purchased. Nineteen per cent did not purchase IVF, and 21% did not purchase GIFT (gamete intrafallopian transfer); these were also the treatments for which selection criteria were more likely to be used. Definitions of the length of time trying, and what constitutes a stable relationship, varied between Authorities.

A report by Kon (1993), also for National Fertility Week, commissioned by the two self-help groups, ISSUE and Child, states that 'Untreated infertility is an enormous social and economic handicap to the nation', leading to loss of productivity and absenteeism (unfortunately no data are provided to support this argument). The report states that there are only six fully-funded, NHS-assisted conception centres in the UK, and it estimates that 90% of IVF children are conceived by private treatment. Kon (1993) quotes figures for a 'take-home baby' of £5000–6000, rising to £23 000 for a woman over 40. The report estimates that the provision of two cycles of IVF/GIFT to 50 couples would involve an extra annual expenditure of about £140 000. Reduction in the use of tubal surgery would then save £20 000–30 000. Extra neonatal care would cost about £30 000.

EFFECTIVENESS AND EFFICIENCY

One consultant in the Kon Report commented that the NHS spent 'an absolute fortune' on fertility treatment but that much of the money was wasted in ineffective treatment, a point that could be made in relation to many other treatments (DoH, 1993). Bulletin 3 of Effective Health Care (1992), based on a comprehensive review of the literature, found that several treatments, such as that for amenorrhoea and IVF with embryo transfer, are effective, but that services are generally poorly organised. IVF with embryo transfer results in maternity rates of about 11% per cycle of treatment, whereas surgery on severely damaged fallopian tubes has a success rate of only 6%; the authors suggest that tubal surgery should be used only for milder disease. Success rates in the larger centres are double those of smaller ones, owing to a wider range of treatments and greater expertise. The report also comments on the resources wasted on duplicate testing when couples change treatment centres and recommends that there should be clear treatment protocols to prevent this happening. A protocol has, for example, been developed in Wakefield and includes aspects of primary care management and a co-op card (NHSME News, 1993). A costing model is developed that includes the extra antenatal and neonatal services generated by multiple births and low birthweight babies. For a population of 250 000 with about 230 consultant referrals per year, the annual cost is estimated as £750 000. Limits to resources, however, may lead to implicit or explicit rationing, as discussed further below. The authors conclude that there is no 'technical fix', such as a formula by which purchasing authorities can decide whether or not to purchase fertility treatment, and that this can make it particularly difficult for staff in the specialist centres, who may have to manage treatment differently, depending on where their patient lives and what their purchasing authority will fund. Purchasers should use maternity rates to compare the reported success of treatment centres, taking into account length of follow-up, length of treatment cycle and patient characteristics. (The live birth rate overestimates success, because of the incidence of multiple births.) The report also calls for well-designed, randomised controlled trials to evaluate the effectiveness of treatments and the need for valid and standardised measures of quality of life for research in this area.

GAUGING PRIORITIES

Effective Health Care (1992) comments that assisted conception is one of the few technologies that has been explicitly rationed in many districts. A much-publicised method of prioritising treatment is the Oregon process, which combines public opinion with an assessment of cost–utility; in Oregon, assisted conception for tubal problems ranked 701 out of 714 conditions considered (Dixon and Gilbert Welch, 1991); generally, both cosmetic surgery and fertility treatment are ranked low. The method has proved to be controversial and may be better for deciding between different treatments for the same problem than for trying to rank different problems; the rankings are very sensitive to how questions are phrased (Bowling, 1992). Pollock and Pfeffer (1993) also urge that all attempts to gauge public opinion on prioritising services should be treated with caution, since people may not realise the implications of their decisions. Current guidance (NHSME, 1994) suggests that purchasers of health care should involve their local community health councils and provide them with information about contracts. Davies (1993), discussing the ACHCEW document *Rationing Health Care: Should CHCs Help?*', says that the government would like to involve community health councils in setting health-care priorities but that the latter are reluctant to be seen to legitimise the decision to leave some health needs unmet. ACHCEW attributes the growing interest in the topic to a perception that the gap between the technically achievable and the affordable is widening and is pushed further up the agenda by the purchaser–provider split, the Patient's Charter (DoH, 1991) and the *Health of the Nation* (DoH, 1992). Traditionally, more implicit mechanisms, such as waiting lists and spreading services thinly, were used to control demand (Hunter, 1991).

Freemantle et al (1992) consider that there is a tension between equity and maximising health gain, since for the latter, only women who stand

most chance of succeeding will be offered fertility treatment. Appleby
(1993) states that limited resources imply trade-offs with other forms of
care and a calculation of the wider opportunity costs of infertility
treatment to society. Economic evaluation is complicated by many factors,
for example what value should be placed on a new life (and whether it is
only a private benefit to the couple or a benefit to society). Costs can also
be problematic, for example estimating the cost of treatment failure, not
only to the NHS but also in terms of emotional distress. Outcomes are also
not simple and involve questions such as what sorts of outcome should be
measured and over what time scale. There is then the problem of
synthesising the material on outcomes into a meaningful whole and using it
to make decisions on which problems should be treated and which should
not. Perhaps the most controversial measure developed has been the
QALY, or Quality Adjusted Life Year, based on the utilitarian principle
that people will try to avoid disability and pain, and trying to assess the
value that they will put on this avoidance. Like the Oregon experiment, the
QALY has been criticised on the grounds that, for many of us, the choices
may be hypothetical and abstract, and the data generated are, therefore, of
dubious validity and reliability.

CONSUMER OPINION

A further element of the new internal market in the NHS is the greater
emphasis on consumer opinion. Owens and Read (1979) represent an early
attempt to gauge patient satisfaction with fertility services; an early review
of patient satisfaction studies in general was conducted by Locker and
Dunt (1978). Since then, the emphasis on consumer satisfaction has
increased, and there is a growing emphasis on commercial concepts, such
as total quality management. Not all evaluations are currently well
designed (Michie and Kidd, 1994); Lyell (1994) cites Jocelyn Cornwell of
the Audit Commission, who states that there is no systematic approach to
what patients want, and there is a tendency to concentrate on waiting times
and 'hotel' services, such as food, rather than standards of clinical care or
communication. Cornwell recommends that all hospitals should have a
plan for information-giving and that service contracts should set out
information requirements.
  Williamson (1992) provides a theoretical framework for understanding
consumerism in health care and discusses the role of pressure groups. Most
consumer pressure groups form alliances with 'proto-professionals', i.e.
professionals who recognise the needs of consumers and can give advice
and help in the interpretation of technical data, put new standards into
practice and act as positive role models for their colleagues. Consumer
groups can also give the professional a platform and a high profile,
providing that the group is not too radical. ISSUE illustrates Williamson's

argument well; both it and the organisation Child have worked closely with a variety of fertility specialists. John Dickson, the director of ISSUE, also outlines the successful campaign to influence the purchasing decisions of district health authorities in Yorkshire and Mersey RHAs (Dickson, 1992) and, more recently, reports on a campaign to influence MPs (*Conceive*, January 1994).

CONCLUSION

As this chapter has shown, fertility treatment receives considerable publicity and results in considerable ethical debate. It is perhaps inevitable that services will vary geographically, since the history of the NHS has been one of trying to achieve a degree of equity for all services, while avoiding centralisation. The purchaser–provider split in the NHS offers both opportunities and threats, since there is a greater emphasis on consumer opinion and also more explicit mechanisms for decision-making in health care; the threat is that fertility services are not generally viewed as a priority.

References

Appleby J (1993) Steptoe ... and sons ... and daughters. *Health Service Journal*, 12 August; 38–9.

Blyth E (1990) Assisted reproduction: what's in it for children? *Children and Society*, **4**(2): 167–82.

Bonazzi M (1993) Italian doctor 'consulted by 50 women'. *Guardian*, 21 July.

Bowling A (1992) Setting priorities in health: the Oregon experiment. *Nursing Standard*, **6**: 28–32.

Bruce N (1990) On the importance of genetic knowledge. *Children and Society*, **4**(2): 183–96.

Byrd W (1992) Quality assurance in the reproductive biology laboratory. *Archives of Pathology and Laboratory Medicine*, **116**: 418–22.

College of Health (1993) *Report of the National Survey of the Funding and Provision of Fertility Services*. London: College of Health.

Conceive (1989) Welwyn Garden City. Serono.

Congress of the United States Office of Technology Assessment (1988) *Infertility: Medical and Social Choices*. Washington, DC: Congress.

Crowe C (1985) 'Women want it': in vitro fertilization and women's motivations for participation. *Women's Studies International Forum*, **8**(6): 547–52.

Crowe C (1990) Whose mind over whose matter? Women, in vitro fertilisation and the development of scientific knowledge. In: McNeil M,

Varcoe I and Yearley S (eds) *The New Reproductive Technologies*, pp. 27–57. London: Macmillan.

Davies P (1993) Damned if they do, damned if they don't. *Health Service Journal*, 27 May: 14.

Dickson J (1992) Campaign for increasing infertility awareness and resources. *Conceive*, **23**: 1.

Dillner L (1994) Rejected concept. *Nursing Times*, **90**(31): 16.

Dixon J and Gilbert Welch J (1991) Priority setting: lessons from Oregon. *Lancet*, **337**: 891–4.

DoH (1991) The Patient's Charter. London: HMSO.

DoH (1992) The Health of the Nation. A Strategy for Health in England. London HMSO.

DoH (1993) *Research for Health*. London: DoH.

Domar A, Zuttermeister P and Friedman R (1993) The psychological impact of infertility: a comparison with patients with other medical conditions. *Journal of Psychosomatic Obstetrics and Gynaecology*, **14**: 145–52.

Douglas G (1991) *Law, Fertility and Reproduction*. London: Sweet and Maxwell.

Edwards J, Franklin S, Hirsch E, Price F and Strathern M (1993) *Technologies of Procreation: Kinship in the Age of Assisted Conception*. Manchester: Manchester University Press.

Edwards R and Steptoe P (1980) *A Matter of Life: The Story of a Medical Breakthrough*. London: Hutchinson.

Effective Health Care (1992) *The Management of Subfertility*. Issue 3. Leeds: Leeds University.

Eichler M (1987) Some minimal principles concerning the new reproductive technologies. In: Overall C (ed.) *The Future of Human Reproduction*. Ontario: The Women's Press.

Finch J (1989) *Family Obligations and Social Change*. Cambridge: Polity Press.

Firestone S (1971) *The Dialectic of Sex*. London: Jonathan Cape.

Freemantle N, Song F and Sheldon T (1992) Tu-be or not tu-be. *Health Service Journal*, 13 August: 24–5.

Glover J (1989) *Fertility and the Family: The Glover Report on Reproductive Technologies to the European Commission*. London: Fourth Estate.

Golombok S, Cook R, Bish A and Murray C (1993) Quality of parenting in families created by the new reproductive technologies: a brief report of preliminary findings. *Journal of Psychosomatic Obstetrics and Gynaecology*, **14**: 17–22

Haimes E (1990) Recreating the family? Policy considerations relating to the 'new' reproductive technologies. In: McNeil M, Varcoe I and Yearley S (eds) *The New Reproductive Technologies*, pp. 154–72. London: Macmillan.

Haimes E (1992) Gamete donation and the social management of genetic origins. In: Stacey M (ed.) *Changing Human Reproduction*, pp. 119–49. London: Sage.

Harding S (1988) Trends in permissiveness. In: Jowell R (ed.) *British Social Attitudes, 5th Report*. Aldershot: Gower.

Harman H (1990) *Trying for a Baby*. London: House of Commons.

HFEA (1991) Code of Practice. London: HFEA.

Human Fertilisation and Embryology Act (1990) London: HMSO.

Humphrey M, Humphrey H and Ainsworth-Smith I (1991) Screening couples for parenthood by donor insemination. *Social Science and Medicine*, **32**(3): 273–8.

Hunter D (1991) Pain of going public. *Health Service Journal*, 20 August: 20.

Jones J (1994a) Mother still knows best? *Observer*, 2 January.

Jones J (1994b) Designer babies repel public, poll reveals. *Observer*, 9 January.

Kon A (1993) *Infertility: The Real Costs*. Birmingham and Middlesex: ISSUE/CHILD.

Leiblum S and Williams E (1993) Screening in or out of the new reproductive options: who decides and why. *Journal of Psychosomatic Obstetrics and Gynaecology*, **14**: 37–44.

Liu A (1991) *Artificial Reproduction and Reproductive Rights*. Aldershot: Dartmouth.

Locker D and Dunt D (1978) Theoretical and methodological issues in sociological studies of consumer satisfaction with medical care. *Social Science and Medicine*, **12**: 283–92.

Lyell J (1994) Be my guest. *Health Service Journal*, 3 March: 14–15.

McKie R (1994) Dangers to test-tube babies totally ignored. *Observer*, 9 January.

Mason J (1990) *Medico-legal Aspects of Reproduction and Parenthood*. Aldershot: Dartmouth.

Mason M-C (1993) *Male Infertility: Men Talking*. London: Routledge.

Mathieson D (1986) *Infertility Services in the NHS: What's Going On?* Report prepared for Frank Dobson MP, House of Commons.

Medical Research Council (1985) *Report of the Inquiry into Human Fertilisation and Embryology: Medical Research Council Response*. London: MRC.

Michie S and Kidd J (1994) Happy ever after. *Health Service Journal*, 3 February: 27.

Nelkin D (1984) *Science as Intellectual Property: Who Controls Research?* London: Collier-Macmillan.

Neuberger J (1994) Mothers' little helper. *Health Service Journal*, 20 January: 21.

NHSME (1994) *The Operation of Community Health Councils*. EL(94)4. Leeds: NHSME.

NHSME News (1993) August. Available from the NHS Executive Communications Unit, Quarry House, Leeds.

Office of Population Censuses and Surveys (1992) *1990 General Household Survey*. London: HMSO.

Owens D and Read M (1979) *The Provision, Use and Evaluation of Medical Services for the Subfertile*. SRU Working paper no. 4. Cardiff: SRU.

Panel on Human Artificial Insemination (Peel Committee) Report (1973) *British Medical Journal*, 1 (supplement): 3–5.

Pfeffer N (1987) Artificial insemination, in vitro fertilisation and the stigma of infertility. In: Stanworth M (ed.) *Reproductive Technologies: Gender, Motherhood and Medicine*, pp. 81–97. Oxford: Basil Blackwell/Polity Press.

Pfeffer N (1993) *The Stork and the Syringe*. Oxford: Polity Press.

Pfeffer N and Quick A (1988) *Infertility Services: A Desperate Case*. London: GLACHC.

Plommer L, Vulliamy E, McIvor G et al (1994) Improvised guidelines on motherhood's brave new world. *Guardian*, 5 January.

Pollock A and Pfeffer N (1993) Doors of perception. *Health Service Journal*, 2 September: 26–8.

Price F (1993) Clinical practices and concerns. In Edwards J, Franklin S, Hirsch E, Price F and Strathern M (1993) *Technologies of Procreation: Kinship in the Age of Assisted Conception*. Manchester: Manchester University Press.

RCOG (1983) *Report of the Royal College of Obstetricians and Gynaecologists Ethics Committee on in vitro Fertilisation and Embryo Replacement or Transfer*. London: RCOG.

Rose H (1987) Victorian values in the test-tube: The politics of reproductive science. In: Stanworth M (ed.) *Reproductive Technologies: Gender, Motherhood and Medicine*, pp. 151–173. Oxford: Basil Blackwell/Polity Press.

Snowden R and Snowden E (1984) *The Gift of a Child*. London: George Allen and Unwin.

Stacey M (1992) Social dimensions of assisted reproduction. In: Stacey M (ed.) *Changing Human Reproduction*, pp. 9–47. London: Sage.

Stanworth M (ed.) (1987) *Reproductive Technologies: Gender, Motherhood and Medicine*. Oxford: Basil Blackwell/Polity Press.

Strathern M (1992) The meaning of assisted kinship. In: Stacey M (ed.) *Changing Human Reproduction*, pp. 148–69. London: Sage.

Sutherland E and McCall Smith A (1991) *Family Rights: Family Law and Medical Advance*. Edinburgh: Edinburgh University Press.

Thomas T and Heberton B (1991) Tin opener for a can of worms. *Health Service Journal*, 8 August: 21.

Walby C and Symons B (1990) *Who am I? Identity, Adoption and Human Fertilisation*. London: British Agencies for Adoption and Fostering.

Waller Report (1983) *Committee To Consider the Social, Ethical and Legal Issues Arising from in vitro Fertilisation: Report on Donor Gametes in in vitro Fertilisation*. Victoria Australia: Government of Victoria.

Warnock M (1984) *Report of the Committee of Inquiry into Human Fertilisation and Embryology.* London: HMSO.

Warnock M (1985) *A Question of Life: the Warnock Report on Human Fertilisation and Embryology.* Oxford: Basil Blackwell.

Weaver S, Clifford E, Gordon A, Hay D and Robinson J (1993) A follow-up study of 'successful' IVF/GIFT couples: social-emotional well-being and adjustment to parenthood. *Journal of Psychosomatic Obstetrics and Gynaecology*, **14**: 5–16.

Williamson C (1992) *Whose Standards?* Buckingham: Open University Press.

Winston R (1993) Menopause for thought. *Guardian*, 21 July.

Yoxen E and Hyde B (1987) *The Social Impact of Biotechnology.* Luxembourg: Office for Official Publications of the European Community.

3

The epidemiology of infertility

Stephen Bennett and Allan Templeton

INTRODUCTION

Epidemiology is the study of groups of individuals and the way in which a particular health problem impinges on the group. This approach to the study of disease was first applied to the investigation of infectious disease epidemics in the nineteenth century, when it was realised that comparisons of affected and unaffected individuals could be used to identify likely causative factors and modes of transmission and to suggest possible therapeutic approaches. Since that time, epidemiological techniques have been widely adopted in all fields of medicine, and information gathered on the incidence or prevalence of a particular problem within the community is obviously of great relevance, not only to the clinicians directly involved, but also to all those concerned with the purchase or provision of health-care services.

Epidemiological studies can be broadly classified into three types. *Descriptive studies* look at the patterns of distribution of disease in populations, including the patterns of incidence or prevalence in different areas or populations and the changes with time. Such studies may demonstrate correlations with social, economic or environmental factors but, in general, do not allow conclusions to be drawn on causation. The bulk of epidemiological studies in infertility are of this general type. *Analytical studies* are used to test the hypotheses generated by descriptive studies and may either be prospective (cohort studies) or retrospective (case –control studies). Only a relatively small number of studies of this type have been reported in the infertility literature. *Interventional studies* are used to assess the benefits obtained by protecting against a suspected harmful environmental agent and, as a result, can prove a causal relationship. Unfortunately, almost no studies of this type have been published in the field of infertility.

In this chapter, we will review the available evidence relating to the epidemiology of infertility, both from this country and from abroad (including evidence for secular changes), and discuss the advantages and disadvantages of various investigative methods.

DEFINITION OF INFERTILITY

There are considerable problems involved in studying the epidemiology of infertility, not least of which is an accurate definition of the condition in the first place. For example, should a couple who have no living children be considered infertile if they have previously had pregnancies that have resulted in miscarriage or stillbirth? On a more philosophical level, should a couple who do not wish to have children but who do not use contraception be considered infertile if they fail to conceive? One possible definition of infertility, which has been widely adopted and which addresses some of these points, is 'a lack of conception following regular, unprotected intercourse'. The length of time that must elapse, however, before a couple are accepted as infertile by this definition varies considerably between different authorities. The World Health Organisation (WHO) recommends a 2-year definition, while the majority of papers published in this field use a 1-year time limit. A second problem arises with defining how frequently intercourse must be occurring before it can be deemed 'regular'. Thirdly, infertility is a condition persisting over a considerable length of time; couples will vary their frequency of intercourse at different times, contraception may be used sporadically to avoid pregnancy at particular times and relationships may break down, with separation of partners and formation of new couples.

Another problem that arises in any study of this condition is how to classify women who successfully conceive after a prolonged length of time, either with their first or subsequent pregnancies. It may seem illogical to classify the parents of a family of four as infertile simply because it took them more than 2 years to conceive each child, but that family may have sought medical help at some stage. Various authors have suggested that infertility should be classified into resolved and unresolved subgroups; the definition of infertility will, however, remain imprecise, since the infertile population consists of not only sterile, but also subfertile, individuals.

METHODOLOGY

While accepting these limitations, there are a number of methods that can be employed to approach the study of infertility in the community. The first of these is an examination of routinely collected national statistics, such as the reports from the Office of Population Censuses and Surveys on the decennial national censuses, and the General Household Survey (OPCS, 1989). The data collected by the censuses give information on marital status and long-term childlessness within marriage, which could formerly be taken as a proxy measurement of the incidence of infertility in the community. Since the advent of oral contraception and the opportunity to plan family size, there has been an increase in voluntary infertility, together with an increase in delayed childbearing. As a result, examination of census data has become a less useful epidemiological method in the study of infertility. Another development that has further reduced the usefulness of this particular approach has been the swing towards childbirth (and hence infertility) outside marriage, representing a large subgroup that cannot be identified by this method.

The General Household Survey is a more detailed, interview-based report obtained by sampling 10% of households on a national basis. This provides information regarding fertility issues, but, like censuses, it shares the same drawback that the data are being collected for other purposes, and hence questions that might be considered pertinent by a specialist in the field of infertility are not covered. In some other countries, notably France and the USA, regular interview-based fertility surveys are carried out on a national basis. Such surveys are obviously far more specific and informative than are census data, and, when repeated, they produce valuable information on secular trends in prevalence, which is of particular value in planning future health-care provision. Unfortunately, no such surveys are performed in the UK, and it is not possible to extrapolate the findings from one country or population to another.

Despite the valuable data that can be produced from interview-based surveys, they have considerable drawbacks, the most important of which is the very high cost associated with the organisation and training of the interviewers. Secondly, they rely heavily on people's perceptions and recall of events that may have occurred a long time previously, and, as a result, they are open to considerable bias, for example as a result of people 'forgetting' a previous pregnancy termination. Thirdly, they are unable to provide any discrimination on the underlying type of infertility, and, unless repeated at intervals, they provide no information on the incidence of infertility or possible causative factors.

Smaller regional surveys are easier to organise and have the advantage of significantly reduced costs. They can be performed on samples drawn either from a defined geographical area or from other populations, such as the patients on a general practice age–sex register. Such studies may be either prospective or retrospective; however, it is important to stress that results from small regional studies must be interpreted with great care, since local demographic factors may make the results inapplicable to the national or, indeed, the wider local situation. In general, therefore, it is not possible to extrapolate the results from such studies to a broader population, and the more limited the population studied, the more likely this is to be the case.

Retrospective studies have been performed on a number of different populations, using a variety of information-gathering techniques. No one approach is ideal, however, and each has its own associated problems. One particular problem common to all retrospective studies of infertility should be briefly considered, and that is the age group that is selected for investigation. The experiences of successive cohorts of women in terms of contraception, sexual relationships and infertility may be very different from those of preceding generations, and it is not therefore, valid to confine a survey to those women who are no longer of childbearing age and then attempt to extrapolate their lifetime experience to current generations. Conversely, if young women are included in the survey, the figures produced may be underestimates, since not all such women will have had the opportunity to test their fertility on either the first or subsequent occasions.

One method used by a variety of authors has been to study the prevalence of a history of infertility among groups of women being treated for other non-related conditions. The major problem associated with this particular approach is the possibility of confounding variables, such as social class, leading to a systematic bias in the study groups. Several studies have reported on the prevalence of a history of infertility among patients attending antenatal or postnatal clinics (Cartwright, 1976), but these studies suffer from the obvious drawback that they will only provide information on episodes of resolved primary or secondary infertility and are unable to provide any information on the prevalence of unresolved episodes. Other populations that have been examined in this way include a group of control and subject women from a study into breast cancer (Greenhall and Vessey, 1990) and women taking part in a cervical screening programme in Finland (Rantala and Koskimies, 1986). This latter study was particularly open to criticism, however, since the uptake of screening was only 60%, with reduced percentages of nulliparous and highly multiparous patients taking part, thereby leading to serious potential biases in the final figures.

An alternative approach has been to investigate a sample of patients drawn from GP age–sex registers or Health Board primary-care registers, with a number of studies having been reported from the UK using this method (Johnson et al, 1987; Page, 1989; Templeton et al, 1990, 1991). In some cases, information was taken directly from the medical records, while in other cases, postal questionnaires or a combination of questionnaire plus record searching was used. On theoretical grounds, such community-based studies should be the most accurate way of detailing the true prevalence of infertility in the population. Unfortunately, a number of factors conspire to corrupt the quality of the information obtained in this way. Firstly, age–sex registers are recognised as being significantly inaccurate, approximately 10% of patient entries being erroneous owing to patients having moved out of the practice area without notifying their GP. This may be of particular importance in terms of determining the prevalence of infertility within a population, since the most mobile sections of the community are likely to be those of a younger age group, who may have more lifestyle risk factors for the development of infertility than do the more settled portion of the community. Secondly, the variable quality of the data recorded may severely limit the accuracy of any conclusions drawn. For instance, whereas marital status is likely to be recorded in the register, information that an unmarried woman is co-habiting is unlikely to be noted unless she has consulted for contraceptive advice. Similarly, unless a patient has presented 'difficulty in conceiving' as a problem, a simple survey of the records is unlikely to be able to pinpoint patients with this problem.

Postal questionnaires offer a more accurate means of identifying patients with fertility problems, and they also enable the investigator to ask detailed questions on contraceptive practice and the pattern of sexual intercourse, thereby permitting an accurate measurement to be made of number of women in the community 'at risk' of pregnancy at any one time. One of the main drawbacks with this type of study, which has already been alluded to, is the inaccuracy of the database from which the sample is drawn. When this is taken in conjunction with the problem of non-response from women who either fail to return the questionnaire or who do not wish to take part in the study, the overall response rate in such studies is usually of the order of 80%. Questionnaire studies also suffer from the dilemma that the more detailed and complex the questionnaire becomes, the greater will be the number of non-responders.

A further method of assessing infertility is to examine the records of patients attending a single specialist fertility clinic over a period of time. This approach will provide detailed information on the underlying types of infertility in that clinic population, but patients presenting to specialist clinics are self-selected and cannot be considered representative of the infertile group within the population as a whole. Even when only those patients from a defined area are considered, the number of patients seen will depend on a number of factors, including patients' access to infertility services, their uptake of such services (which will, in turn, be affected by the demographic characteristics of the local population), the number of referrals made to other clinics and patients' expectations of what such services can offer. While such data are, therefore, of interest in terms of changing referral patterns, they cannot produce an accurate assessment of the prevalence or incidence of infertility in the general community.

Prospective studies of infertility present their own particular problems, since it is, in general, difficult to identify and follow large groups of women who are attempting to conceive. Some data have, however, been reported from patients enrolled in the Oxford Family Planning Association contraceptive study who ceased using contraception with a view to becoming pregnant (Vessey et al, 1978). Although the women enrolled in this study cannot be considered representative of the UK population as a whole, since they were recruited from white, married women aged between 25 and 39 attending family planning clinics, the large size of the studied population ensures that the results obtained are likely to be accurate, at least for this particular subgroup of women.

PREVALENCE OF INFERTILITY

Textbooks generally quote a figure of 10% for the prevalence of infertility in the population. This figure was derived from a theoretical mathematical projection published in 1960, and current evidence suggests that it is probably a considerable underestimate of the true scale of the problem.

Over the past 12 years, a number of studies have been published reporting estimated prevalence rates for infertility problems in Western developed countries. The principal reports during this time have been listed in Table 3.1, and while it is difficult to make comparisons between the results from the different studies, in view of the widely differing populations studied, methodologies employed and definitions used, it is remarkable how similar the conclusions from these studies have been. In the great majority of reports, a prevalence rate of around 15% has been calculated, with only a single paper (Greenhall and Vessey, 1990) reporting rather higher prevalence rates of 20% and 28% in their studied populations. The most accurate figures on infertility prevalence rates are likely to be those obtained from the national fertility surveys performed in Denmark, France and the USA. Somewhat surprisingly, the results from the two clinic-based studies in this series were similar to those obtained from the population-based studies; since not all the infertile couples in a region would be expected to present for investigation, the similarity of the results suggests that either the population-based studies were underestimating the true prevalence of infertility or that the clinic-based studies were dealing with an unrepresentative population. The third possibility is that only a small percentage of infertile couples do not present to specialised clinics, and there is some evidence to support this suggestion; a recent study (Templeton et al, 1991) showed that, among a cohort of 36–40-year-old women, fewer than 5% of those with primary infertility had not consulted a doctor, compared with 27.9% of those from an older cohort of 46–50-year-old women. Even in this study, however, significant numbers of women with secondary infertility had not made use of available medical services.

Table 3.1 Epidemiological studies into the prevalence of infertility

Authors	Year	Country	Time Definition (years)	Study Type	Infertility Rate (%)
Rachootin and Olsen	1981	Denmark	2	Population	16.1
Hull et al	1985	U.K.	1	Clinic	17.0
Rantala and Koskimies	1986	Finland	1	Population	15.4
Hirsch and Mosher	1987	U.S.A.	1	Population	14.1
Page	1989	U.K.	2	Population	13.7
Greenhall and Vessey	1990	U.K.	1	Population	24.2
Templeton et al	1990	U.K.	2	Population	15.2
Thonneau et al	1991	France	1	Clinic	14.1
Webb and Holman	1992	Australia	1	Population	19.1

The relative frequencies of primary and secondary infertility vary among the studied populations, with reported prevalence rates ranging from 4 to 13% for primary infertility and from 4 to 17% for secondary infertility. The clinic-based studies report higher percentages of primary infertility compared with secondary, but this probably reflects the well-documented observation that couples with primary infertility are more likely to consult a doctor than are couples with secondary infertility (Rachootin and Olsen, 1981; Hirsch and Mosher, 1987; Templeton et al, 1990). No clear-cut pattern emerges from the reports relating to the population-based studies on this point, with one study (Templeton et al, 1990) suggesting that primary infertility is more common, three studies (Rachootin and Olsen, 1981; Rantala and Koskimies, 1986; Page, 1989) suggesting that the prevalences are about equal, and two studies (Hirsch and Mosher, 1987; Greenhall and Vessey, 1990) suggesting that secondary infertility is, in fact, more common. The prevalence of infertility within any given community will of course, also depend on the desired family size: the larger the typical family size, the greater the likelihood of any one woman experiencing an episode of infertility and the greater the relative importance of secondary infertility. In the UK, where the average family is small, the popularity of surgical sterilisation procedures will also tend to mask the true prevalence of secondary infertility.

It is well recognised that a significant number of women will conceive spontaneously following an episode of infertility, and the prevalence of resolved and unresolved infertility subgroups has been calculated in some of these studies. Such resolved episodes will obviously be more common in those studies using a 1-year definition of infertility, since any such episodes that resolve between 12 and 24 months would not be classified if a 2-year definition were used. A further percentage of women will successfully conceive following infertility treatment, particularly good results being obtained in the subgroup of women with ovulatory dysfunction treated with medical ovulation induction agents and those with tubal damage treated with in vitro fertilisation. Results from clinic-based studies (Bernstein et al, 1979; Collins et al, 1983) suggest that between 40 and 60% of pregnancies occurring to couples being investigated for infertility result from treatment, with a similar percentage occurring spontaneously. The influence of infertility treatment on figures for the prevalenzce of resolved infertility episodes in a population has not been satisfactorily addressed by epidemiological studies to date, although it is somewhat disconcerting that Templeton et al (1990) found a higher pregnancy rate among couples with primary infertility who did not consult a doctor than among those who did!

The prevalence of long-term involuntary childlessness is, of course, considerably less than the overall prevalence of infertility and appears to be of the order of 3–4% of the population in industrialised countries.

This chapter has so far been confined to data from the developed world, but infertility is, of course, a worldwide problem. Indeed, the personal impact of infertility may be even greater in cultures in which a woman's social status is entirely dependent on her bearing children. Epidemiological statistics are, of course, much harder to obtain in developing countries. Census data (if available) tend to be less accurate and less complete, while the availability of medical services is often patchy and of variable quality. Data collected from modern clinics with advanced diagnostic facilities are unlikely to be representative of the situation in the country as a whole. Population-based studies, on the other hand, may be hampered not only by the lack of a database from which to draw a representative sample, but also by the lack of written records, high illiteracy rates and migrant populations. As a result of these difficulties, few good epidemiological data are available regarding the prevalence of infertility in such countries. However, local prevalence rates as high as 50% have been reported in some sub-Saharan African countries (Belsey, 1976). The available evidence suggests that these high rates result from an increased prevalence of tubal damage secondary to pelvic infection. A recent WHO multicentre study demonstrated that patients attending clinics for investigation of infertility in Africa were far more likely to have an infection-attributable cause for their problem than were their counterparts in the developing countries of Asia or Latin America (Cates et al, 1985). Indeed, nearly 50% of the African women investigated had bilateral tubal blockage (three times the proportion found in these other regions). While infections due to postabortal or puerperal sepsis and pelvic tuberculosis contribute significantly to the high incidence of pelvic infection, there is a considerable body of evidence implicating sexually transmitted disease as the major cause of tubal damage, *Neisseria gonorrhoeae* and *Chlamydia trachomatis* being the principal organisms responsible. It is known that very high prevalence rates of these organisms are found in some African communities. In one reported study (Arya et al, 1973), the prevalence of gonorrhoea in a random sample of Ugandan women from a district with low fertility rates was 18%. Other studies have shown that up to half the infected men from such high prevalence regions have asymptomatic infection. Clearly, such men will be less likely to obtain treatment and will thus put their female partners at risk of pelvic infection; furthermore, as studies from the preantibiotic era have shown, untreated gonorrhoea will progress in 17–30% of cases to epididymitis, with subsequent childlessness secondary to obstruction in 42% of cases with bilateral infection. This particular complication is seldom seen where the infection is treated promptly with appropriate antibiotics. The implication of gonorrhoea as the causative organism in many of the cases of female tubal occlusion is thus further supported by the high prevalence of obstructive azoospermia found among African men investigated for infertility (Cates et al, 1985), a cause that accounts for only a minority of cases in the developed world (Hull, 1992). Further circumstantial evidence is provided both by studies that have shown a correlation between areas with a high prevalence of infertility and areas with a high prevalence of gonorrhoea (Arya et al, 1980) and by earlier studies demonstrating a decline in local infertility rates in many African countries following the introduction of mass antibiotic treatment campaigns for the eradication of gonorrhoea and yaws (Sherris and Fox, 1983). Owing to the difficult methodology involved in laboratory culture or serological testing for *Chlamydia trachomatis* there have, until recently, been few data available concerning the relative contribution made by this organism to the problem of tubal infertility in Africa. These technical difficulties are compounded by the often asymptomatic nature of chlamydial salpingitis, but recent studies (e.g. De Muylder et al, 1990) suggest that *Chlamydia trachomatis* and *Neisseria gonorrhoeae* are of equal importance.

TRENDS IN PREVALENCE

Although the number of patients seen at infertility clinics has increased dramatically over recent years, there is considerable doubt as to whether this represents a true increase in the underlying prevalence of the condition or simply reflects an increased proportion of infertile couples making use of medical services, together with the expected demographic increase in the numbers of young adults reaching their reproductive years as a result of the 'baby boom' of the 1950s and 60s and the effect of delayed childbearing, leading to increasing numbers of women attempting conception in their later, less fertile years (Aral and Cates, 1983)

Direct evidence for a change in prevalence rates can only be obtained from repeated surveys of the same population, and hence the data from the National Surveys of Family Growth in the USA are the only readily available source of information; a review incorporating data from the 1988 survey has concluded that there is no evidence for any recent change in the underlying rate of unresolved infertility in the USA (Mosher and Pratt, 1991).

Indirect evidence on changing prevalence rates can be obtained from studies of different cohorts of women in the same population. In the UK, two studies using this approach (Johnson et al, 1987; Templeton et al, 1991) have produced findings similar to those of the American surveys, with no evidence for increasing levels of involuntary infertility. Such studies, however, may be relatively insensitive in determining recent changes in prevalence rates. This is possibly why the well-documented increases in the prevalence of pelvic inflammatory disease (Westrom, 1980; Robinson et al, 1981) and the associated condition of ectopic pregnancy (Flett et al, 1988), which occurred following the 'sexual revolution' of the 1960s in both the UK and other Western industrialised countries, have not so far been translated into demonstrable increases in involuntary infertility rates. Interestingly, recent epidemiological studies from Sweden and the USA (Westrom, 1988; Cates et al, 1990) have shown a dramatic decrease since the early 1970s in the incidence of gonorrhoeal genital infection, together with the associated conditions of acute salpingitis and pelvic inflammatory disease. In Sweden, there has also been a concomitant decrease in the incidence of chlamydial infection; this has not been the case in the USA, where, as a result, chlamydial genital infections have since 1972 outnumbered gonorrhoeal infections.

The long time interval that must elapse between starting any therapeutic manoeuvre and the benefit becoming apparent in terms of infertility prevalence rates is the main reason for the lack of interventional epidemiological studies in the field of infertility. As a result, surrogate markers for infertility that can be more readily monitored have often been used in clinical studies. One such marker for male infertility is the routine semen assay, and considerable interest has been generated over the past few years by work that suggests there has been a global decline in semen quality over the last 50 years (Carlsen et al, 1992; Ginsburg et al, 1994). While a wide range of environmental toxins is known to have adverse effects on testicular function, suspicion is currently focused on synthetic oestrogens and chemicals with oestrogenic activity, which accumulate in the food chain and can be isolated both from food stuffs and drinking water (Sharpe and Skakkebaek, 1993). It is suggested that such substances might be affecting the male fetus in utero; however, it should be stressed that there are, as yet, no good experimental data to support this hypothesis.

Many other physical and dietary factors have been put forward as possible risk factors for the development of subsequent infertility, including smoking, high alcohol intake, high caffeine intake and exposure to psychological stress. It is, however, extremely difficult to disentangle the various confounding demographic variables when studying the influence of such factors, and the published clinical studies have produced conflicting results. Moreover, such studies can at best only show an association with infertility, without being able to prove a causal relationship. Good epidemiological studies, on the other hand, are conspicuous by their absence. At the present time, therefore, it is not possible to assess the significance of such factors in the history of an infertile couple.

Another lifestyle factor that has engendered considerable debate in recent years is the association between use of an intrauterine contraceptive device (IUCD) and pelvic infection. The use of this method of contraception is associated with higher rates of pelvic infection, compared with use of the oral contraceptive pill or barrier methods. Grimes (1992) argues that this is not because the IUCD increases the risk of such infection, but rather because the other methods confer a degree of protection; in other words, it is the sexual activity that is the risk factor, rather than the use of an IUCD. Other researchers maintain that there is, nonetheless, an increased risk of pelvic inflammatory disease with IUCD use, although the risk is less with the newer, medicated IUCDs (Buchar et al, 1990). The picture is clouded in some studies by the unreliability of the diagnosis of pelvic inflammatory disease.

CONCLUSION

In conclusion, therefore, it would appear that, using a 2-year definition, the prevalence rate of infertility in the UK population is 15%. However, up to half of these couples may conceive spontaneously or with medical help, leaving 8% of the population who do not achieve their desired family size. Of these, 4% have never experienced a pregnancy.

The increasing prevalence of pelvic inflammatory disease and ectopic pregnancy observed during the 1970s and 1980s now appears to have levelled out, and there is no evidence that the background prevalence of infertility has changed as a result. Whether the postulated secular deterioration in semen quality will result in any such change remains to be seen.

Despite this stability in prevalence rates, however, the demand for infertility services may continue to rise, as a result of greater uptake of medical services by infertile couples. The planning of future infertility health care can now be based on sound information in relation to prevalence and uptake of services.

References

Aral S O and Cates W (1983) The increasing concern with infertility. *Journal of the American Medical Association*, **250**(17): 2327–31.

Arya O P, Nsanzumuhire H and Taber S R (1973) Clinical, cultural, and demographic aspects of gonorrhoea in a rural community in Uganda. *Bulletin of the World Health Organization*, **49**: 587–95.

Arya O P, Taber S R and Nsanze H (1980) Gonorrhea and female infertility in rural Uganda. *American Journal of Obstetrics and Gynecology*, **138**: 929–32.

Belsey M A (1976) The epidemiology of infertility: a review with particular reference to sub-Saharan Africa. *Bulletin of the World Health Organization*, **54**: 319–41.

Bernstein D, Levin S, Amsterdam E, and Insler V (1979) Is conception in infertile couples treatment-related? A survey of 309 pregnancies. *International Journal of Fertility*, **24**: 65–7.

Bushan H, Villard-Mackintosh L, Vessey M, Yeates D and McPherson K (1990) Epidemiology of pelvic inflammatory disease in parous women with special reference to intrauterine device use. *British Journal of Obstetrics and Gynaecology*, **97**: 780–8.

Carlsen E, Giwercman A, Keiding N, and Skakkebaek N E (1992) Evidence for decreasing quality of semen during past 50 years. *British Medical Journal*, **305**: 609–13.

Cartwright A (1976) *How Many Children?* London: Routledge.

Cates W, Farley T M M and Rowe P J (1985) Worldwide patterns of infertility: is Africa different? *Lancet* **ii**: 596–8.

Cates W, Rolfs R T and Aral S (1990) Sexually transmitted diseases, pelvic inflammatory disease, and infertility: an epidemiological update. *Epidemiological Reviews* **12**: 199–217.

Collins J A, Wrixon W, Janes L B and Wilson E H (1983) Treatment-independent pregnancy among infertile couples. *New England Journal of Medicine*, **309**(20): 1201–6.

De Muylder X, Laga M, Tennstedt C, Van Dyck E, Aelbers G N M and Piot P (1990) The role of Neisseria gonorrhoeae and Chlamydia trachomatis in pelvic inflammatory disease and its sequelae in

Zimbabwe. *Journal of Infectious Diseases*, **162**: 501–5.

Flett G M M, Urquhart D R, Fraser C, Terry P B and Fleming J C (1988) Ectopic pregnancy in Aberdeen 1950–1985. *British Journal of Obstetrics and Gynaecology*, **95**: 740–6.

Ginsburg J, Okolo S, Prelevic G and Hardiman P (1994) Residence in the London area and sperm density. *Lancet*, **343**: 230.

Greenhall E and Vessey M (1990) The prevalence of subfertility: a review of the current confusion and a report of two new studies. *Fertility and Sterility*, **54**(6): 978–83.

Grimes D A (1992) The intrauterine device, pelvic inflammatory disease, and infertility: the confusion between hypothesis and knowledge. *Fertility and Sterility*, **58**(4): 670–3.

Hirsch M B and Mosher W D (1987) Characteristics of infertile women in the United States and their use of infertility services. *Fertility and Sterility*, **47**(4): 618–25.

Hull M G R (1992) The causes of infertility and relative effectiveness of treatment. In: Templeton A A and Drife J O (eds) *Infertility*. London: Springer–Verlag.

Hull M G R, Glazener C M A, Kelly N J et al (1985) Population study of causes, treatment, and outcome of infertility. *British Medical Journal*, **291**: 1693–7.

Johnson G, Roberts D, Brown R et al (1987) Infertile or childless by choice? A multipractice survey of women aged 35 and 50. *British Medical Journal*, **294**: 804–6.

Mosher W D and Pratt W F (1991) Fecundity and infertility in the United States: incidence and trends. *Fertility and Sterility*, **56**(2): 192–3.

Office of Population Censuses and Surveys (1989) *1987 General Household Survey*. London: HMSO.

Page H (1989) Estimation of the prevalence and incidence of infertility in a population: a pilot study. *Fertility and Sterility*, **51**(4): 571–7.

Rachootin P and Olsen J (1981) Social selection in seeking medical care for reduced fecundity among women in Denmark. *Journal of Epidemiology and Community Health*, **35**: 262–4.

Rantala M and Koskimies A I (1986) Infertility in women participating in a screening program for cervical cancer in Helsinki. *Acta Obstetricia et Gynecolcgica Scandinavica*, **65**: 823–5.

Robinson N, Beral V and Ashley J S A (1981) Trends in pelvic inflammatory disease in England and Wales. *Journal of Epidemiology and Community Health*, **35**: 265–70.

Sharpe R M and Skakkebaek N E (1993) Are oestrogens involved in falling sperm counts and disorders of the male reproductive tract? *Lancet*, **341**: 1392–5.

Sherris J D and Fox G (1983) *Infertility and Sexually Transmitted Disease: a public health challenge*. Population Reports Series L 4. Baltimore: Johns Hopkins University.

Templeton A, Fraser C and Thompson B (1990) The epidemiology of infertility in Aberdeen. *British Medical Journal*, **301**: 148–52.

Templeton A, Fraser C and Thompson B (1991) Infertility – epidemiology and referral practice. *Human Reproduction*, **6**(10): 1391–4.

Thonneau P, Marchand S, Tallec A et al (1991) Incidence and main causes of infertility in a resident population (1 850 000) of three French regions (1988–1989). *Human Reproduction*, **6**(6): 811–16.

Vessey M P, Wright N H, McPherson K and Wiggins P (1978) Fertility after stopping different methods of contraception. *British Medical Journal*, **i**: 265–7.

Webb S and Holman D (1992) A survey of infertility, surgical sterility and associated reproductive disability in Perth, Western Australia. *Australian Journal of Public Health*, **16**(4): 376–81.

Westrom L (1980) Incidence, prevalence, and trends of acute pelvic inflammatory disease and its consequences in industrialized countries. *American Journal of Obstetrics and Gynecology*, **138**: 880–92.

Westrom L (1988) Decrease in incidence of women treated in hospital for acute salpingitis in Sweden. *Genitourinary Medicine*, **64**: 59–63.

4

Investigation and treatment

Alison Taylor, Anwar Soubra and Peter Braude

INTRODUCTION

As discussed in the previous chapter, subfertility is a common problem, affecting about 15% of the population or 1 in 6 couples. It must be stressed that most couples presenting with difficulty in conceiving are not absolutely *in*fertile (with no chance of achieving a pregnancy together) but are usually *sub*fertile (having a reduced chance of conceiving spontaneously). However, for many of these couples, to be subfertile represents a major life crisis that can put them under severe emotional and psychological stress. This can profoundly influence many areas of their life together as a couple, as well as their relationships with family, friends and work colleagues. Thus, couples who are concerned about their fertility should be interviewed with sensitivity and understanding. It is important that the couple are seen together and that both partners are investigated, as there may be contributory factors in both that could influence the selection of therapy.

Ideally, couples presenting with subfertility should be seen in a dedicated clinic arranged, if possible, for a time when antenatal patients and general gynaecology patients who may be seeking sterilisation or termination of pregnancy do not share the same waiting room. An appropriate amount of time for consultation should be allocated for each couple (at least half an hour), and investigations should follow a clear protocol. The basic investigations can be performed reasonably quickly, enabling a diagnosis to be reached and management plans to be instituted promptly, which may help to limit the distress that patients feel. Throughout the investigations, couples should be informed of the reasons behind each test and the implications of the results. Experienced fertility nurses can play a vital role, from enhancing the organisation of investigations and integrating the various stages of management, to providing information counselling and support for couples.

MAIN CAUSES OF SUBFERTILITY

The most common causes of subfertility are spermatozoal defects, anovulation, tubal disease and unexplained subfertility (Figure 4.1). A significant proportion of couples will have more than one cause for their subfertility. The proportion of couples who have unexplained infertility will depend, in part, on the extent of the investigations performed.

Figure 4.1 Causes of subfertility

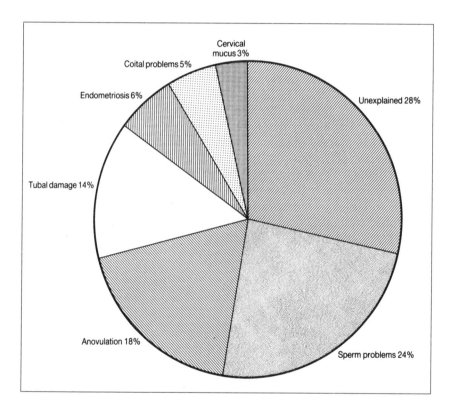

INVESTIGATION OF SUBFERTILITY

The investigation of a subfertile couple consists of taking a history, the relevant physical examination and carrying out specific investigations. These latter may be initiated by the GP or the fertility nurse. The diagnosis and management of subfertility can often be reached more quickly if preliminary results are available at the time of the first visit to the secondary referral centre.

History and physical examination

General enquiries should include age, occupation and a general medical and social history of both partners. Some occupations may involve shift work or time away from home, making it more difficult for intercourse to take place regularly. Rarely, men may be in a job that exposes them to toxic chemicals that can impair spermatogenesis. The duration of the relationship, contraceptive history and length of time trying to conceive should be recorded.

Female history

Of particular interest in the female history are regularity of menstrual cycles and a complete history of any previous pregnancies. The father of these pregnancies should be noted, as should whether the conceptions were spontaneous or followed fertility treatment, and the outcome of all pregnancies. Any history that may suggest possible tubal damage, such as pelvic inflammatory disease, sexually transmitted disease, previous abdominal or pelvic surgery or the use of an intrauterine contraceptive device, should be sought. A history of galactorrhoea may indicate hyperprolactinaemia. It is important to ask about changes in weight in women with oligomenorrhoea or amenorrhoea. Once a rapport has been established with the patient, she may be more receptive to questions about coital frequency, any coital difficulties or pain on intercourse (dyspareunia).

Male history

The male partner should be asked about any problems with testicular descent in childhood, severe testicular trauma, mumps orchitis or sexually transmitted diseases. A full history of all previous pregnancies fathered by him should be recorded. The frequency of intercourse is noted, and any problems with impotence or premature ejaculation should be excluded. Social history regarding cigarette smoking, alcohol intake and the use of drugs must also be elicited from both partners, as excessive consumption may reduce the chances of conception.

Examination

Although physical examination of the couple is often unremarkable, general and pelvic examination should be carried out on the woman, together with a genital examination of her partner.

For the woman, height, weight and the presence of excess body hair (hirsutism) should be recorded. This is an opportunity to perform a breast examination and to instruct the patient about self-examination. On examination of the abdomen, any tenderness and sites of previous surgical scars are noted. At pelvic examination, cervical smears and culture swabs may be taken, as appropriate. Bimanual examination may reveal tenderness, reduced mobility of pelvic structures, reflecting the presence of adhesions, masses in the adnexa or nodules in the pouch of Douglas, which may suggest the presence of endometriosis.

In the male partner, a genital examination is carried out to exclude the presence of varicocele and to assess testicular size, preferably noting the volume using an orchiometer.

SPECIAL INVESTIGATIONS

The initial investigations that should be performed for all couples are listed in Table 4.1. Apart from the tests for tubal patency, these tests can be organised by the couple's GP, and, if the results are available at the time of their first visit to a subfertility clinic, a diagnosis may be made and treatment started more promptly.

Table 4.1 Basic initial investigations for patients presenting
with subfertility

1. Hormonal	
Follicular phase (day 5–9)	• FSH
	• LH
	• TSH
	• prolactin
	• testosterone
Luteal phase (day 21 in a 28 day cycle)	• progesterone
2. Rubella serology	
3. Semen analysis x 2, at least 4 weeks apart	
4. Test of tubal patency	• hysterosalpingogram
	• laparoscopy and dye

Assessment of ovulation

The role of the ovary is to mature and release oocytes and cyclically to produce the hormones oestrogen and progesterone. These activities are the result of repetitive follicular maturation, ovulation and corpus luteum formation, followed by corpus luteum regression and menstruation if pregnancy does not follow. Normal ovulation requires an intact and normally functioning hypothalamic–pituitary–ovarian axis. Briefly, the hypothalamus produces gonadotrophin releasing hormone (GnRH), which stimulates the release of the gonadotrophins, follicular stimulating hormone (FSH) and luteinising hormone (LH), from the pituitary. FSH stimulates the growth and maturation of follicles in the ovaries, which begin to produce the hormone oestrogen. Usually, in each cycle, one follicle becomes the dominant follicle that will go on to ovulate as the other follicles regress. Rising oestrogen levels have a negative feedback effect on the production of FSH and LH from the pituitary. At mid-cycle, however, there is a surge in the LH level, which triggers the final maturation and release of the oocyte from the dominant follicle. LH also stimulates the production of progesterone by the follicle, which becomes a corpus luteum. Under the influence of oestrogen in the first half of the cycle prior to ovulation, the endometrial lining of the uterus becomes thicker. After ovulation, progesterone alters the endometrium to make it ready for an implanting embryo. If pregnancy occurs, the early embryo produces human chorionic gonadotrophin (hCG), which maintains continued production of progesterone from the corpus luteum to support the implanting embryo until the placenta takes over production of progester-one. If a pregnancy does not occur, the corpus luteum regresses, progesterone production falls and menstruation starts.

Dysfunction at any of the levels, from the hypothalamus to the ovary, can result in anovulation. In general, menstrual cyclicity will be impaired, with either irregular cycles, oligomenorrhoea (infrequent periods) or amenorrhoea (absence of periods for more than 6 months). However, regular cycles are not always ovulatory.

The hypothalamic–pituitary–ovarian axis can be investigated in several ways, outlined below.

Follicular phase hormonal profile

A serum hormone profile is performed in the follicular phase of the cycle, usually between days 5 and 9, where day 1 is the first day of menstruation. The time of the mid-cycle surge of LH should be avoided. Levels of FSH, LH, prolactin, oestradiol, thyroid stimulating hormone (TSH) and testosterone will be helpful in diagnosis.

Measurement of FSH. The serum FSH level should be less than 10 iu/l, and the main purpose of its measurement is to exclude premature ovarian failure, which can be diagnosed by finding a significantly raised FSH (greater than 20 iu/l). A slightly raised FSH level (11–20 iu/l) may indicate ovaries that are beginning to fail and that are likely to be resistant to ovulation induction. Women who are perimenopausal may still menstruate. However, if the FSH is significantly raised, they need careful counselling, to the effect that ovarian failure is, unfortunately, irreversible and will not respond to ovulation induction therapy. These patients may wish to consider other options, such as adoption, egg donation, surrogacy or remaining childless. Ovarian failure is a devastating blow to any woman who is trying to conceive, and supportive counselling should be offered. Hormonal replacement therapy (HRT) should be advised to counteract bone mineral loss and to reduce the risk of ischaemic heart disease.

Measurement of LH. LH also rises in ovarian failure, but is accompanied by a rise in FSH. In anovulatory patients, an elevated LH level (greater than 10 iu/l) in the presence of a normal FSH level is suggestive of the polycystic ovarian syndrome (PCOS) (see below). Low FSH and LH levels are less common but indicate dysfunction at the hypothalamic or pituitary level (hypogonadotrophic hypogonadism).

Measurement of oestradiol. Oestrogen levels reflect follicular development; however, the range for normal oestradiol values at each point in the menstrual cycle is highly variable. A low (less than 60 pg/ml) oestradiol level in association with a raised FSH indicates ovarian failure.

Measurement of testosterone. In hirsute or obese patients with anovulation, measurement of serum testosterone may be helpful in the diagnosis of PCOS. If the level is substantially raised, serious disorders such as an androgen secreting ovarian or adrenal tumour need to be excluded.

Measurement of prolactin (PRL) and thyroid stimulating hormone (TSH). Hyperprolactinaemia is a common cause of secondary amenorrhoea. If hyperprolactinaemia is found, underlying causes, such as hypothyroidism or administration of dopamine antagonist drugs (e.g. phenothiazines), should be excluded. In hypothyroidism, increased secretion of thyrotropin releasing hormone (TRH) stimulates the release of prolactin as well as TSH from the pituitary. In the absence of hypothyroidism, a pituitary adenoma is sought using imaging techniques, such as computerised tomography (CT) scanning or magnetic resonance imaging (MRI) of the pituitary fossa. Most small to moderately sized pituitary prolactinomas can be successfully treated with the dopamine agonist bromocriptine. If large tumours are suspected, further investigation in cooperation with an endocrinologist should be organised.

Luteal phase progesterone measurement

A rise in the serum progesterone level in the second half (luteal phase) of the cycle to more than 30 nmol/1 suggests that ovulation has occurred. This is commonly measured on day 21 of a 28-day cycle. However, if the cycles are generally longer than 28 days, measurement should be made later in the cycle. The time between ovulation and the onset of menstruation is thought to be fairly consistent, at around 14 days, and in cycles longer than 28 days, it is the follicular phase of the cycle that is variable. Therefore, if the progesterone level is to be measured in the middle of the luteal phase of the cycle, the blood sample should be taken approximately 7 days before the next period would be due (e.g. day 28 of a 35-day cycle).

Detection of an LH surge

Ovulation is triggered by a surge in LH, and this rise can be detected by measuring the LH in blood or urine. Commercially prepared home testing kits are now available from pharmacies, enabling simple detection of the LH surge by testing a urine sample. This can be used to time procedures such as donor insemination. Some patients also like to use them to time intercourse around ovulation, especially if they have a slightly irregular cycle or one that is longer than 28 days.

Temperature charts and changes in cervical mucus

Around the time of ovulation, the cervical mucus becomes thinner in consistency and is secreted in greater quantity. Some patients may notice a clear watery or mucoid vaginal discharge at mid-cycle. However, it can be an unreliable sign, and patients who do not notice this are not necessarily anovulatory.

Indirect evidence of ovulation can be obtained by use of basal body temperature (BBT) charts, showing a rise in temperature after ovulation (abiphasic pattern). Use of BBT charts has been criticised, however, because women who are ovulating may have monophasic graphs, and charts can be very difficult to interpret. They are often found to be a nuisance by those asked to fill them in, concentrate attention too much on the fertility problem and are no longer recommended.

Ultrasound scanning

The role of ultrasound in the field of reproductive medicine has expanded considerably with advances in the specialty. Serial ultrasound scans of the ovaries can accurately follow the growth of the dominant follicle (follicle tracking) and its subsequent collapse, indicating ovulation. It may not be a practical method of screening for ovulation in all patients with subfertility if ultrasound facilities are limited. It is, nevertheless, the only safe way to monitor cycles that are undergoing ovulation induction with gonadotrophins, to ensure that a limited number of dominant follicles are developing and to reduce the risk of ovarian hyperstimulation syndrome (OHSS). Follicle tracking may also be helpful in diagnosing the rare entity of luteinised unruptured follicle syndrome (LUFS), in which ovulatory levels of progesterone exist but the preovulatory follicle fails to rupture and release the egg. Since this phenomenon has been observed in both fertile and infertile women, its significance as a cause of subfertility remains to be established (Speroff and Kase, 1989). Ovarian ultrasound scanning is also an important tool in the diagnosis of polycystic ovarian syndrome. Ultrasonography of the ovaries may be carried out transabdominally through a full bladder, or, alternatively, a better view of the ovaries can be obtained using a transvaginal probe, for which the bladder needs to be empty.

Tests of tubal patency

A history of pelvic inflammatory disease, septic abortion, intrauterine contraceptive device use, ruptured appendix, previous tubal surgery or ectopic pregnancy raises the possibility of tubal damage, hence the necessity to assess tubal status early in subfertility investigations.

Laparoscopy

Laparoscopy should be viewed as the primary tool for tubal investigation. In addition to assessing tubal patency, laparoscopy can reveal the presence of adhesions or endometriosis, and all abnormalities should be clearly documented. The advent of videolaparoscopy has meant that a visual record can be kept, in the form of photographs or a video recording. If tubal blockage is found, the extent of damage can be accurately assessed, which is important when contemplating whether or not tubal surgery would be of benefit. If appropriate skills, equipment and time are available, it may be possible to divide the adhesions laparoscopically (adhesiolysis) at the time of diagnostic laparoscopy. Laparoscopy can be performed as an outpatient procedure in a day surgery unit, and patients are generally fit to go home within a few hours of the operation. Patients can be told of the operative findings before discharge but may not be able to remember all they are told, having had a general anaesthetic. They should, therefore, be offered a follow-up appointment in the subfertility clinic reasonably quickly, when a full discussion of the results of all investigations and treatment options can take place. The main disadvantages of laparoscopy are that it requires a general anaesthetic, that there is a risk of perforating bowel at the time of inserting the laparoscope and that the procedure can be technically difficult in obese patients. Postoperatively, patients may complain of abdominal pain and discomfort around the chest and shoulders, owing to gas trapped under the diaphragm.

Hysterosalpingography (HSG)

If tubal pathology is noted at laparoscopy, or demonstration of tubal patency has been inconclusive, HSG may be of benefit. It is also useful in identifying the level of block if surgery is being contemplated. In addition, HSG can identify abnormalities within the uterine cavity, such as polyps, fibroids or septa, which cannot be identified at laparoscopy, unless hysteroscopy is performed at the same time. The other advantages of HSG are that it can be performed without general anaesthesia and it can be used as a method of checking tubal patency in obese patients. It can, however, be a painful procedure for the patient, especially where the tubes are blocked.

Rubella serology

It is sensible to check for evidence of rubella immunity in any woman who is trying to conceive, because of the risks of fetal abnormality associated with rubella that is acquired in the first few weeks of pregnancy. If a patient is found not to have antibodies to rubella, she should be immunised and advised to avoid intercourse for one month, before the rubella serology is rechecked.

Semen analysis

As discussed in Chapter 2 semen samples can be highly variable, so it is prudent to obtain two semen specimens at least one month apart, especially if the first specimen was subnormal. Where possible, in order not to duplicate investigations unnecessarily, semen analyses should be performed in the laboratory that serves the fertility clinic to which the couple may be referred. A leaflet explaining how to obtain and deliver a semen sample to the laboratory should be given to the couple. This will explain that the period of abstinence should ideally be between 48 and 72 hours, since prolonged abstinence can depress the percentage of motile spermatozoa and their viability. The sample should be collected by masturbation directly into a wide-mouth, sterile, plastic specimen pot, taking care not to lose the first few drops of the ejaculate, which are rich in spermatozoa. Lubricant jellies, condoms or coitus interruptus should not be used in obtaining a semen specimen. The normal values for semen analyses according to WHO criteria are given in Table 4.2.

Table 4.2 Normal values for semen analysis (WHO, 1992)

Volume	$\geqslant$ 2 ml
Liquefaction time	Within 30 min
Concentration	$\geqslant$ 20 million/ml
Total count	$\geqslant$ 40 million
Motility	$\geqslant$ 50% class a + b* motility Including $\geqslant$ 25% class a* motility
Morphology	$\geqslant$ 30% normal forms
White blood cell count	< 1 million/ml

*Classification of motility:
Class a – rapid linear progressive motility.
Class b – slow or sluggish progressive motility.
Class c – non-progressive motility.
Class d – immotile.

Interpretation of semen analysis

Volume. Most of the ejaculate consists of secretions from the seminal vesicles and prostate gland. Thus, the ejaculate volume reflects accessory gland function. A very low volume may also suggest the possibility of retrograde ejaculation into the bladder, in which case a postejaculatory sample of urine should be centrifuged and examined for the presence of sperm. A large volume of ejaculate may suggest accessory gland infection.

Liquefaction. Semen rapidly coagulates after ejaculation, before liquefying within 30 minutes, to become watery in consistency. Although subfertility cannot be clearly linked to highly viscous semen, high viscosity may lead to laboratory errors in performing the semen analysis.

Concentration. Although the lower limit of a normal sperm count is arbitrarily set at 20 million spermatozoa per millilitre, pregnancies have been achieved with considerably lower concentrations. Semen samples with counts lower than 20 million/ml are described as *oligozoospermic.* The likelihood of achieving a spontaneous pregnancy appears to be greatly reduced with counts below 10 million/ml (severe oligozoospermia).

Motility. Actively motile sperm should be able to swim with a forward progressive motion. Semen with sperm showing poor motility is described zas *asthenozoospermic.* Motility is an important criterion because it correlates well with fertilising capacity. Since sperm motility decreases with time after ejaculation and varies with temperature, these two variables should be well controlled when assessing motility. As well as reporting the proportion of motile sperm, the semen analysis should also make some assessment of the forward progression.

Morphology. *Teratozoospermia,* or poor sperm morphology, is associated with low fertilising ability and hence subfertility.

Impaired spermatogenesis often manifests itself with a combination of defects, which may include all three of the above (*oligoteratoasthenozoospermia*).

Bacteriological screen. The presence of more than 1 million white blood cells per millilitre of ejaculate may be indicative of infection. The source and nature of the infection should be sought and treated.

Postcoital test (PCT)

The PCT provides information about both the receptivity of cervical mucus and the ability of sperm to reach and survive in the mucus. Although this test has been used extensively over the years, it still lacks uniformity in the way in which it is performed and interpreted. Whether or not the result of a PCT alters the therapy that should be offered to a couple is heatedly debated. Ideally, a PCT test should be carried out just before ovulation, when the cervical mucus changes to become thin, copious and most readily penetrated by sperm. A PCT that is poorly timed will give a negative result. A PCT should be performed in a cycle that is being monitored with ultrasound follicle tracking and/or urine analysis for the LH surge. At the time of ovulation, the couple are advised to have intercourse at home. The woman is advised that she can wash or shower but should not take a bath. Within the next 12 hours, the woman attends the clinic, where a small sample of cervical mucus is removed from the cervix, placed on a slide under a cover slip, and examined for motile sperm using a microscope. There is still no consensus on the number of motile sperm per high power field (HPF) that denotes a normal PCT, although most consider $\geq$ per HPF to be normal. Not surprisingly, patients may find this test embarrassing and dislike having sex to order.

MANAGEMENT OF SUBFERTILITY

Having completed investigations, the first steps in the management of subfertility are to explain to the couple the interpretation of the results, arrive at a diagnosis and give some indication of prognosis without treatment, before considering different therapeutic options. Good communication is essential and can reduce the stress that patients may feel. By involving them in the decision-making process, patients are less likely to feel that the situation is completely beyond their control. The treatment options available should be discussed, with a realistic appraisal of:

1.   the ability of proposed therapy to increase the chance of conception in a treatment cycle over and above the chance of spontaneous conception;

2.   any disadvantages or risks of treatment.

Figures 4.2 and 4.3 depict a scheme for a systematic approach to the management of female and male factor subfertility respectively.

A plan of management can then be formulated with the couple, according to factors such as their age and how actively they wish to pursue invasive treatment. Unfortunately, the most appropriate form of therapy (e.g. IVF) may not always be readily available, and subfertile patients are often, therefore, offered less clinically appropriate treatment.

The management of each couple should be reviewed regularly. If a pregnancy does not occur within an agreed time, progression from simpler therapies to more invasive and potentially more stressful treatment may be considered. Clinicians must be wary of dangling increasingly sophisticated 'carrots' for vulnerable patients, who, in their desperation to achieve a pregnancy, may be prepared to try anything. Some patients feel pressurised

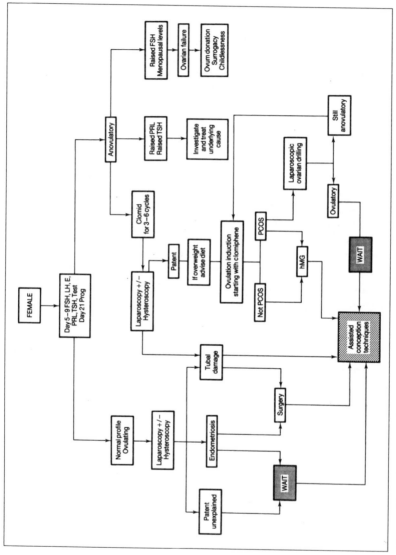

Figure 4.2 A systematic approach to the investigation and management of female subfertility

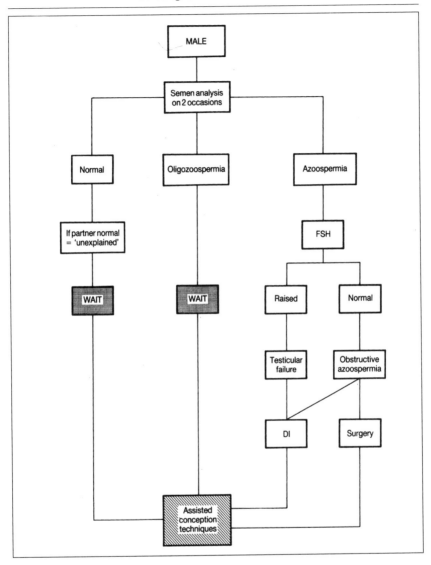

Fig 4.3 A systematic approach to male subfertility investigation and management

into continuing active treatment, while others may need careful counselling to consider alternative options, such as adoption or remaining childless. Trained counsellors may be able to offer invaluable help and support in these situations.

In the authors' experience, the presence of a dedicated fertility nurse in the subfertility clinic greatly enhances the service offered to patients at all stages of management. Some of valuable roles they play are in:

- the initiation of preliminary investigations and coordination of results;
- data collection for patients, enabling easy audit of different treatment modalities;
- performing PCTs;
- coordination of treatment cycles, such as intrauterine insemination (IUI);
- ultrasound scanning;
- semen preparation for IUI.

Perhaps most importantly of all, patients value having access to someone who knows them, provides support and can answer questions about treatment that may have arisen since a clinic visit.

The management of specific subfertility problems will now be considered.

Management of anovulation

Correction of underlying causes

Before committing patients to any form of ovulation induction, it is wise to seek and treat any underlying causes of anovulation (see Table 4.3), such as hyperprolactinaemia, hypothyroidism and disorders of weight.

Hypothyroidism. In the small proportion of cases of hyperprolactinaemia that are due to hypothyroidism, correction of hypothyroidism with thyroxine replacement often results in spontaneous resumption of ovulation.

Hyperprolactinaemia. This can be treated with dopamine agonists, for example bromocriptine. Common side-effects are nausea, diarrhoea, dizziness, postural hypotension, headache and fatigue. These side-effects can be minimised by starting the patient on a low initial dose of bromocriptine of 1.25 mg at bedtime, to be increased gradually up to the usual dose of 2.5 mg twice daily.

After 1 to 2 weeks on this dose, the prolactin level should be reassessed, and if it is not within the normal range, the dose of bromocriptine may be increased further. Ovulatory menses and pregnancy are achieved in 80% of patients with hyperprolactinaemia, usually with the resumption of ovulatory cycles within 4–6 weeks of treatment (Yuen, 1992). If ovulation does not occur within 2 months of therapy that has effectively suppressed the prolactin level, ovulation induction with clomiphene can be added.

Weight. In anovulatory patients who are either extremely obese or severely underweight, attaining a normal body mass index alone may be enough to achieve resumption of spontaneous ovulation. Body mass index can be calculated as weight in kilograms $\div$ (height in metres)^2 and, should ideally be between 19 and 25 kg/m^2. However, even if a normal weight for height is not reached, a change of weight in the right direction is often all that is needed to re-establish ovulation, and this should be encouraged.

Table 4.3 Causes of anovulation

Ovarian causes
Polycystic ovaries
Ovarian failure
• Genetic, e.g. Turner's syndrome
• Autoimmune
• Iatrogenic, e.g. radiotherapy or chemotherapy

Hypothalamic–pituitary causes
Hyperprolactinaemia (pituitary adenoma)
Functional
• Weight loss
• Exercise
• Stress
• Idiopathic
Kallman's syndrome (hypogonadotrophic hypogonadism with anosmia)
Hypopituitarism
• Large pituitary tumour
• Iatrogenic, e.g. ablative therapy
• Sheehan's syndrome

Other endocrinological conditions
Hypothyroidism
Adrenal disorders
• Congenital adrenal hyperplasia
• Cushing's disease
• Adrenal tumour

Induction of ovulation

In the past, a woman with anovulation had little hope in conceiving. Now, however, clinicians have many preparations available for the induction of ovulation, from simple oral agents, such as clomiphene, through to gonadotrophins and GnRH. Providing anovulation is the only problem causing subfertility, ovulation induction therapy can enable a couple to expect their chances of conception to be similar to that found in the general population (Hull, 1992). If anovulation is found on initial investigation by the GP, it would not be unreasonable for the couple to commence ovulation induction with clomiphene (see below) while they are awaiting a subfertility clinic outpatient appointment.

Antioestrogens. Clomiphene is available as 50 mg tablets. It has a structural similarity to oestrogen that allows its uptake and binding by oestrogen receptors in the hypothalamus and pituitary. This prevents the normal negative feedback effect of oestrogen and hence allows further endogenous FSH and LH secretion. Clomiphene does not directly stimulate ovulation, but it induces a sequence of events leading to ovulation.

Clomiphene generally is started at a dose of 50 mg per day for 5 days, beginning in the first 5 days of a spontaneous or induced cycle. If a day 21 progesterone level is anovulatory in the first cycle of treatment, the dosage is increased to 100 mg a day for 5 days, and the day 21 progesterone level is checked again. Once ovulatory levels are achieved, treatment should be continued for at least six cycles. Ovulation can be expected in the interval between 5 and 10 days after the last dose of clomiphene. The couple should be advised to have intercourse every 2–3 days around the time of mid-cycle. If clomiphene does not achieve ovulation, or pregnancy has not happened after 6 months of ovulatory cycles, ovulation induction with gonado-trophins should be used.

Women with low oestrogen levels, such as those who are hypogonado-trophic, are less likely to respond favourably to clomiphene. Obese anovulatory women can also be resistant to clomiphene therapy and may need higher doses of clomiphene; this may be due to high androgen levels. Advice about weight loss is, therefore, essential and can either result in spontaneous resumption of ovulation or improved therapeutic response to clomiphene.

In properly selected patients, 80% can be expected to ovulate, and around 40% become pregnant (Gorlitsky et al, 1978). All patients started on ovulation induction therapy should be warned about the increased risk of multiple pregnancy. The multiple pregnancy rate is about 5–8%, the majority of which (90%) will be twin pregnancies, although higher order pregnancies occasionally occur. The abortion rate and the incidence of congenital abnormalities are not increased.

Side-effects do not appear to be dose related. The most common problems are vasomotor flushes (10%), abdominal distention, bloating pain or soreness (5%), breast discomfort (2%), nausea and vomiting (2%), headaches (1.5%) and visual disturbances (1.3%). Significant ovarian enlargement and hyperstimulation are uncommon and rarely occur within the 5-day course. Maximal enlargement of the ovary usually occurs several days after discontinuing clomiphene. If the patient is symptomatic, an ultrasound scan is indicated. Ovarian enlargement will usually dissipate rapidly, but significant ovarian hyperstimulation syndrome (OHSS) can occur, particularly in patients with polycystic ovaries.

Gonadotrophins. Gonadotrophins are now or will be available in several forms:

- human menopausal gonadotrophin (hMG), extracted from the urine of postmenopausal women and containing equal amounts of FSH and LH;
- highly purified FSH, which has little or no LH activity;
- pure 'recombinant' FSH that is manufactured using molecular biology techniques, rather than being urinary derived, which will be available in the future.

Currently, however, there is little evidence to suggest the superiority of one form over the other. Gonadotrophins are inactive orally and must therefore be given by injection. hMG is administered by intramuscular injections, while the purer forms of gonadotrophin can be given subcutaneously.

Gonadotrophin therapy is expensive and carries an increased risk of complications, such as OHSS and multiple pregnancy. Prior to starting treatment, patients should have been fully investigated to demonstrate tubal patency and an acceptable semen quality.

Proper instruction and counselling of the couple is crucial, and the fertility nurse can play a very useful role in this respect. The couple need to understand the necessity for frequent monitoring and the risks involved in such treatment. The patient or her partner may be taught to administer the injections. The couple should also be informed that they will be advised about the optimum time for intercourse and the possibility that more than one course of treatment may be necessary.

There is no ideal fixed regimen for gonadotrophin use. Variable regimen tailored to the cause of anovulation, age and therapeutic response of each patient produce the best results. Follicle stimulation is achieved by 7–14 days of daily or alternate day gonadotrophin administration, usually beginning with two ampoules a day. Response is monitored by ultrasound scans of the ovaries for follicle size and number, sometimes in conjunction with serum oestradiol measurement. Patients should not receive gonadotrophin therapy without adequate ultrasound monitoring. Patients with polycystic ovaries should be stimulated cautiously, because their ovaries have a greater tendency to multiple follicular development and OHSS. These patients are usually started on a smaller dose, such as one ampoule or less per day, and they should be closely monitored. Older patients, on the other hand, have less sensitive ovaries and may need to start on three ampoules of gonadotrophins daily.

The aim of ovulation induction is the development of a single dominant follicle each cycle, although this is rarely achieved other than with a prolonged, low-dose regimen. When the ovaries contain a maximum of three follicles measuring $\geqslant$ 17 mm in diameter, 5000–10 000 units of hCG are given as a single intramuscular dose to simulate the natural LH surge and induce ovulation 36–48 hours later. hCG should be withheld if more than three large follicles are present (to reduce the risk of higher order pregnancies) and where more than 10 small follicles are visualized on scan, in order to minimise the risk of hyperstimulation.

More than 90% of patients with competent ovaries will ovulate in response to gonadotrophins, and a pregnancy rate of 50–70% is usually achieved after an average of 3–4 ovulatory cycles (Brown et al, 1987). Prior to the use of careful ultrasound monitoring, the multiple pregnancy rate was about 30%; currently, it is about 15%.

GnRH. The main advantages of using GnRH lie in the fact that it leads usually to unifollicular development and it is difficult to produce ovarian hyperstimulation. Futhermore, the multiple pregnancy rate with GnRH is no greater than that in the general population.

GnRH as gonadorelin is administered by a programmable minipump, ensuring that physiological levels and patterns of FSH and LH secretion are achieved. Because the internal feedback mechanisms between the ovary and pituitary operate normally, follicular growth and development occur in a way similar to that usually seen in a natural cycle. Induction of ovulation with GnRH is most successful in patients with amenorrhoea owing to a hypothalamic defect resulting in low gonadotrophin production by the pituitary. In these patients, a pregnancy rate of 30–35% per treatment cycle can be achieved (Martin et al, 1990).

Superactive GnRH analogues. The superactive GnRH analogues, such as buserelin, are used in a different way. They act by initially producing a stimulatory effect or flare of FSH and LH release. Continued administration of GnRH analogues, however, results in pituitary desensitisation and no further release of gonadotrophins. These two actions are used in the superovulation regimes employed in assisted conception techniques such as IVF and GIFT. The initial flare of gonadotrophin secretion can be used in an 'ultrashort' regimen of superovulation to recruit follicles that are then further stimulated by the administration of hMG. Prolonged pituitary desensitisation can be exploited to suppress the occurrence of a spontaneous LH surge, thus preventing ovulation prior to egg collection.

Risks of medical ovulation induction: OHSS

OHSS can occur in various degrees of severity (Golan et al, 1989). In mild cases, it includes ovarian enlargement, abdominal distension and weight gain. The severe form of the syndrome is life threatening and consists of ascites, electrolyte imbalance, hypovolaemia, oliguria and pleural effusion. The ovaries enlarge extensively, with many follicular cysts. The basic pathology underlying this syndrome is a shift of fluid from the intravascular space into the abdominal cavity, probably due to increased capillary permeability secondary to very high levels of oestrogen. Serious clinical complications include hypercoagulability leading to thromboembolism and renal failure owing to decreased renal perfusion. Some patients, particularly those with polycystic ovaries, have an increased tendency to develop OHSS. Careful monitoring and prevention is vital because, once OHSS is established, there is no curative treatment, and therapy is supportive until the condition resolves spontaneously. If monitoring suggests that an excessive number of follicles have developed and/or the serum oestradiol level is too high, hCG should be withheld and intercourse avoided until the follicles have regressed. The rationale behind this is, firstly, that hCG itself gives the ovaries a further stimulus and, secondly, that if the cycle results in the patient conceiving, endogenous hCG produced by the early implanting embryo can further exacerbate the situation.

In severe cases, hospitalisation is necessary, strict fluid balance being monitored by accurate input–output charts and daily weight. Haematological investigations that may need repeating daily include urea and electrolytes, haematocrit, serum albumin, total proteins and a coagulation profile. A chest X-ray may be required to exclude a pleural effusion. Intravenous fluid replacement, including a colloid such as human albumin solution, will help to maintain the urine output. Paracentesis may become necessary if the patient has difficulty breathing, urine output is poor or the patient is very uncomfortable and distressed.

Surgical ovulation induction

Before gonadotrophins were available for the induction of ovulation ovarian wedge resection was a method of restoring ovulation in women with polycystic ovaries. Until recent times, this method was still used in patients who were resistant to medical ovulation induction. Such a procedure, however, carries the disadvantages of major abdominal surgery, especially the development of postoperative pelvic adhesions, and was hence discouraged. Laparoscopic ovarian drilling using diathermy or laser has recently been advocated as an alternative, less invasive approach. Initial results of this procedure have been encouraging with respect to resumption of ovulatory cycles (86%) and spontaneous pregnancy rates (77%) (Armar and Lachelin 1993). Further studies are needed, however, to clarify whether or not there are risks, such as pelvic adhesion formation.

Management of tubal factors

Tubal pathology accounts for approximately 14% of cases of subfertility, although, in some populations, this proportion may be higher. Sexually transmitted diseases, particularly chlamydial and gonococcal infections, can cause tubal damage and subsequent infertility. The fallopian tube is not just a conduit for eggs, sperm or zygotes; it is also a reproductive organ in which several functions must be ensured to lead to an intrauterine pregnancy. Even tubes that are apparently minimally damaged can be functionally incompetent. The chance of achieving a spontaneous pregnancy reduces with increasing severity of tubal damage, and if conception occurs, the incidence of ectopic pregnancies is higher than in the general population.

Tubal surgery

The fallopian tube is a very delicate organ. When attempting tubal surgery, the aim is not only to restore patency, but also to ensure resumption of tubal function. Evidence has accumulated to support the fact that microsurgical tubal surgery is superior to conventional surgical techniques. Currently, several tubal microsurgical techniques are available, including salpingostomy, fimbrioplasty, salpingolysis, tubal anastomosis and tubal implantation. All of these techniques have the following basic principles in common: adequate surgical exposure and the use of magnification, secure haemostasis, irrigation of tissues to prevent them drying out, avoidance of any unnecessary tissue damage, meticulous closure of peritoneal surfaces and the use of fine, non-reactive suture material. However, for microsurgery to be successful, it requires proper training, equipment and continuing experience. Therefore, microsurgery should be limited to a few centres and should only be performed by surgeons with the necessary expertise.

Results of tubal microsurgery are also influenced by factors such as the age of the patient and the type of tubal pathology. Repetitive tubal microsurgery has a poor prognosis; hence, the best chance of success lies in the first operation. Thus, proper patient selection is probably one of the key factors affecting success rates of tubal surgery. The success rates of microsurgery vary with the severity of tubal disease. It is evident that the best chances of achieving a pregnancy after tubal surgery for minimal disease lie in the first year following surgery (Hull 1992). When tubal surgery is contemplated, the tubal status should be meticulously assessed by laparoscopy and hysterosalpingography before a decision is reached. The location and extent of tubal damage, previous tubal surgery and associated pelvic disease should all be considered as factors affecting the treatment. Severe pelvic adhesions immobilizing the tubes, or a hydrosalpinx with an ampullary diameter of greater than 20 mm, are unlikely to benefit from surgery. If the patient is older than 40 years, the operation is more likely to be associated with a poor prognosis. An acceptable semen quality should be documented before attempting tubal microsurgery. If there is a combination of tubal disease and suboptimal semen analyses, IVF may be a more appropriate choice of therapy for the couple. Evidence of ovulation should also be sought preoperatively, or there should at least be no contraindication to ovulation therapy such as ovarian failure. If the patient has not conceived by 1 year after surgery, IVF should be considered.

Prevention of tubal damage

It is clear that tubal surgery is not successful in many cases, especially where there is moderate to severe damage. Prevention of tubal damage might be a more effective tool to deal with the problem. It can be accomplished by the early diagnosis and appropriate treatment of pelvic infection before any irreversible functional damage has taken place.

Taking care to use an aseptic technique at the time of insertion of an IUCD and the use of prophylactic antibiotics to cover procedures such as termination of pregnancy may minimise the risk of infection following these interventions.

Surgery or IVF?

IVF and tubal microsurgery are alternative options for the management of subfertility secondary to tubal damage. There are many factors to consider when choosing which is the most appropriate form of treatment, the most important being the likelihood of success with each technique. The choice is also made according to age of patient, type of pathology, other contributory subfertility factors and often, regrettably, the availability of the service.

Management of male factor subfertility

In male factor subfertility, the cause of impaired spermatogenesis is usually unknown; hence, specific therapy is not available. In addition, the wide biological variation of semen parameters that can occur normally within an individual makes objective assessment of general therapies difficult. Thus, the treatment of male factor subfertility represents one of the biggest challenges in reproductive medicine. After clinical and laboratory investigations have been carried out, patients with male factor subfertility tend to fall into one of the following groups:

1. *Primary testicular failure with azoospermia and elevated gonadotro-phin (FSH and LH) levels.* Pharmacological treatment in this category is of no benefit, and the option of donor insemination (DI) should be broached. (This is discussed further in the section on assisted conception.)

2. *Secondary testicular failure due to gonadotrophin (FSH and LH) deficiency.* These comprise 5–10% of oligozoospermic males, and cases respond well to gonadotrophin replacement or treatment with GnRH.

3. *Idiopathic oligozoospermia (normal FSH and LH levels).* Various different medical therapies have been used to treat idiopathic male subfertility, but none has been shown to be effective (Wang et al, 1983). Generally, some form of assisted conception treatment, such as IVF, is needed to improve the chances of conception.

4. *Oligozoospermia (normal FSH and LH) associated with various andrological abnormalities,* such as varicocele, vas deferens obstruction, retrograde ejaculation, acute or chronic infection and disorders of the accessory sex glands. It may be possible to correct anatomical problems, such as vas deferens obstruction, by microsurgical techniques, and the management of varicocele is discussed below. Infections should be treated, but, as with the idiopathic oligozoospermia group, most men in this group need some form of assisted conception technique to improve their chances.

Surgical treatment of varicocele

The relationship between varicocele, disordered spermatogenesis and subfertility is controversial. Patients with varicoceles show a spectrum of semen abnormalities. The conventional treatment for varicocele is surgical ligation of the spermatic vein above the internal inguinal ring, although embolisation of the spermatic vein using interventional radiological techniques is becoming more widely available. The results of studies are conflicting; the role of varicocele as a cause of male subfertility and the benefits of surgical treatment need further investigation and assessment.

Other methods of management

If male subfertility is not amenable to medical or surgical treatment, assisted conception techniques, such as IUI, DI or IVF, should be considered. These will be discussed later in this chapter. Men with mildly impaired semen samples who have been trying to conceive for less than 2 years may achieve a pregnancy spontaneously if allowed more time; however, the needs of each couple should be individually assessed.

Assisted conception techniques

Assisted conception techniques include the various methods of artificial insemination, in vitro fertilisation and embryo transfer (IVF–ET), GIFT and other variations based on these techniques. All assisted conception procedures share the same basic principles, which are:

- induction of multiple follicular development;
- preparation of a sample of motile sperm;
- the bringing together of gametes (sperm and oocytes) in order to improve the likelihood of fertilisation.

IVF–ET is the only assisted conception technique that bypasses the fallopian tubes and can be offered as a treatment for tubal infertility, while all other techniques depend on the presence of functioning tubes. The most commonly used abbreviations for the various assisted conception techniques are listed in Table 4.4.

Table 4.4   Assisted conception techniques

AIH	Artificial insemination using husband's sperm
DI	Donor insemination
IUI	Intrauterine insemination
DIPI	Direct intraperitoneal insemination
IVF–ET	In vitro fertilisation and embryo transfer
GIFT	Gamete intrafallopian transfer
ZIFT	Zygote intrafallopian transfer
TET	Tubal embryo transfer (same as ZIFT)
ICSI	Intracytoplasmic sperm injection
SUZI	Subzonal injection of sperm
PZD	Partial zona dissection

Artificial insemination using husband's or partner's semen (AIH)

AIH involves placing the entire ejaculate near or into the cervix. There is no clear evidence that AIH has any advantages over sexual intercourse (Hughes et al, 1987), except for some limited indications, including hypospadias in the male and vaginal anomalies in the female, retrograde ejaculation (Braude et al, 1987), spinal cord injury, impotence in the male and vaginismus in the female. Other than for these rare indications, there seems to be no role for AIH in the effective management of subfertility.

Donor insemination (DI)

Male infertility that is not amenable to IVF treatment, together with the difficulties encountered in adopting a baby, have increased the demand for DI. Although DI is technically a simple procedure, it carries with it serious emotional, ethical and legal implications, which need careful consideration. Both couples considering DI and men volunteering to donate semen samples should have access to a trained independent counsellor.

Indications for donor insemination are given below.

Sperm abnormalities. Azoospermia, severe oligozoospermia, gross terato-zoospermia or severe asthenospermia are common indications for donor insemination. However, even with quite markedly impaired spermatogenesis, fertilisation can sometimes be achieved in vitro with IVF. New assisted fertilisation techniques, such as intracytoplasmic sperm injection (ICSI) (Van Steirteghem et al, 1993), offer hope to these men of fathering a child of their own genetic make-up. Ideally, therefore, these avenues should be explored before considering DI.

Genetic indications. DI may be appropriate where there is a high likelihood of a genetic disorder being transmitted via the male gamete. Alternatively, where a medical condition in the pregnancy may be exacerbated by the male genotype, for example, where a woman has had a previous fetal loss secondary to Rhesus (Rh) isoimmunisation, and her partner is homozygous for the Rh factor, donor insemination from an Rh-negative donor can be used. Genetic counselling may help couples to assess their risks of passing on serious disorders to their offspring, and, for some couples to whom this risk appears unacceptably high, DI may be considered.

Before initiating DI, the couple should be properly counselled, and an informed consent must be obtained from both partners. Among other things, counselling should discuss the possible implications of DI on the relationship, and the couple should be asked to consider seriously whether, and when, they intend to inform the child of the nature of the conception. It should be made clear to them that in the UK, under terms of the Human Fertilisatioin and Embryology Act 1990, the male partner, rather than the donor, would be the legal father of the resulting child, if he has consented to treatment.

As a rule, the donor should remain anonymous to the couple. However, non-identifying characteristics, such as height, hair colour, eye colour and blood group, may be supplied in order to help in the matching process. In recruiting the donor, careful family, medical and social histories must be obtained. Periodic testing of the donors for gonorrhoea, syphilis, herpes, chlamydia and mycoplasma should be performed. Donors must be routinely screened for hepatitis B, cytomegalovirus and HIV infection, and this is repeated at 3–6 monthly intervals.

DI can be carried out in cycles with spontaneous or induced ovulation. Fresh semen is no longer used, because of the risks it carries in the transmission of infection, particularly HIV. All donated samples are stored for a minimum of 6 months while the donor is checked for anti-HIV antibodies. The insemination is carried out around the time of ovulation, which can be monitored using urinary LH kits or by ultrasound. The semen is usually placed in the cervical canal using a sterile plastic catheter, or it can be inserted higher into the uterine cavity (IUI).

DI does not guarantee a pregnancy, and success rates are slightly lower with frozen samples than were previously achieved with fresh samples. Cumulative pregnancy rates after six cycles vary between 60–80%, over 50% of pregnancies occurring in the first three cycles of treatment (Glezerman, 1993). Therefore, if pregnancy has not occurred after six cycles of treatment, the couple should be re-evaluated, or a combination of IVF and DI should be considered.

Intrauterine Insemination (IUI)

The aim of IUI is to increase the number of motile spermatozoa in the uterus and fallopian tube at the time of ovulation. This is achieved by introducing a fine catheter through the cervix into the uterine cavity and injecting a prepared semen sample. The semen preparation involves thorough washing to remove the seminal plasma, which is rich in prostaglandins and can cause painful uterine cramps, together with a technique such as the 'swim-up' method or the use of Percoll® density gradients to concentrate the most motile and morphologically normal sperm. The insemination is performed at the time of ovulation, which is usually monitored by ultrasound follicle tracking. There is conflicting evidence on whether IUI in natural cycles increases the chance of conception over timed intercourse (Kirby et al, 1991). However, if it is combined with controlled superovulation to produce a maximum of three mature follicles, pregnancy rates of around 15% per cycle have been reported (Dodson and Haney, 1991).

Indications for IUI include oligospermia (reduced seminal volume of less than 1 ml), oligozoospermia, asthenozoospermia, increased seminal viscosity and delayed liquefaction, anatomical abnormalities such as hypospadias or vaginal anomalies, functional abnormalities such as impotence, retrograde ejaculation or vaginismus and sperm–mucus interaction problems. A trial of superovulation and IUI is worthwhile before proceeding to IVF for patients with unexplained subfertility.

Direct intraperitoneal insemination (DIPI)

DIPI involves the injection of a prepared sperm suspension through the posterior vaginal fornix into the peritoneal cavity, to be picked up by the fallopian tubes. It is not a commonly used technique, but pregnancy rates of 16–17% per cycle have been reported (Evans et al, 1991).

In vitro fertilisation and embryo transfer (IVF–ET)

As discussed in chapter 2 the number of IVF programmes has increased dramatically, and success rates have improved, so that IVF should now be regarded as a standard part of infertility treatment. Unfortunately, in the UK, NHS provision for subfertility treatment is poorly funded, and IVF is not readily available to many couples. The number of indications for IVF has increased over the years, to include tubal disease, male factor subfertility, unexplained subfertility, endometriosis, cervical factor subfertility and anovulation. IVF involves the accomplishment of several steps, as outlined below.

Superovulation. IVF can be performed in natural cycles; however, the pregnancy rates per cycle are greater if stimulation of multiple follicular development (superovulation) is employed. In the past, stimulation protocols for IVF have utilised clomiphene alone, combinations of clomiphene and hMG, or gonadotrophins alone. Currently, most drug regimens rely on the various available forms of gonadotrophin to effect multiple follicular development. The introduction of a superactive GnRH analogue prior to and throughout hMG stimulation has provided additional advantages. The GnRH analogues (e.g. buserelin) are administered either by subcutaneous injection or nasal spray. When started in the luteal phase of the pretreatment cycle and continued for approximately 14 days prior to starting gonadotrophins (long regimen), GnRH analogues lead to pituitary desensitisation with depletion of endogenous FSH and LH, hence rendering the ovaries quiescent. This allows cycle programming and gonadotrophin stimulation to be started on any day, according to a fixed schedule. It also prevents a premature LH surge, which could cause ovulation or premature luteinisation of follicles. Alternatively, the initial flare of endogenous FSH and LH release produced in the first 48 hours of GnRH analogue administration can be used in the ultrashort regimen of superovulation to initiate follicular recruitment. Further stimulation is continued with gonadotrophins.

The doses of gonadotrophin used are usually higher than those for simple ovulation induction. Superovulation is monitored by checking serum or urinary oestradiol levels and ultrasound scanning of the ovaries, the dose of gonadotrophins being tailored according to the response. Stimulation with gonadotrophins is usually continued until at least three follicles achieve a diameter of $\geqslant 17$ mm, at which time final maturation of the oocytes is promoted by a single intramuscular injection of hCG. Approximately 10–15% of IVF cycles are cancelled prior to the egg collection, either because of a poor response or, alternatively, owing to an excessive response and hence an increased risk of OHSS.

Egg collection. Egg collection is performed 34–36 hours after the hCG injection, before ovulation occurs. Oocyte retrieval is accomplished by aspiration of the follicles, either laparoscopically, or transvaginally under ultrasound guidance. The transvaginal approach has become the preferred method and can be performed under sedation rather than a general anaesthetic. The fluid from each follicle is microscopically examined for an oocyte by an embryologist. Each oocyte that is found is transferred to a culture drop and kept under carefully controlled conditions in an incubator at 37° C.

Insemination of oocytes and in vitro culture of embryos. The semen sample is produced by masturbation and is prepared to separate the most motile and morphologically normal sperm from the ejaculate. Approximately 100 000 motile sperm are added to each dish containing an oocyte and are incubated overnight. The oocytes are examined for signs of normal fertilisation (i.e. the presence of two pronuclei) the following morning, at about 18 hours postinsemination. The proportion of oocytes that fertilise varies and may be lower where there are severe abnormalities of the semen sample. In these cases, there is also a higher chance that none of the oocytes will fertilise. For couples who have encountered the disappointment of complete failed fertilisation after conventional IVF, or whose semen samples are so poor that conventional IVF is not justified, the new assisted fertilisation techniques, such as ICSI, may offer hope (Van Steirteghem et al, 1993).

After fertilisation has been confirmed, zygotes are cultured in vitro for a further 24–48 hours until they are replaced in the uterus.

Embryo transfer. Most embryo transfer procedures are performed at approximately 48 hours after the egg collection, when the embryos have reached the four cell stage of development. Embryos are transferred to the uterine cavity transcervically in a tiny volume of culture fluid, by means of a fine plastic catheter. Patients need careful counselling about the risks of multiple pregnancies when they are considering the number of embryos to transfer. In the UK, under the terms of the Human Fertilisation and Embryology Act 1990, the maximum number of embryos that can be transferred in one cycle is three. Surplus embryos can be frozen (cryopreserved) for replacement in later unstimulated cycles, if transfer of the fresh embryos fails to result in a pregnancy. Following embryo transfer, most IVF units give patients extra luteal support with progesterone suppositories or injections.

Overall success rates of IVF–ET

Comparison of results between centres can be difficult because data are presented in different ways and patient selection criteria may also vary. Pregnancy rates can be reported per cycle started, per egg collection or per embryo transfer procedure, but perhaps the most meaningful figure for patients is the 'take home baby rate'. Major factors that adversely affect success rates are the severity of sperm disorders and the female partner's age being greater than 40 years.

In their Annual Report of 1992, the HFEA published IVF treatment data collected from 64 assisted conception units in the UK (HFEA, 1992). Overall, the average pregnancy rate per IVF cycle started was 17.3% (range 2.7–45.0%); the average live birth rate was 12.5% per cycle (range 2.1–33.3%) and the overall multiple pregnancy rate was 25.6% (21.9% being twins, 3.6% triplets and 0.1% quadruplets). The overall congenital malformation rate for babies born following IVF is not increased over the background rate for the general population.

Gamete intrafallopian transfer (GIFT)

GIFT is a more recent alternative to IVF–ET (Asch et al, 1985) and is only possible if the woman has at least one patent and healthy tube. The superovulation regimens used for GIFT are the same as those for IVF. The difference, however, lies in the way in which the gametes are replaced and the site of fertilisation. Egg retrieval can be accomplished either laparoscopically or transvaginally, as in IVF, and is performed under general anaesthesia, as this is required for the laparoscopic transfer of the gametes to the fallopian tube. A maximum of three eggs are transferred, together with a small amount of medium containing motile sperm, under direct vision laparoscopically into the fallopian tube. Advocates of GIFT claim that it has the advantage that fertilisation and early embryo development occur as they would do naturally in vivo. The disadvantage, however, lies in the inability to obtain information relating to the sperm–egg interaction and the fertilising ability of the sperm. Many assisted conception units would not, therefore, offer GIFT as a first-line treatment to couples who have no documented evidence of previous fertilisation, preferring IVF, which will yield more information. Nevertheless, GIFT may be a more acceptable alternative for couples who, for religious or moral reasons, may find the creation of embryos in vitro unacceptable. Reports on GIFT are mostly limited to relatively small series of cases, but reported pregnancy rates per cycle are 26–36% (Hull, 1992).

Zygote intrafallopian transfer (ZIFT)

In ZIFT, or tubal embryo transfer (TET), the superovulation regimen, egg retrieval and fertilisation are performed in the same way as for IVF; however, once the eggs are fertilised (i.e. at the two pronucleate stage), they are transferred into the fallopian tube laparoscopically, the day after oocyte retrieval. The main disadvantage of ZIFT is that two operative procedures are required. Success rates of up to 48% per transfer procedure have been claimed (Devroey et al, 1989). The theoretical advantages are that early embryo development takes place where it would naturally and that, in contrast to GIFT, information is obtained about fertilisation.

Egg donation

Egg donation may be required for women who have undergone a premature menopause, where the ovaries have been surgically removed or damaged by chemotherapy or radiotherapy, for women born without normal ovaries (e.g. Turner's syndrome) and for women who are at significant risk of passing on a serious genetic disorder to their children.

To obtain sperm for donation from male donors is technically simple, as a single ejaculate from a fertile donor will contain millions of spermatozoa. It is rather more complicated to obtain eggs for donation, as egg donors have to undergo an egg collection procedure, and, in order to obtain more than one egg, the donors have to undergo the same drug stimulation regimen as do patients going through IVF, which carries the risk of OHSS. Also, egg donors should ideally be under the age of 35, because of the increased risks of genetic abnormalities, such as Down's syndrome, with advancing maternal age, yet have completed their own family. These factors combine to mean there is always a severe shortage of egg donors.

Once eggs have been obtained from a donor, they can be fertilised by the sperm of the recipient's partner, as in conventional IVF, or replaced into the fallopian tube of the recipient, together with her partner's sperm, as in GIFT. However, to protect against the risks of HIV, the safest course of action is to fertilise the oocytes, store the frozen embryos and replace them once repeat testing has established that the donor is free from HIV infection. The disadvantage is that the chances of success are not as good as if fresh oocytes or embryos are used. If the woman who is going to receive the embryos has ovarian failure, she will need to be given HRT to ensure that the endometrium is appropriate for implantation to occur and to support the early pregnancy.

As with DI, all parties involved must have access to trained counsellors to consider all the implications of this type of treatment.

CONCLUSIONS

Subfertility is a common problem and can profoundly alter the lives of affected couples. Ideally, patients should be seen in a dedicated subfertility clinic, where a sympathetic approach, combined with a reasonably rapid and systematic protocol of investigation, can minimise the stress for these couples. Good communication is essential at all stages of management, and a team approach, using the skills of fertility nurses and trained counsellors in conjunction with clinicians, is likely to benefit patients. Although treatment of many causes of subfertility has become more successful in the past decade, unfortunately no therapy can guarantee conception. A pregnancy rate of 30% per treatment cycle, which would, for example, be good for many IVF units, leaves 70% coping with devastating disappointment, sometimes recurrently. An important role of personnel working with subfertile patients is to provide support throughout treatment, particularly at the time that they consider stopping active treatment, and help them to see this decision in a positive light, rather than as a failure.

References

Armar N A and Lachelin G C L (1993) Laparoscopic ovarian diathermy: an effective treatment for anti-oestrogen resistant anovulatory infertility in women with the polycystic ovary syndrome. *British Journal of Obstetrics and Gynaecology*, **100**(2): 161–4.

Asch R H, Ellsworth L R, Balmaceda J P and Wong P C (1985) Birth following gamete intrafallopian transfer. *Lancet*, **ii**: 163.

Braude P R, Ross L D, Bolton V and Ockenden K (1987) Retrograde ejaculation: a systematic approach to non-invasive recovery of spermatozoa from post-ejaculatory urine for artificial insemination. *British Journal of Obstetrics and Gynaecology*, **94**: 76–83.

Brown J B, Pepperell R J and Evans J H (1987) Disorders of ovulation. In: Pepperell R J, Hudson B and Wood C (eds) *The Infertile Couple*. London: Churchill Livingstone.

Devroey P, Staessen C, Camus M, De Grauwe E, Wisanto A and Van Steirteghem A C (1989) Zygote intrafallopian transfer as a successful treatment for unexplained infertility. *Fertility and Sterility*, **52**(2): 246–9.

Dodson W and Haney F (1991) Controlled ovarian hyperstimulation and intrauterine insemination for treatment of infertility. *Fertility and Sterility*, **55**: 457.

Evans J, Wells C, Gregory L and Walker S (1991) A comparison of intrauterine insemination, intraperitoneal insemination, and natural intercourse in superovulated women. *Fertility and Sterility*, **56**(6): 1183–7.

Glezerman M (1993) Artificial insemination. In: Insler V and Lunenfeld B (eds) *Infertility Male and Female*. London: Churchill Livingstone.

Golan A, Ron–El R, Herman A, Soffer Y, Weinraub Z and Caspi E (1989) Ovarian hyperstimulation syndrome: an update review. *Obstetrical and Gynecological Survey*, **44**(6): 430–40.

Gorlitsky G A, Kase N G and Speroff L (1978) Ovulation and pregnancy rates with clomiphene citrate. *Obstetrics and Gynaecology*, **51**: 265.

HFEA (1992) *Annual Report*. London: HFEA.

Hughes E G, Collins J P and Garner P R (1987) Homologous artificial insemination for oligoasthenospermia: a randomized controlled study comparing intracervical and intrauterine techniques. *Fertility and Sterility*, **48**(2): 278–81.

Hull M G R (1992) Infertility treatment: relative effectiveness of conventional and assisted conception methods. *Human Reproduction*, **7**(6): 785.

Kirby C A, Warnes G M and Flaherty S P (1991) A prospective trial of intrauterine insemination of motile spermatozoa versus timed intercourse. *Fertility and Sterility*, **56**: 102–7.

Martin K, Santoro N, Hall J, Filicori M, Wierman M and Crowley W F (1990) Management of ovulatory disorders with pulsatile gonadotrophin-releasing hormone. *Journal of Clinical Endocrinology and Metabolism*, **71**: 1081.

Speroff L, Glass R H and Kase N G (1989) *Clinical Gynecologic Endocrinology and Infertility*. Baltimore, Maryland: Williams and Wilkins.

Van Steirteghem A C, Nagy Z, Joris H et al (1993) High fertilisation and implantation rates after intracytoplasmic sperm injection. *Human Reproduction*, **8**(7): 1061–6.

Wang C, Chan C W, Wong K K and Yeung K K (1983) Comparison of the effectiveness of placebo, clomiphene citrate, mesterolone, pentoxyfylline, and testosterone rebound therapy for the treatment of idiopathic oligospermia. *Fertility and Sterility*; **40**: 358–65.

World Health Organisation (1992) *WHO Laboratory Manual for the Examination of Human Semen and Sperm–Cervical Mucus Interaction*, 3rd edn., p. 44. Cambridge: Cambridge University Press.

Yuen B H (1992) Etiology and treatment of hyperprolactinemia. *Seminars in Reproductive Endocrinology*, **10**(3): 228–35.

5

The development of the nurse's role

Jane Denton

INTRODUCTION

The aim of this chapter is to consider the role of the infertility nurse. The current position will be examined and the opportunities and uncertainties identified. Finally, the ways in which the role should be developed to fulfil training and organisational needs will be discussed, taking into account factors that are influencing changes in nursing generally.

Over the past few years, advances in scientific knowledge and increasing clinical skills have resulted in rapid developments in the treatment of infertility. Although there have been references to infertility and various remedies throughout history, it is only now, through the new technologies, that it has become established as a medical subspecialty.

Infertility is a unique field, both in terms of the clinical and scientific methods used and the fact that the main aim of the treatment is to produce new life. Patients are not ill in the strictly defined sense; psychological effects of involuntary infertility, however, may have long-term consequences that are underestimated, but, as yet, there have been no studies fully to assess this.

The other factor that differentiates treatment in this field is that, in the UK, the majority of the assisted conception procedures are carried out in private clinics.

Staff from all disciplines working in the specialty have developed their roles through hands-on experience and adaptation within their own teams, to provide the treatment services that are now available. As a result of this individualised approach, there is diversity between units in the roles of all staff, particularly in that of the nurse.

The technology has raced ahead, leaving other aspects of the treatment services evolving more slowly. Clinicians, scientists, nurses and counsellors are identifying the training needs of those working in the field, and appropriate courses and training pathways are being developed. Professional bodies have been established, such as the British Infertility Counselling Association (BICA) and the Association of Clinical Embryologists (ACE), and, in response to their professional needs, infertility nurses have established a membership group, the Fertility Nurses Group (FNG), within the RCN. The formation of this group is a good point at which to start to look at the nurse's role.

THE CURRENT POSITION

In 1987, a group of infertility nurses met informally at RCN Headquarters to consider the professional requirements within the specialty. The main concerns were the lack of specific training and educational opportunities and the need for professional guidance in an area fraught with moral issues and ethical dilemmas, in which a completely new nursing role was developing. It was decided that the first step should be to establish more precise details of the range of tasks undertaken and also to identify the areas of concern. To achieve this, the FNG carried out a questionnaire survey (RCN Fertility Nurses Group, 1990). The questionnaire was circulated to 100 infertility units, which were selected on the basis of how they were funded; 50 were in the NHS and 50 were completely private centres. A further division was made in each section, by selecting 25 that specialised in infertility and 25 that combined infertility with other gynaecological treatments. The overall response rate was 59%.

The analysis confirmed the diversity of the nurse's role, with wide variation in everything from clinical tasks to job titles. It indicated that the majority of infertility nurses were Registered General Nurses (RGNs), and about half of these also had a midwifery qualification. Most of them had received postbasic training but considered that this was insufficient to prepare them for their current role. There was a demand for a specialised training course, preferably away from the working environment.

It appeared that the teaching they had received was provided by medical colleagues in over half the cases, and only a small number had any training input from nurses. Ten per cent had training from members of other disciplines, such as ultrasonographers. It was inevitable that training should be on this basis, as there were no other sources available. However, the important factor was that two-thirds of nurses considered that they were inadequately prepared for their role.

According to the survey, the majority of nurses moved into caring for the infertile as a result of their medical colleagues choosing to expand the type of treatment available, which ultimately extended the nurse's role; an example of this would be ovulation induction offered as part of the services in a gynaecology outpatients clinic.

Most of the nurses in the specialist units had previously worked in gynaecology or midwifery. In the rest of the centres surveyed, caring for infertility patients was only part of the nurses' role, as they also worked in other areas, including obstetrics, gynaecology, general surgery and endocrinology. As previously mentioned, one of the most striking things about the infertility nurse's role is its variability. Infertility nurses can be divided initially into those who incorporate their work with infertile patients with other treatment, for example nurses working in a general gynaecology outpatients department with perhaps an infertility clinic once a week, and those who work in dedicated units. The types of treatment offered in the specialist units vary. Some may only provide DI, others only in vitro fertilisation, and some provide a comprehensive infertility service incorporating all types of treatment. There has been a further step in the differentiation as a result of the licensing requirements resulting from the Human Fertilisation and Embryology Act 1990; details of licensable activities are given in Chapter 8. The HFEA Code of Practice (HFEA, 1993) is an excellent model for good practice, which could be adapted for use with all infertility treatment, although the unlicensed centres do not have the same legal obligation to adhere to it.

The FNG survey indicated that most units employ between three and six nurses, while 16% of the units have more than six nurses. However, it is clear from wide discussion with members of the FNG that many infertility clinics have only one or two nurses.

There is generally some confusion over nursing titles, as confirmed by a survey commissioned by the Department of Health (Butterworth, 1994), which called for clarification. Infertility is no exception, and this issue must be addressed. The conventional 'staff nurse' and 'sister' titles are used in some cases, while in others, 'nurse coordinator' is common. To further confuse the issue, in some units, the doctors are referred to as coordinators. Nurses with the same title, but working in different clinics, are likely to have very different jobs. For instance, the nurse coordinator in one clinic that offers IVF may be responsible for organising appointments and ensuring that patients understand the instructions from the doctors, and may act as a chaperone but have no clinical role, while a nurse with the same title in another clinic may directly supervise the monitoring of cycles, perform ovarian scans, assist with egg retrieval procedures and embryo transfers and also be involved in some of the counselling. In some clinics, nurses may act only as chaperones, while in others, they perform intracervical and intrauterine inseminations, embryo transfers and ultrasonography. Others carry out some of the tasks traditionally attributed to laboratory staff, such as semen analysis, preparation and cryo-preservation of semen samples and various diagnostic tests. Some nurses are trained as embryologists and combine this with their other nursing tasks. The provision of counselling for the infertile, and who should provide it, has provoked much debate between nurses, counsellors and clinicians involved with treatment services. Nurses contribute to the counselling process to differing degrees, but this part of the role requires clarification and definition. The title of the nurse, therefore, gives limited information about her role.

There is also a variation in the management of units, and more information about this is required. The range of types of unit, from those that are part of a large NHS Trust to those that are privately owned and dedicated to infertility work, inevitably results in different management structures. The main issue, according to anecdotal information from infertility nurses, is that the managers in all types of units do not, in many cases, understand the nurse's role, as they do not have sufficient knowledge of the specialty. In some cases, nurses are directly responsible to the medical director of the unit. There have been reports of difficulties arising in such cases, when doctors are not familiar with UKCC guidelines for practice and nurses have no other management support for issues relating to their role. However, in some units, mainly private ones, nurses have become specialist managers, as their roles evolved in conjunction with the service provided by the clinic.

SOME AREAS OF CONCERN WITH THE NURSE'S ROLE

An outstanding factor frequently reported by infertility nurses is their feeling of professional isolation; there are several reasons for this. Some such nurses work in private centres, which are physically self-contained and wholly dedicated to infertility services. They have no connection with the provision of any other health care, so there is no access to the support, management and training structures available in larger private and NHS hospitals. Interestingly, even within the environment of a large hospital, infertility nurses find that there is often a lack of knowledge and understanding of their role and the functions of the whole infertility unit from colleagues working in different areas and also from managers. This may be even more apparent in infertility units where there are only one or two nurses. They often feel that there is nobody with sufficient knowledge of the specialty with whom they can discuss problems arising from some aspect of their work. This raises the fundamental point that these nurses are pioneering a new and unique role, to which principles of nursing are applied but which incorporates few of the traditional tasks. The complexities of the clinical treatment and the inevitable jargon that evolves in any medical specialty, combined with scientific research that presents society with complex moral dilemmas, may seem daunting to those who do not work in the field, and, as a result, they may find it difficult to appreciate exactly what the work entails. Networking will help to alleviate the sense of isolation, so it is important to take every opportunity to communicate with colleagues, not just infertility nurses but also other health-care professionals with common interests. Practice nurses, midwives and gynaecology nurses may all come into contact with infertility patients, and sharing ideas and, where possible, solving problems are likely to result in better care for patients. Joining professional organisations and attending conferences and study days increases knowledge of developments in the specialty, and collective approaches to professional problems are more likely to have effective results.

The clinical work may present problems if nurses are unsure of what they should be undertaking. As there is, at present, no standardised training and peer assessment, nurses are usually taught by doctors to carry out procedures such as IUI and embryo transfer. Doctors may be anxious for the nurse to take on this delegated task, and the nurse, feeling pressurised, may do so before she is competent and confident, which is contrary to the UKCC's Code of Professional Conduct (UKCC, 1992a). Many nurses perform ultrasound examinations to monitor growth of the ovarian follicles, and, again, they are taught on an *ad hoc* basis by doctors or sometimes ultrasonographers. Some courses are available in general ultrasonography, but these do not focus on developing the skills of closely monitoring the growth of ovarian follicles. There is no standard form of assessment of a nurse's competence in scanning. Some nurses also have the responsibility of making decisions about whether to continue with injections of gonadotrophins, based on the rate of growth and size of the follicles. This raises the issue of accountability and legal protection, which will be addressed later in the chapter.

A development over the past few years in the provision of treatment is the growth in the number of clinics offering 'transport IVF' (Kingsland et al, 1992). This involves patients having treatment up to the point of egg retrieval at a 'satellite centre'; the eggs are then transferred in an incubator to the main centre, usually by the partner, although in some cases a member of staff does this. The embryology work and embryo transfer are all carried out at the main centre. Where transport IVF is offered, it is essential that nurses in both the satellite and main centres ensure that their roles are clarified, and excellent communication is of paramount importance.

ETHICAL ISSUES

The developments in reproductive technology have presented society with some challenging moral dilemmas (Bromham et al, 1988), which must be considered by the multidisciplinary team in the development and implementation of policies. Although the Human Fertilisation and Embryology Act 1990 has given a practical interpretation of some of the ethical problems, such as embryo research, teams working in infertility units are constantly faced with ethical decision-making. The selection of patients for treatment is a controversial issue, although in some cases, this is taken out of the direct control of units if the health authorities are funding treatment, either by block contracts or extra-contractual referrals. Selection criteria are established by each health authority, but these vary greatly and continue to provoke wide debate. A survey commissioned by ISSUE illustrates the inconsistencies in the present procedures (College of Health, 1993). Units treating self-funding patients must have a selection process. The HFEA Code of Practice stipulates that 'Centres should take all reasonable steps to ensure that people receiving treatment and any children resulting from it have the best possible protection from harm to their health. Before providing any woman with treatment, centres must also take account of the welfare of any child who may be born or affected as a result of the treatment' (HFEA, 1993: Section 3.1). The Code of Practice gives guidance on how to make this assessment, and, as with the rest of the Code, this provides an excellent basis for use by all infertility units, not just the licensed centres. As scientific and clinical advances are made, further ethical problems are presented. One such issue is the treatment of postmenopausal women (see Chapter 2), and as research continues to cross scientific boundaries, society must address the questions raised about the morality of the work.

All members of the multidisciplinary teams must consider their personal values and beliefs and ensure that these are compatible with their roles. It is essential for each nurse to consider her own personal ethical stance. She needs a sound theoretical basis on which to make decisions on ethical matters that can be applied in everyday practice, and this must be addressed in training programmes. Furthermore, consideration must be given to future ethical problems likely to arise with scientific progress. Every nurse has a duty to herself to make sure she is comfortable with the work in which she is participating. Part of the recruitment process for all staff in infertility units should include discussion about the ethical issues; managers should clarify exactly what the work entails and discuss conscientious objection. The Human Fertilisation and Embryology Act 1990 makes provision for anybody who can show a conscientious objection to any of the activities carried out in licensed centres not to be obliged to participate.

THE WAY FORWARD

Infertility is an exciting area for all professionals involved. The enthusiasm shown by the response to conferences, workshops and study days for infertility nurses, and discussions on these occasions, indicates a strong commitment to developing the nursing role in the specialty. It is difficult to assess the number of nurses in this field, but, at the time of writing, the FNG has 800 members. The HFEA has 104 licensed centres (HFEA, 1994), with an approximate average of two nurses each. It is difficult to assess how many other nurses are involved, but a further survey of infertility nurses is planned to gather more information.

The two main areas that need to be developed in infertility nursing are training and education, and general organisational policies. In addition, the two broad categories of infertility nurse must be considered. These are, firstly, nurses working full time in dedicated infertility units and, secondly, those such as practice and gynaecology nurses who are involved with some aspects of the care of infertility patients as part of a wider role. Nurses working full time in infertility in dedicated units are developing their own network, through such organisations as the FNG and the British Fertility Society (BFS), which was founded by clinicians but has now opened its membership to nurses, counsellors and scientists. Regular meetings held by these organisations facilitate multidisciplinary communication. This networking should be extended to include the 'part-time' infertility nurses to enhance the overall service to the infertile.

EDUCATION

The first step in considering how training for infertility nurses should be structured is to review the current situation for all nursing education. The Project 2000 reforms (UKCC, 1986) are the basis for the changes that are being implemented. A framework for postregistration education and practice, known as PREP (UKCC, 1990), was developed, and this is now known as the Standards for Education and Practice following Registration. This sets out standards required to maintain an effective registration, a model for practice and a framework for education to prepare for practice. All nurses will be required to undertake a minimum of 5 days study for professional development every 3 years for effective registration (UKCC, 1994). It is stressed that consideration should be given to the relevance of the subject matter, the qualifications and experience of the leaders or speakers, and the objectives and evaluation of any formal study undertaken to fulfil the UKCC requirements. Guidance will be sent to all practitioners renewing their registration, with requirements to be met at the time of their next renewal, which will be three years later. This will allow adequate time for them to prepare to meet the UKCC's standards.

It is fortuitous that education and training for infertility nurses is also at a developmental stage, and the model evolved by the UKCC clarifies the direction that infertility training must take. The next step is to look at how this can be implemented.

Firstly, let us consider the category of nurses who are not working in infertility full time. These are mainly gynaecology, practice and family planning nurses. A recent survey of practice nurses (Atkin et al, 1993) revealed that 30% in fundholding and 31% in non-fundholding GP practices have a family planning qualification, and, overall, 75% carry out cervical smears. These nurses should have some knowledge of all aspects of infertility, as they are potentially one of the first points of contact for women raising concerns about their fertility. There is a case for basic information about infertility and its treatment to be included· as a core feature in their training programmes. The argument against this is that there is a strong case for infertility services to be provided predominantly in specialised tertiary units (Effective Health Care, 1992), which would result in these nurses having less involvement with infertility patients. However, even if this situation arose in the future, these nurses would still need to have some knowledge of the emotional impact and the clinical treatments involved with infertility, to enable them to support these couples, with whom they are likely to have contact at some stage during the course of their work. For this reason, some information about infertility should be included in core curricula.

The second category is the full-time fertility nurses. The HFEA Code of Practice (HFEA, 1993) requires that licensed centres should employ at least one nurse or midwife with current effective UKCC registration. It also requires all staff taking part in specialist activities to receive regular updating, but, at the moment, there is no further specification of the form that this should take.

Since the 1970s, there has been much discussion about the development of specialisation in nursing. The PREP proposals recognise that there is a clear distinction between being engaged in specialist practice and simply working in a specialty. Specialist patient requirements call for additional education for safe and effective practice (UKCC, 1994).

The specialist nursing practice qualification will reflect the additional knowledge and skill acquired by practitioners and will be recorded against their names in the register. The areas of specialist nursing practice for which a postregistration programme is required have been defined and are divided into critical, acute and continuing care nursing. These are not watertight categories, as there are elements of each in some aspects of practice, and the UKCC will continue to review the list. Gynaecology is included, but infertility nursing is not.

The preparation for specialist nursing practice concentrates on four areas: clinical nursing practice; care and programme management; clinical practice development; and clinical practice leadership. The content of the education programmes and learning outcomes are specified. This may be particularly challenging with infertility, because the small specialist teams and the nurse's role do not allow for development on the basis that is outlined. For example, in an infertility unit with only one or two nurses, it would be difficult to acquire and implement leadership skills relating to support, supervising other nurses and teaching and overseeing student placements.

As discussed earlier in the chapter, the role of the nurse varies considerably between each unit. Those who have worked in the field for some time and gained considerable experience, through learning from doctors and developing their own roles through practice, describe themselves as having an extended role, in some cases as clinical nurse specialists. It is arguable, however, that some of these tasks should be the responsibility of other members of the team. Laboratory work, such as preparation of semen samples for insemination, is undertaken by some nurses, as is some of the counselling. Nurses take this on with the best intentions, considering that they are providing their patients with continuity of care; however, this may not always be the case, as they may not have the time or experience to provide the highest standards of care and service in several different areas. There may also be pressure from lack of resources or the efforts to cut the costs to self-funding patients by staff taking on these additional roles. Professional boundaries should only be crossed when the nurse is aware and confident of her abilities and has time to fulfil all her duties effectively.

As some nurses consider themselves to be practising at the 'specialist nurses' level, their roles should be used as the basis for developing the training that will ultimately meet the requirements for qualification as specialist infertility nurse practitioners. In these cases, their knowledge and experience should be evaluated through assessment of prior experiential learning (APEL), to ascertain what further training is required for accreditation. More information must be gathered about the infertility nurse's role and common tasks and responsibilities identified to provide a basis for the future educational needs.

In the meantime, education programmes should aim to provide nurses with a comprehensive knowledge of all aspects of infertility and also teach them how to develop their roles rationally and objectively within multidisciplinary teams to provide safe and effective practice. The first course to be established is the RCN Institute of Advanced Nursing Education Assisted Conception Nursing Care Course. Within the academic framework, the course leads to 60 credit points at level 2, so could contribute towards a Diploma or Honours degree in Nursing. The curriculum covers reproductive physiology, ethics, research and issues in nursing practice, sociological, political and legal perspectives, psychology and issues relating to counselling. The course will be reviewed as necessary with the aim of contributing towards the UKCC qualification in specialist practice. It is hoped that further such courses will be established in the near future.

Advanced practice has been the source of much debate and the title of clinical nurse specialist and consultant applied to this level of practice. To function as an advanced practitioner, the nurse is likely to need additional knowledge and skills at Masters degree level. Advanced practice will be concerned with adjusting the boundaries of practice and contributing to health policy. Nurses working at advanced level will be involved with practice development and clinical supervision, leadership in clinical practice, audit development and research.

The next few years will be a transitional period in which these reforms are established. The Council recognises that close liaison is necessary to ensure that the learning outcomes and programme content are applicable to the specific speciality. Infertility nurses must ensure that they contribute to the process of identifying appropriate and feasible education programmes and outcome criteria that comply with the UKCC standards, through channels such as the RCN FNC.

The ENB has established a Framework and Higher Award for Continuing Professional Education for Nurses, Midwives and Health Visitors. The aim of the Framework is to provide a flexible system that will enable practitioners to work towards the ENB Higher Award. Each nurse can plan an individual programme of professional development related to her practice, based on the 10 key characteristics that have been identified. The versatility of this system is particularly useful for infertility nurses.

COUNSELLING AND TRAINING

The importance of nursing education incorporating communication and counselling skills has been recognised and addressed throughout the Project 2000 reforms. This is particularly relevant to infertility, as counselling plays a crucial part in the care of infertile patients as discussed in the Chapters 8 and 9 on the HFEA and counselling. The HFEA Code of Practice gives very helpful and specific guidance about the provision of counselling, which should ideally be used as a model in all infertility units and not just licensed centres. Who should fulfil the counselling role and the training necessary for this is a subject that has provoked much debate. The FNG survey referred to earlier revealed that, in over half the units, nurses were the main counsellors. However, only one-quarter of nurses had received any counselling training, and 93% believed that they needed training. In response to this, short courses and workshops have been organised, and while these are of value, it should be recognised that they probably do not provide sufficient counselling skills training. When selecting a course, nurses should take into consideration the credit points and academic level to ensure that, as far as possible, postregistration training requirements are met.

As discussed in Chapter 9, the nurse is likely to be involved in giving information to the couple, which can overlap with implications counselling. Counselling skills training will enhance the ability of the nurse to understand the difference between these two areas and also to be aware of her own limitations. She will also need to recognise when a couple require the help of a counsellor and have the necessary skills to convey this to them in a sensitive and positive way, to ensure, as far as possible, that they accept counselling. There are many generic communication and counselling skills courses that are suitable, and, ideally, all infertility nurses should undertake such a course as soon as possible. Suitable courses have been identified, and a list is available from the British Infertility Counselling Association. The King's Fund Centre report (1991) suggested a model for training, and a Working Group facilitated by the HFEA is currently considering the way forward.

DEVELOPING THE ROLE

Yet another area of current debate relates to 'extended' and 'enhanced' roles. Clay (1987) uses the definitions of an 'extended' role being one not included in basic nurse training and comprising tasks undertaken by a doctor but which may be delegated to a nurse who has received appropriate training and has been assessed as competent, and an 'enhanced' role as a one that is expanded round the needs of the patient, rather than simply taking on delegated tasks.

The Scope of Professional Practice (UKCC, 1992b) says that the term 'extended role' is no longer suitable and gives guidance based on a set of principles that 'provide the basis for ensuring that practice remains dynamic and is able readily and appropriately to adjust to meet changing care needs'. In the past, 'official' recognition of the extended role has been by certification. The UKCC believes that this concentration on activities can detract from an holistic approach to nursing care. This makes it clear that the ultimate responsibility is upon the practitioner to determine her own individual competence and to be prepared to refuse to undertake a task if she is not confident (Dimond, 1994). This is very pertinent to infertility, as more nurses are being trained by doctors to carry out such procedures as IUI. Initially, doctors have had to train nurses, but as nurses become experienced, they can begin to take over the training. However, it is essential that UKCC requirements are complied with and, if necessary, advice is sought from professional bodies about how this should be implemented. It is likely that there will be an increasing need for professional guidelines, such as those already issued by the FNG on IUI and embryo transfer.

ACCOUNTABILITY AND PROTOCOLS

All nurses must be aware of the issues surrounding accountability and use the UKCC Code of Professional Conduct (UKCC 1992a) as a basis for their actions. Infertility nurses may be particularly vulnerable when accepting delegation of tasks if they are working in isolation, with managers with no nursing experience. As already discussed, the techniques and roles of the doctor and the nurses are evolving with the advances in the specialty. Rapid changes in a busy unit may lead to insufficient consideration of the task undertaken by the nurse, who must bear in mind that she should 'acknowledge any limitations in [her] knowledge and competence and decline any duties or responsibilities unless able to perform them in a safe and skilled manner' (UKCC, 1992b). In addition, as previously discussed, the nurse may be working in isolation, with senior colleagues unable to assist as they lack suffcient detailed knowledge of the speciality. The nurse is accountable for her own actions, and, as Pyne (1992) says, 'nobody else be they medical practitioner, senior colleagues or manager can bear their accountability for them'. This raises the importance of having protocols. These are used in health care to assist diagnosis, improve medical care of a disease, manage or reduce costs and provide legal protection (*Nursing Standard*, 1993). The HFEA Code of Practice (HFEA, 1993) requires licensed units to have an 'effective system for monitoring and assessing laboratory clinical and counselling practice'. Emphasis is also placed on continuous assessment and review to improve practice and the quality of the service offered. There is a temptation, particularly in small clinics with one doctor and one nurse, to assume that each knows exactly what the other is doing and to regard protocols or written standard procedures as unnecessary. This is a dangerous assumption, and the nurse should have written details of all the procedures she performs, which should be regularly reviewed to ensure they reflect current practice. There may be frequent changes in clinical management of patients as more research is published and techniques refined. Appropriate protocols also provide evidence of good safe practice should any medicolegal issues arise.

CLINICAL SUPERVISION AND PERFORMANCE REVIEW

Supervision in counselling is recognised as being very important in allowing counsellors to share their working practice and continue to develop their skills to provide a better service for their clients. A similar system for nurses is another topic that is currently being debated. The terms 'clinical supervision', 'mentorship' and 'preceptorship' are being used more widely, but, as Faugier and Butterworth (1994) have observed, there is some confusion about their meaning. In the past, qualification was viewed as an end in itself, and qualified nurses were deterred from obtaining the professional supervision and support they needed as it was regarded as a weakness or 'inability to cope'. Clinical supervision is usually associated with a management activity, and, as Platt-Koch (1986) says, 'To many nurses, supervision means observation by an administrative supervisor who inspects, directs, controls and evaluates the nurse's work'. However, Butterworth and Faugier (1992) describe it as 'An exchange between practising professionals to enable the development of professional skills'. The aim of supervision is to encourage the development of knowledge and competence and to enable practitioners to assume responsibility for their own practice, which will result in the delivery of safe and effective care.

Nurses at all levels require supervision, and ways of achieving this are currently being examined (Faugier and Butterworth, 1994). The UKCC has issued a position statement on clinical supervision for consultation and this should be finalised in late 1995. The reported diversity in the infertility nurse's role and the isolation felt by many (Walker, 1994) suggest that supervision would be particularly appropriate. Individual performance review, previously referred to as staff appraisal, is another term that is becoming familiar. In the developing framework for nursing, this will be increasingly undertaken by the clinical supervisor and should be a valuable tool in assisting individual practitioners to reach their full potential and also maintain high standards of care. Managers and senior nurses in infertility units, if not already doing so, should be establishing effective mechanisms to achieve this. Even in small units, it is beneficial to take time objectively to examine the role of the nurse and how it is changing, and this can only be realistically carried out if a specific procedure is followed.

THE MULTIDISCIPLINARY TEAM

The other important facet is the infertility nurse's role within the multidisciplinary team. The fact that the title 'coordinator' is increasingly used indicates that the nurse's role is seen as pivotal. The nurse usually liaises with other members of the team to organise management of the patient's treatment and also participates in clinical care to varying degrees.

As in many medical specialties, in dedicated infertility units, small teams work closely together. However, this alone does not lead to effective team working. Poulton and West (1993) suggest that team effectiveness is a combination of team performance and team viability. Performance is achieving agreed goals and providing an acceptable service to the patients; viability relates to the satisfaction of the team members, the clarity of their roles and processes such as communication.

Excellent communication is one of the key requirements. A mechanism for regular formal meetings and a commitment from all the team members is essential. This provides the opportunity to review all aspects of the service, from the policy issues to difficulties with individual patients. Protocols should be discussed, new ones drawn up and established ones reviewed in accordance with changes in practice. Nurses should contribute to the decision-making process, to ensure that any changes comply with their own practice and to enable them to provide the highest standards of care for their patients. All members of the team must have an understanding of each other's role, to enable them to have an overview of the treatment processes and also to appreciate and anticipate any difficulties that may arise, either in the provision of care or in the relationships between team members.

The professional boundaries of the team members must also be established and respected. This is a subtle process, and although protocols and job descriptions to some degree prescribe these, good communication and mutual respect for professional expertise is of paramount importance. This applies particularly if the nurse is undertaking information-giving and also contributing to the implications counselling (see Chapter 9). It should be recognised that she needs sufficient time and an appropriate setting, and she should not be expected to fulfil other clinical demands at short notice during the specific time that has been allocated for counselling.

Managers also need to be aware that compatibility of team members is important, and this should be considered when recruiting staff. The work is intense and emotionally demanding, and great commitment is required from everybody. It is potentially very destructive if there is poor communication and lack of cooperation within the team.

The team should also collectively address ethical issues and take into account individual views when formulating unit policy. The quality of the service provided depends on the efficient functioning of the team.

ASSESSING QUALITY OF CARE

'Clinical audit involves systematically looking at the procedures used for diagnosis, care and treatment, examining how associated resources are used and investigating the effect care has on the outcome and quality of life for the patient' (DoH, undated).

The health service reforms have focused attention on audit as a means of assessing the service provided, in order to identify areas that can be improved, with resulting cost-effective, high-standard care. The infertility units in the private sector are likely to have some mechanisms in place for audit as part of their business plans. The centres licensed by the HFEA are required to monitor treatments and success rates and have mechanisms for quality control in clinical and laboratory services. For these reasons, infertility units are already, to varying degrees, monitoring their services.

Each unit will need to identify a leader for the audit process, who may be a nurse. If not, nurses should be involved with the process, examining the cost-effectiveness and value of the service at the clinical team level as part of business planning. Audit should develop a culture of continuing evaluation and improvement of clinical effectiveness, focusing on patient outcomes (DoH, undated) The process should be seen as constant evaluation of quality of care.

Standard-setting and patient involvement should contribute to achieving high standards. The FNG has produced Standards of Care (RCN Fertility Nurses Group, 1993) (Table 5.1), which are intended as a broad base for nurses to adapt to their own practice situation. The Working Group recognised that, as infertility treatments progress, the Standards of Care will require frequent review, which should be reflected in the infertility units.

Table 5.1 Standards of Care for Fertility Nurses
(RCN, Fertility Nurses Group 1993)

Five main topics of concern to infertility nurses were identified and standards written on the following topics:

- Professional development and responsibilities
- Safety
- Patient care
  Subtopics – Care of the individual's needs within the couple
            – The role of the male partner
- Counselling
  Subtopics – Information-giving
            – Support counselling
- Ethical matters

At least one nurse coordinator has evaluated the service through a questionnaire to patients (Latarche, 1993), and other nurses may find this approach valuable.

Although introducing clinical audit and standard-setting has initial resource implications, the resulting benefits to the service should compensate for this.

CONSUMER ISSUES

The Health Service reforms have raised awareness of the rights and needs of patients. The Patient's Charter (DoH, 1991) specifies 10 patient rights and 9 standards that should be achieved. Some are more relevant to infertility than are others, such as the right to be given a clear explanation of any proposed treatment with the risks and alternatives before agreeing to proceed. Again, the licensed centres are already obliged to do this through the Human Fertilisation and Embryology Act 1990 and the HFEA Code of Practice. A further issue already addressed through the HFEA Code of Practice is the complaints procedure for patients. This is also being reviewed in the NHS. A recent report, *Being Heard* (Wilson,

1994), which is currently subject to consultation, makes recommendations to reform the NHS complaints system, which is, at present, slow and cumbersome. Nurses are often the first to be aware of a patient's discontent and, in many cases, can resolve the situation by dealing with it speedily and effectively, with apologies, explanations and assurances to investigate the cause and, where possible, rectify the situation. In Chapter 9, the reactions of infertility patients are described, and it is not unusual for strong feelings of anger to result in complaints, some of which may seem irrational at the time. The mechanisms already described in this chapter have an important function in the case of complaints. Counselling skills training will help communication with the patients; the necessity for standard procedures, with explicit protocols and accurate record-keeping, provides evidence of safe and appropriate practice; support from colleagues will be provided if the multidisciplinary team is functioning effectively.

CONCLUSION

Infertility is an exciting area of nursing. Although it is becoming recognised as a specialty, the challenge remains for those in the field to use the changes in education and professional development to ensure that the role continues to evolve in a way that provides a high standard of care for patients and fulfils their own professional needs. It is likely that there will only ever be a relatively small number of nurses in the specialty, which increases the need for networking to share ideas and learn from the experiences of peers. Those who are breaking new ground now are shaping the future for infertility nursing, and they must make sure that they are leading the way and not being swept along in the wake of the new technology.

References

Atkin J, Lunt N, Parker G and Hirst M (1993) *Nurses Count: A National Census of Practice Nurses.* York: Social Policy Research Unit, University of York.

Bromham D, Dalton M and Jackson J (1988) *Philosophical Ethics in Reproductive Medicine.* Proceedings of the First International Conference of Philosophical Ethics in Reproductive Medicine, Leeds.

Butterworth C A (1994) *A Delphi Survey of Optimum Practice in Nursing, Midwifery and Health Visiting.* Manchester: Manchester University.

Butterworth C A and Faugier J (eds) (1992) *Clinical Supervision and Mentorship in Nursing.* London: Chapman & Hall.

Clay T (1987) *Nurses, Power and Politics.* London: Heinemann.

College of Health (1993) *Report of the National Survey of the Funding and Provision of Infertility Services.* London: College of Health.

DoH (1991) *The Patient's Charter*. London: HMSO.

DoH (undated) *The Evolution of Clinical Audit*. London: HMSO.

Dimond B (1994) Legal aspects of role expansion. In: Hunt G and Wainwright P (eds) *Expanding the Role of the Nurse*. Oxford: Blackwell.

Effective Health Care (1992) *The Management of Subfertility*, Issue 3. Leeds: Leeds University.

Faugier J and Butterworth C A (1994) *Clinical Supervision: A Position Paper*. Manchester: School of Nursing Studies, University of Manchester.

HFEA (1993) *Code of Practice*. London: HFEA.

HFEA (1994) *Third Annual Report*. London: HFEA.

King's Fund Centre (1991) *Counselling for Regulated Infertility Treatments*. London: King's Fund Centre.

Kingsland C, Aziz N, Taylor C, Manasse P, Haddad N and Richmond D (1992) Transport in vitro fertilisation – a novel scheme for community based treatment. *Fertility and Sterility*, **58**: 153–8.

Latarche E (1994) Quality of service. *Conceive*, **26**: 8–9.

Nursing Standard (1993) Protocols: guidance for good practice. *Nursing Standard*, **8**(8): 29.

Platt-Koch L M (1986) Clinical supervision for psychiatric nurses. *Journal of Psychological Nursing*, **26**(1): 7–15.

Poulton B C and West M A (1993) Primary health care team effectiveness: developing a constituency approach. *Health and Social Care*, **2**: 77–84.

Pyne R (1992) Accountability in principle and in practice. *British Journal of Nursing*, **1**(6): 301.

RCN Fertility Nurses Group (1990) *Report of a Professional Survey*. London: RCN.

RCN Fertility Nurses Group (1993) *Standards of Care for Fertility Nurses*. London: RCN.

UKCC (1986) *Project 2000: A New Preparation for Practice*. London: UKCC.

UKCC (1990) *The Report of the Post-Registration Education and Practice Project*. London: UKCC.

UKCC (1992a) *Code of Professional Conduct for the Nurse, Midwife and Health Visitor*, 3rd edn. London: UKCC.

UKCC (1992b) *The Scope of Professional Practice*. London: UKCC.

UKCC (1994) *The Future of Professional Practice – The Council's Standards for Education and Practice Following Registration*. London: UKCC.

Walker P (1994) New educational horizons for assisted conception nursing. *British Journal of Midwifery*, **2**(6): 281–7.

Wilson A (1994) *Being Heard: A Report of a Review Committee on NHS Complaints Procedures*. Leeds: DoH.

6

The nurse's role
in specific treatments

Deborah Kiddy, Liz Corrigan and Sandra Cant

INTRODUCTION

As discussed in Chapter 5, the nurse's role in the infertility clinic may vary considerably. It may be confined to venepuncture, chaperoning and giving advice, but, with training and experience, it can be expanded, to the benefit of both the clinic and the patient. In this chapter, three experienced nurses discuss their roles in respect to three different types of treatment: ovulation induction, IVF and associated techniques, and DI.

HEALTH PROMOTION

It is important that any couple wishing to have a baby are given advice about the health issues that can affect the chance of conception, the risk of miscarriage and the health of the ensuing child. Advice should cover the risk of rubella infection, hepatitis B and C and toxoplasmosis. Diabetes screening is also advisable.

A woman trying to conceive should have a healthy, well-balanced diet. The Department of Health advises all women to take 0.4 mg folic acid per day and to continue this dose for the first trimester of pregnancy, to reduce the risk of having a baby with a neural tube defect. This dose is available over the counter at pharmacies and is best taken on its own rather than in a multivitamin preparation. If a woman has had a previous pregnancy resulting in a neural tube defect, it is recommended she take 5 mg folic acid per day (available only on prescription) for the same time period. If the woman is epileptic, this dose of folic acid may affect the dose of anticonvulsant therapy required, so discussion with a doctor is advised prior to starting folic acid supplements. It is also recommended that a diet including foods with a high folic acid content should be followed (DoH, 1992).

Alcohol can affect male and female fertility and contribute to miscarriage, so couples should be advised to restrict their intake. Smoking may make both men and women less fertile; it has been reported that smoking is associated with a one-third reduction in fertilisation of eggs in in vitro fertilisation (Rosevear et al, 1992), and it would, therefore, be expected to affect natural monthly fecundity similarly, as observed by Baird et al (1985). Passive smoking also has deleterious effects on a woman trying to conceive; in addition, women who smoke run a higher risk of miscarriage. Many women report disorders of their menstrual cycle after stressful life events, but it is difficult to assess the effect of stress on ovulation. It helps if women are not asked to keep basal body temperature charts to assess whether their cycles are ovulatory, as this is an investigation that can raise stress levels, reminding the women of their infertility. It is a good idea for couples with infertility, and particularly those undergoing investigation or treatment, to find ways of relaxing. It can be part of the nurse's role to facilitate communication between the couple, as this may alleviate stress and can sometimes be lacking.

OVULATION INDUCTION

At the beginning of treatment to induce ovulation, the treatment protocols should be discussed with the couple. The mechanism of action, side-effects and efficacy of drugs to be used should be explained, as should any procedures, for example vaginal ultrasound scan. Information leaflets are useful adjuncts to verbal information. The number of cycles of treatment to be given, with realistic expectations regarding the likelihood of success, and any potential risks, should be discussed. (Many couples think, if anovulation has been the problem, that the first time the woman ovulates, she will conceive. Unfortunately, the human race is not a particularly fertile one, and this does not usually occur.) Although this should be discussed by the clinician, it is often necessary for the nurse to repeat such details. The nurse is often perceived as having more time than clinicians, and, therefore, patients will often ask her more questions, which means that she should be both available and approachable. It is important in an ovulation induction programme to give continuity of care to patients, by ensuring they are seen by the same staff as much as possible. In this specialty, as in other areas of nursing, it is of great importance to be precise in one's language and explain terminology carefully.

As in all infertility treatment, it is important that both partners should be involved. The male partner should be encouraged to be present at any consultation and treatment, if the couple so desire. He sometimes likes to feel more involved, so may, for example, help with the daily injections or changing the subcutaneous needle for the pulsatile GnRH pump. Sexual intercourse 'on demand' can, at best, take the spontaneity out of a relationship and can cause sexual problems; it is important that couples realise that this is common while undergoing infertility investigation and treatment. Such matters should be discussed as appropriate in an open but non-obtrusive and professional manner.

Weight loss-related amenorrhoea

Weight loss-related amenorrhoea is found in women with marked weight loss and sometimes persists in women who have partially regained their weight. Ultrasound images of the ovaries of such patients demonstrate a 'multifollicular' pattern (Adams et al, 1985), in which there are several follicles but no increase of stroma. In both groups of women, treatment of the underlying problem, i.e by an increase in body weight, needs to be addressed initially before ovulation induction is commenced. Dietary advice may suffice, but counselling and/or psychotherapy is often required. It has been shown that women who are underweight when they conceive run a significantly higher risk of having an underweight baby than do women of normal weight (van der Spuy et al, 1988). It is important, therefore, that the patient is aware of the implications and is given support and advice through what may well be a protracted period of time. All women undergoing ovulation induction should have a normal body mass index, i.e. in the range 19–25 kg/m^2, calculated as weight in kilograms/ (height in metres)^2.

Treatment of hypothalamic amenorrhoea – pulsatile GnRH therapy

Treatment with pulsatile GnRH is a physiological method of ovulation induction that results in restoration of normal fertility in hypogonado-trophic subjects. Patients should be advised of potential problems prior to GnRH treatment, when they should be taught about the working of the pump and infusion. GnRH is administered via a minipump, which can often be worn on a belt, in a pocket or attached to a bra. Although the thought of wearing an infusion pump and having a subcutaneous cannula in situ 24 hours a day can be daunting, most patients quickly become accustomed to it. Patients may be taught to look after and change the subcutaneous cannula and infusion themselves, and, if they are able to do so, they can then have freedom from the pump between pulses (usually administered at 90-minute intervals) for a bath, to swim or to exercise. Careful monitoring using pelvic ultrasound should be performed, particularly in the first cycle of treatment, when multiple follicles and, therefore, multiple pregnancy are more likely to occur. Fewer visits to the hospital are necessary with this treatment, compared with gonadotrophin therapy, because it is more physiological and has fewer complications. If multiple follicles occur, appropriate advice should be given (see 'Monitoring with ultrasound' below). The nurse can give the appropriate advice, monitor such treatment and, if it is agreed by her medical colleagues and a suitable protocol is followed, make concomitant decisions. The protocol should be signed by the clinician in charge and included in the nurse's personal file.

Polycystic ovaries (PCO)

Polycystic ovary syndrome (PCOS) is associated with anovulation, hirsutism, obesity and infertility. PCOS is the most common cause of anovulatory infertility, accounting for 73% of such cases (Hull, 1987). The heterogeneous nature of PCOS has led to much debate over its diagnosis.

Pelvic ultrasound

High resolution pelvic ultrasonography can now readily demonstrate the characteristic morphological features of polycystic ovary (PCO). The ultrasound definition of the polycystic ovary, using the transabdominal route, is (a) that it contains eight or more follicles in one plane (2–8 mm in diameter and characteristically distributed peripherally, although they may be situated throughout the stroma), (b) the presence of increased stroma and (c) an increase in the size of the ovary (greater than 9 mm) (Adams et al, 1986). Two of these three criteria should be met for the diagnosis to be made.

Pelvic ultrasound is one of the main tools in the diagnosis of PCO and in monitoring ovulation induction treatment. It demands a high degree of expertise, but if trained and with adequate experience, a nurse may undertake ultrasound scanning. It is crucial that the nurse is familiar with normal pelvic anatomy, and back-up must be available, so that when pathology is found, she may refer the patient for further examination. There are occasional courses in obstetric and gynaecological scanning that may be appropriate, and further information is available through the British Medical Ultrasound Society (see Appendix).

The patient with PCO should be reassured that the condition is benign and that the symptoms, if any, are treatable. Approximately one in five women has PCO (Polson et al, 1988). A diagram is useful in explaining the condition, discussing normal ovulation and the situation in PCO when lots of small follicles are arrested in development and ovulation does not occur.

The term 'PCO', itself should be explained, as it frequently conjures up the image of 'cysts', which will have to be removed, and/or of an abnormality that may become malignant. Polycystic ovaries have been demonstrated before puberty (Brook et al, 1988), and they can be detected after the menopause. There is often a positive family history of PCO.

Weight

Women with PCO are often overweight. Weight reduction in any obese patient should be encouraged for health reasons; PCO is also associated with insulin resistance, and anovulatory women with PCO have demonstrated a greater degree of hyperinsulinaemia and are more insulin resistant than their weight-matched controls, a difference that is amplified by obesity. Obese women with PCO are at risk of developing non-insulin-dependent diabetes mellitus. Many such women have an abnormal lipid profile, and they may be at an increased risk of developing atherosclerosis and cardiovascular disease in later life. All women with PCO should, therefore, receive advice on diet, exercise and smoking, which can be given by or supported by the nurse.

Obese women with PCO have a greater incidence of menstrual irregularities than do their weight-matched counterparts with normal ovaries. In addition, the author's group has found that calorie restriction in obese women with PCO resulted in a marked improvement in clinical and endocrine function in women losing more than 5% of their initial body weight, with return of ovulation occurring in some subjects, as demonstrated by conceptions in some patients who had complained of infertility (Kiddy et al, 1992). Other studies have also reported a return of spontaneous ovulatory cycles and improvement in response to ovulation induction with clomiphene citrate (Harlass et al, 1984). In patients with PCO and infertility, therefore, it is particularly important to encourage weight reduction before ovulation induction treatment is commenced.

Clomiphene therapy

The first-line treatment of PCO is clomiphene citrate. It is the authors' practice to monitor the first cycle of therapy using serial ultrasound scanning (see *Monitoring with ultrasound* below) and mid-luteal phase progesterone measurements, to ensure that the ovaries are responding adequately (but not over-responding) to the dose. If, on ultrasound scan, more than three follicles are present, equal to or greater than 15 mm in diameter, the risk of multiple pregnancy can be minimised by advising the patient to use contraception. If ovulation has not occurred, review of the treatment is required, although the same protocol may well be followed in a subsequent cycle. Results should be discussed with the patient, and the nurse may be in a good position to do this, as she may be providing day-to-day care. It is crucial that measures are taken to minimise the risk of multiple pregnancy (Botting et al, 1990; Levene et al, 1992) (see below).

Gonadotrophin therapy

Guidelines for the use of gonadotrophic hormone preparations have been produced by the Royal College of Obstetricians and Gynaecologists (1994).

If patients are clomiphene resistant, ovulation induction may be attempted using hMG or FSH. Such treatment should be given under close supervision, with monitoring of ovarian response by serial ultrasound scanning and serum oestradiol measurements. It is important to be aware that women with PCO have an increased risk of developing OHSS, which can be life threatening. Conventional doses of gonadotrophins have been associated with an increased rate of multiple pregnancy and OHSS. A low-dose protocol to reduce this risk has been developed (Polson et al, 1987). In this group of women, the aim is a single dominant follicle, and a low-dose protocol minimises the number of cycles abandoned due to multifollicular development and multiple pregnancies (Hamilton-Fairley et al, 1991). It is essential that patients' attention is drawn to the intense nature of the treatment and its monitoring. Normal life is disrupted and patients may well require extra time off work.

The intramuscular or subcutaneous (in the case of 'high-purity FSH') injections may be administered by the patient or her partner following adequate teaching and supervision of the correct technique (UKCC, 1992c). This allows a more relaxed approach to treatment and is more convenient for the patient, compared with the alternative of having to attend the hospital or GP for injections. This may, in turn, reduce the amount of time needed to be taken off work and can, therefore, alleviate stress.

Monitoring with ultrasound

Scans should be performed approximately twice a week, more often in some cases, particularly when approaching ovulation. The thickness of the endometrium and the number and size of any follicles greater than 10 mm in diameter in each ovary should be recorded. If a follicle of 18 mm with no more than two additional follicles of 15 mm is present, release of the follicle is triggered by a single dose of hCG. If there are three or more follicles of 15 mm or more, the treatment cycle should be discontinued and, as spontaneous ovulation may occur, the patient should be advised to avoid intercourse or use a barrier method of contraception to minimise the risk of multiple pregnancy. It is of benefit in such circumstances if prior warning has been given of a possible or probable over-response, as the patient can then be more prepared for disappointment at abandoning the cycle of treatment. Multiple pregnancy should, as far as possible, be avoided, because of the high rates of infant mortality and morbidity associated with it (Levene et al, 1992) and the social problems experienced by families with triplets or higher order multiple births (Botting et al, 1990). The patient should be advised of the symptoms of OHSS and should contact the team if problems arise. In any case, the patient should be assessed 1 week later, when the ovaries are usually at their maximum size. If hCG is given, an ultrasound scan, to assess endometrial thickness and the presence of a corpus luteum, and serum progesterone measurement are performed 8 days later to confirm ovulation. Menses are due 1 week later and a pregnancy test may be done if they do not occur.

Superovulation and Intrauterine insemination (IUI)

Superovulation and IUI are sometimes offered as a treatment option in cases of unexplained infertility or mild male infertility. The ovaries are stimulated with exogenous gonadotrophins, sometimes with the addition of clomiphene. It is crucial that the patient's response to treatment is carefully monitored with ultrasound and serum oestradiol measurements. As noted earlier, the use of ultrasound in monitoring the ovarian response is the only way of ascertaining the number of follicles present. The treatment cycle should be abandoned if more than three preovulatory follicles are present, because of the risk of OHSS (see Chapter 4) and multiple pregnancy (discussed above).

The IUI procedure is, by its very nature, an intrusive one, and it should be performed with sensitivity; if the couple so desire, it should be permissible for the male partner to be present. The procedure can, in the authors' experience, be quite straightforward and pain free for the patient, although it may in some cases be quite painful. Complications are rare.

IUI may be performed by nurses and is indemnified by the RCN. It is imperative that protocols for training and practice are used by all nurses. The nurse should have a thorough knowledge of the anatomy of the pelvis. She should understand the importance of the preparation of the semen sample and have a thorough knowledge of any drugs to be used and the method of monitoring. There should be a routine for the preparation of the semen sample (by a trained technician) and a means of identifying the correct sample for each patient. It is suggested that the nurse who is learning the technique of performing IUI needs to observe a minimum of three IUIs and then perform three, or more if necessary, under supervision until assessed as being competent and confident. Again a comprehensive written protocol should be followed, which includes criteria on stimulation regimens, monitoring and timing of insemination. Copies of such protocols should be signed and included in each nurse's personal file. There must be a doctor available to take over from the nurse in the event of any technical difficulties arising from the insemination or in case of emergency. The nurse should decline to perform IUI if she is concerned about any aspect of the procedure.

The role of the nurse

The nurse involved in ovulation induction can play an important role. She can coordinate the ovulation induction programme. She can monitor the response by taking blood samples for hormone assay, she may perform ultrasound scanning (providing she is adequately trained to perform follicle tracking) and make decisions regarding drug dose and timing of induction of ovulation, or, if over-response has occurred, the discontinuation of treatment in that cycle, if agreed by her medical colleagues. She may perform IUI. It is extremely important that, for any treatment, a protocol is followed, and a copy of each protocol should be signed by the clinician in charge and included in the nurse's personal file. The responsibilities of the nurse must be clearly defined and appropriate to her level of training and experience. The nurse should be involved in team discussions of patients and their treatments and should voice her opinion, particularly if she disagrees with decisions, as discussed in Chapter 5.

Ongoing support

This type of treatment, which involves frequent visits to the hospital, can by its very nature, be stressful, and it is important that couples or individuals have access to someone to talk to at all times during working hours, either in person or on the telephone. There are particular situations in which support is especially required, including when cycles are 'abandoned' (careful use of terminology being required here so that patients do not feel that they are being abandoned because the treatment has not worked) and, of course, when a patient comes to the end of the course of treatment. There may be alternative treatment options to be discussed, or it may be that a couple have come to the end of treatment and may be helped to come to terms with their infertility. A positive outcome of treatment need not be a live baby, but the fact of having come through treatment and then being able to divert their attention to other life goals. This can be very difficult to do, and trained counsellors are often required to help. It is important that the nurse realises when such intervention could be beneficial and refers the couple to an appropriate counsellor.

IVF AND ASSOCIATED TECHNIQUES

The normal route of referral to the specialist centre is via local hospital outpatient clinics or the GP's surgery. Couples may have to wait some time for their initial consultation: 6 weeks is acceptable, but for some, any wait is too long. Ideally, they should then be in their treatment cycle[1] within 3 months. While waiting for their consultation and treatment, the couple may become very anxious, owing to isolation and uncertainty. Anxiety can be relieved by contact with the centre; consequently, at this time it is appropriate to inform couples of patient support groups, contact numbers and the counselling support that is available at the centre.

Patient information

Before the initial consultation, it is essential that the couple receive as much written information about the centre as possible. They will have time to absorb this initial information, which should be both readable and informative. Hence, when they attend, they will be well informed and able to ask appropriate questions and cope with the added information.

The Human Fertilisation and Embryology Act 1990, Section 13(b), Schedule 3, para. 3(1)(b) states that the couple must be given 'such relevant information as is proper'. It should be given verbally and supported by easily understood written information. The most important information a couple will require is their chance of having a baby after the treatment; the HFEA requires centres to include their own live birth rate per treatment cycle.

The HFEA has produced booklets that answer questions and provide general information; the topics covered are *The Role of the HFEA*, *Treatment Clinic: Questions To Ask*, *Sperm and Egg Donors and the Law* and *Egg Donation*. All booklets should be available in licensed centres and can also be obtained from the HFEA.

Other useful and informative aids are videos and audio cassettes on assisted conception, which can be viewed or listened to, either with other couples or in the comfort of their own homes. These can keep couples in touch with their own and other couples' feelings. They are available from centres. *In Vitro Fertilisation: the Next Step* is a video produced by the HFEA, and there are others made by individual centres or other health professionals.

---

[1]   In this text, a treatment cycle is defined as being from the beginning of down-regulation to the beginning of a period (or confirmation of pregnancy) following embryo transfer. As a general rule, unless otherwise indicated, the text refers to both IVF and GIFT.

Financial cost

As most couples, at present, have to pay for their treatment, the cost will also be discussed in their preparatory literature, ensuring that the couple are aware of any hidden charges. For example, if the usual method of egg recovery is by ultrasound using sedation, there may be extra costs for a laparoscopy and general anaesthetic if this method is inappropriate. The direct financial cost to the couple ranges from no cost if the treatment is funded by the NHS to over £2000 if it is funded by the patient.

The costs should be set out clearly for the couple to see and understand, with clear indications of whether these may change. Many couples have to borrow the money to ensure that they have sufficient funds; consequently, they must be quite certain that they wish to undertake such a commitment. The financial strain may cause friction between the couple, and they may find themselves in debt.

Statistics show that couples in the favourable group who persist for up to four cycles of IVF have a 60% chance of taking home a baby (Hull et al, 1992). This chance is acceptable for some but too low for others. After a considerable financial outlay, the couple may show disappointment and dissatisfaction with the treatment centre if they are unsuccessful.

Selection criteria

Each centre will have its own selection criteria for accepting couples for assisted conception (Hull, 1990). The most favourable indications are couples diagnosed with tubal damage (IVF only), prolonged unexplained infertility and minor endometriosis. Other favourable qualifying requirements are women under 40 years, normal regular menstrual cycles, normal basal LH and FSH levels, no immunological evidence of recent chlamydia infection in women, normal uterus and a sperm recovery and 24-hour survival at 37°C of at least one million motile spermatozoa.

If the couple have been referred to the specialist centre but are not suitable for IVF, alternative treatments may be offered, but smaller centres may need to refer on to other specialists. This may cause further frustration to the couple, and the need for this referral should be identified as soon as possible to avoid further wasted time.

Initial consultation

When a couple arrive for their initial consultation, they must be welcomed and made to feel relaxed. They may be apprehensive and insecure and need to build up confidence at this stage. A full medical history should be taken, and all previous investigations should be checked and more carried out only if necessary. In Chapter 4, it explains that most investigations would have been performed during the initial diagnostic phase. It is important that the nurse is aware of and understands the essential tests.

For the woman:

- Antibody assay:
  - *Chlamydia trachomatis*
  - Hepatitis B and C
  - HIV
  - Rubella
- Hormone assays:
  - LH and FSH (during the first week of a menstrual cycle)
- Routine:
  - Haemoglobin (full blood count if anaemic)

For the man:

- Antibody assay:
  - Hepatitis B and C
  - HIV
- Specialised tests
  - Semen analysis (to ensure that the sperm are suitable for IVF or confirm that donor sperm are to be used). If donor sperm are necessary, specific counselling will be required.

Some clinics insist on antibody testing all couples for HIV, whereas other clinics only test couples known to be at risk. It is essential that the couple have specific counselling beforehand, and skilled counsellors should be available if the test proves to be positive.

Investigations can, in themselves, be very stressful. Couples need to understand the wording and how to interpret the results. The discussion should be very clear and pitched at the right level for the individual person. It is not uncommon for couples to ask for the exact results rather than accept vague answers such as 'satisfactory'.

A diagnostic ultrasound scan may be carried out at this stage to ensure that the ovaries and uterus appear normal. If they are not, steps can be taken to identify and rectify problems early.

The following implications of treatment (Hull, 1993) should be discussed at this stage, and the nurse should be aware of their significance:

- *Failure to complete treatment*, owing to inadequate follicular response, premature ovulation, failure to recover or fertilise eggs or failure to freeze or to thaw embryos.
- *Freezing of embryos*: the chance of success, the disposal of unwanted embryos or what should happen to the embryos in the event of one or both partners' death.
- *Operative risks*: anaesthesia, surgical damage to viscera or vessels, possible laparotomy and infection.
- *OHSS*: pain, swelling, need for admission and treatment (see Chapter 4).
- *Multiple pregnancy*: twins, triplets, higher order births and domestic pressures. Other issues include the risk to babies of prematurity, embryo reduction and the risk of pregnancy loss balanced against the risk of higher order birth (see Chapter 7).
- *Ectopic pregnancy*: the rate is 1 in 12 for couples with tubal disease having IVF, but for others and for GIFT, the risk is extremely low.
- *Miscarriage*: the rate is no higher than that in the general population.
- *Congenital abnormality*: related to age. There is nothing to suggest an increased incidence of congenital abnormality with IVF or GIFT; however, the norm in the general population will apply.

Consent

At this stage, the consent forms for treatment should be discussed. Official forms often appear daunting and confusing, and the patient should be reassured and offered help if necessary. An example of the HFEA consent form can be seen in Figure 6.1.

It is important to inform couples that a decision made at this stage (if not already put into action) can be altered if circumstances change. For example, couples may decide to use their embryos only for themselves, but after achieving a pregnancy, they may then wish to donate their freeze-stored embryos to another couple. The forms should be carefully explained and then given to the couple to take away, read, understand and return at a later date, either completed and witnessed or to be completed and witnessed with the help of the staff.

CONSENT TO TREATMENT INVOLVING EGG RETRIEVAL AND/OR EGG OR EMBRYO REPLACEMENT

Name of centre: ....

Address: ....

Full name of woman: ....

Address: ....

This consent form is in two parts. These may be signed separately. When frozen embryos are being replaced they should be signed separately.

Part I

1. I consent to (delete/complete as applicable):
    i. be prepared for egg retrieval;
    ii. the removal of eggs from my ovaries with the aid of:
        (a) laparoscopy
        (b) ultrasound
    iii. the administration of any drugs and anaesthetics which may be found necessary in the course of the procedure(s);
    iv. the mixing of the following (tick each column as required):

    ( ) my egg(s)   ( ) with the sperm of my husband/partner

    ( ) eggs donated by   ( ) with sperm donated by
    ....

    ( ) an anonymous donor's   ( ) with an anonymous
        egg(s)   donor's sperm

2. I understand that if the donor has given effective consent under the Human Fertilisation and Embryology Act 1990, the donor will not be the legal parent of any resulting child.

3. I have discussed with ....the procedures outlined above. I have been given information orally and in writing about them.

4. I have been given a suitable opportunity to take part in counselling about the implications of the proposed treatment. (For GIFT using donated sperm or eggs, or any IVF treatment).

Patient's signature: .... Date: ....

Figure 6.1 HFEA (91)7 Form for consent for the use of eggs and the storage of embryos. Reproduced with kind permission of HFEA.

Part II

1. I consent to:

    i. the placing in my uterus or fallopian tube(s), as may be appropriate, of not more than:
        (tick as applicable)

        (a) 1( )   egg(s) mixed with sperm
             2( )
             3( )

        (b) 1( )   embryo(s)
             2( )
             3( )

    ii. the administration of any drugs and anaesthetics which may be found necessary in the course of the procedure(s).

2. I understand that only the egg(s) from one woman and sperm from one man will be used in any one treatment cycle.

3. I have discussed with .... the procedures outlined above. I have been given information orally and in writing about them.

4. Other remarks (if required): ....
    ....

    Patient's signature: .... Date: ....

5. All the information listed in paragraph 4.4 of the Human Fertilisation and Embryology Authority's Code of Practice has been given to the patient. The patient has been offered a suitable opportunity to take part in counselling about the implications of the proposed treatment.

    Doctor's signature: .... Date: ....

Figure 6.1 contd.

6. I am the husband of .... and I consent to the course of treatment outlined above. I understand that I will become the legal father of any resulting child.

7. Any other remarks: ....

    ....

Signature of husband: .... Date: ....

Full name in block capitals: ....

Address: ....

....

(NOTE: the centre is not *required* to obtain a husband's consent in order to make the treatment lawful, but where donated sperm is used, it is advisable in the interests of establishing the legal parenthood of the child. See paragraphs 5.6–5.8 of the Code of Practice).

Male partner's acknowledgement

8. I am not married to .... , but I acknowledge that she and I are being treated together, and that I will become the legal father of any resulting child.

7. Any other remarks: ....

    ....

Signature of male partner: .... Date: ....

Full name in block capitals: ....

Address: ....

....

(NOTE: the centre is not *required* to obtain a partners acknowledgement in order to make the treatment lawful, but where donated sperm is used, it is advisable in the interests of establishing the legal parenthood of the child. See paragraphs 5.6–5.8 of the Code of Practice).

Figure 6.1 contd.

Preparation for treatment cycle – information-giving

When all the test results requested at consultation are available, the couple should be informed, the results clearly explained and the recommended treatment advised. IVF, for example, may be preferable to GIFT to test the fertilising capacity of sperm, especially if there is a suspected sperm problem, but GIFT would be advised in women over 40 with healthy tubes, as in most centres, this gives a higher chance of success, possibly due to the natural environment, in which fertilisation takes place.

Referring doctors should also be fully informed of the decision; however due to the restrictions on confidentiality (Human Fertilisation and Embryology Act 1990), it is necessary either to get the consent of the couple to enable centres to correspond with unlicensed practitioners (HFEA, 1993) or, if this is not obtained, to correspond through the couple.

The basic information is the same for couples undergoing IVF or GIFT; the practical difference is that for GIFT, the eggs and sperm are transferred directly to the fallopian tubes, usually by laparoscopy, and there is, therefore, no embryo transfer (some centres collect the eggs via ultrasound and then perform a laparoscopy to transfer the eggs and sperm).

The nurse will remind the couple of the side-effects of the drugs and how they should be administered. If they wish to administer their own injections, it is usually the nurse who teaches the woman or her partner. There must be a protocol for this teaching process and a record in the patient's notes stating that this has been followed. The nurse must ensure that the couple understand the need for the correct dose and administration, because, if it is not correct, it may jeopardise the treatment cycle or lead to hyperstimulation, which can, in rare cases, be fatal. The drug is either given by intramuscular or subcutaneous injection. There are home videos available to demonstrate subcutaneous injections, and leaflets outlining both intramuscular and subcutaneous techniques. As previously discussed teaching the woman to self-administer the injections can be of advantage to the couple, as it will give them more freedom.

The treatment cycle

Details will vary according to local practice but down-regulation (see Chapter 4) will normally start 1 week before the earliest expected period or soon after ovulation and continue up to and including the day of administration of hCG.

Once her period arrives, the woman will contact the nurse and will then be given instructions on when to start the hormone injections to stimulate the ovaries. (While on buserelin, the start can be at any time, thus avoiding starting too many people on the same day and the knock on effect of having too many ready for operation on the same day.) The couple will have a rough idea of the start date because they will have to make arrangements at work for time off. If the injections are not self-administered, they can be given at the centre, their GP's surgery or their local hospital.

A semen sample (unless donor sperm is used) may be checked at the start of this cycle for infection, so that, if necessary, antibiotic treatment can be given before and up to egg collection, to avoid risk of bacterial contamination of the eggs.

Ultrasound scanning of the ovaries (most scans now being carried out using a vaginal probe) and serum oestradiol assessment will be carried out, depending on local practice. In many centres, nurses perform the scans. This is a very responsible procedure and only appropriate for nurses who have been trained and have an aptitude for the technique. It provides continuity of care and the opportunity for the nurse to interact with her patient. It is essential to audit this procedure to ensure standardisation; the best practice is for one nurse to follow the patient through from the initial provision of information to embryo transfer (see below).

It is acceptable to carry out the first scan and blood test on day 8 after the start of the injections. The dose of gonadotrophin will need to be increased if there is no adequate follicular response, and further monitoring will be required. At this stage, a further semen sample will be required, to check suitability of sperm preparation.

Egg collection

Most women are admitted to hospital on the morning of egg collection, and the partner will produce his semen sample. This is the most important part that he has to play, and the stress should not be underestimated. Some men fail, and it may be necessary to anticipate this and arrange freezing of sperm in advance to relieve the anxiety.

The most common procedure is vaginal, ultrasound-guided egg collection (see Chapter 4), with either intravenous sedation or a light anaesthetic. Although the procedure is simple, the stress and anticipation make the couple anxious, and they need much support and understanding at this stage.

Embryo transfer

If the eggs fertilise, they are returned to the uterus approximately 2 days later. To the couple, embryo transfer is the most important part of treatment. After suitable training, it is now acceptable for nurses to perform embryo transfer, and it has been shown that it may be of benefit to the couple (Barber et al, 1991), to improve continuity of care. The woman may go home soon afterwards and return to normal activity the following day.

The HFEA stipulates that a maximum of three embryos be replaced, to minimise the risk of multiple births (HFEA, 1993). The couple should be counselled and given the opportunity to explore the implications and discuss how many embryos they wish to have replaced well before this time. They must balance their chance of conception against the risk of multiple birth, which carries the serious risk of premature birth and possible consequent damage. In addition, they must recognise the tremendous strain that is put upon the family (including other children) when the babies arrive and the amount of after-care that they will require.

Support

The stress of waiting for the initial consultation can be overwhelming. Once the couple have been seen, there are new hopes and expectations. Discussion is essential to ensure that expectations are realistic.

At each stage of treatment, anxiety is increased. The treatment cycle is often a welcome relief, as the couple at last feel that they are doing something. However, it is also very stressful, involving time off work and unexpected response to treatment. It raises questions on semen quality, the number of eggs, fertilisation and embryo transfer. There is also the stress of unexpected change in clinic practice, such as changes related to rest after embryo transfer. Change may, in itself, make the patient feel insecure, unless the reason is fully explained and understood.

For some couples there is also a special need to have staff – nurse, doctor or scientist – they are familiar with. For these couples, continuity of care is essential.

Anxiety and uncertainty may lead to 'difficult' behaviour (Stockwell, 1972) as a way of trying to maintain control in an uncertain situation. These couples are often recognisable from the start, appearing demanding and regularly changing appointments or routines. Despite warning them that the things they insist are right for them may be detrimental to their treatment, the nurse may, when problems arise, feel responsible and feel that she should have managed the situation differently. It is helpful to discuss these problems with other colleagues who have had similar experiences.

Unsuccessful treatment cycles

The fear of failure (not achieving a pregnancy) may be constantly on the couple's minds. When failure occurs at this stage, it is equally, if not more, devastating than if fertilisation had never occurred. This feeling is similar to bereavement, but, unlike bereavement, there is no obvious loss, and the patient is not given permission to grieve (Baram et al, 1988; Greenfeld et al, 1988). Anger is another common way of expressing feelings. The couple are angry with the people whom they need most, and, although this is painful, the nurse has to recognise it.

The follow-up after an unsuccessful treatment cycle is very important. Ideally, the patient will contact the clinic advising the onset of a period and talk to her support nurse: counselling should be offered and a follow-up appointment be given to see the doctor. A letter from the nurse is a good way of keeping in contact with the patient and provides an opportunity for her to talk, as patients often feel lonely and isolated. This isolation can also be relieved by contact with a patient support group. These groups fill a necessary gap in the service (see Chapter 10). Where a centre covers a large geographical area, couples may be prevented from meeting; however, a network of telephone numbers may resolve this and allow couples to discuss problems with others in similar situations.

Successful treatment cycles

The method of pregnancy diagnosis is often dependent upon geographical siting (a reliable urinary pregnancy test can be performed at home or in a clinic). When the couple have a positive pregnancy test, a scan (which is often performed by the nurse) should, ideally, follow 3 weeks later. The pregnancy, once confirmed, is treated as 'normal'. Some couples choose not to tell their obstetrician that they have conceived through assisted conception treatment to ensure that they are treated as 'any other patient', and others keep it secret because they do not wish other people to know that their baby was not conceived in the 'normal' way. Most realise the necessity of keeping practitioners fully informed. Because the babies are so precious, the anxiety of the couple will continue and may influence their antenatal care. Some couples feel a sense of loss when they become 'just another pregnant woman', even feeling neglected and wondering whether this is really what they want, although research indicates that adjustment to parenthood resembles that of other parents (Golombok et al, 1993; Weaver et al, 1993).

Frozen embryo transfer

Extra eggs can be frozen at the two pronucleate or embryo stage and then replaced in a subsequent cycle. These may be natural or hormone replacement cycles, according to local practice, and the nurse will coordinate this. The woman may be down-regulated and then substitution therapy given. With this method, oestradiol valerate is given in the first half of the cycle, followed by progesterone. There is minimal monitoring and nursing involvement, but the specific day for embryo transfer can be planned and carried out in the normal way. The couple will be in constant contact with the nurse to ensure that everything is going to plan. The substitution therapy will continue, and a pregnancy test is carried out 3 weeks after embryo transfer. If it is negative, the drugs are stopped and a period will start shortly after. If it is positive, the dose of substitution therapy will be adjusted according to hormone levels, and the woman is then weaned off this in about 4 months. The consent to the embryo transfer procedure is the same as that for fresh embryo transfer, and the support needed is the same, as expectations are as high.

It is essential to know the outcome of all treatment cycles, to ensure that the HFEA has complete records. It is important that these registration forms are discussed with the couple at the onset of treatment, so that they are aware of the information given and its importance. They should also realise that the information will remain confidential. Anyone over the age of 18 (or 16 if contemplating marriage) has a right to seek information about their genetic origins from the HFEA. No identifying information about the donor will be given, but the HFEA has yet to make regulations about what is provided (see Chapter 8).

DONOR INSEMINATION (DI)

DI has a valuable part to play in the management of male infertility and, to some degree, in the absence of a male partner.

As with other treatments, it is important that this form of treatment should always be offered in the context of choice for the couple. Even with poor quality semen, the possibility of successful fertilisation by in vitro methods is increasing, which can be a viable, if expensive, alternative. Acceptance of their childless future can also be a positive choice for some couples.

Selection

Should a couple decide that DI is the option they wish to follow, what factors must be considered? Couples do not have to pass a 'selection' process, but it is true to say that there are qualities in a couple that would make them more suitable for DI (Schover, 1994).

It is not necessary for the couple to be married, but it is important that they are in a happy and stable relationship. This would be difficult to define, and certainly if a couple have been through the daunting process of infertility investigations, followed by the diagnosis of male infertility, happiness may not be a word that would immediately spring to mind. The stability of their relationship may have been tested severely during the investigation period, and if they are to go on to consider the option of DI, communication becomes increasingly important. The couple who are able to talk openly and explore the issues from one another's point of view are more likely to reach the decision that is right for them. At this stage, it is important that decisions are not rushed and that time is taken to work through the various factors.

It is also important that the couple have, to some degree, 'come to terms' with their diagnosis. 'Come to terms' is a phrase that does not realistically reflect the slow process of acceptance of an infertility diagnosis. Couples may accept that they are not likely to achieve a pregnancy, but that is not to say that they do not wish that this was not so. For the majority of couples, the element of hope is never abandoned. In fact, for the majority of couples, there will always be a chance that natural spontaneous conception can occur, although that chance may be very slight.

DI can also have a place in the treatment of single women and lesbian couples who are considering embarking on a pregnancy. Other options available to them include having intercourse with a male in an attempt to conceive or self-insemination using a syringe and a sample of semen donated by a male friend. Both these methods carry a risk of passing on transmissible disease, including HIV. Probably the most responsible method is DI at a licensed clinic, and in the UK, DI should not be carried out elsewhere (see Chapter 8).

The HFEA Code of Practice states that where there is no legal father, the doctors and counsellors must assess the woman's ability to meet the child's needs fully, including the need for a father. Each clinic has its own policy about whether to treat single or lesbian women; cases are often considered on an individual basis, and the clinic may consult its own ethics committee if necessary. The nurse should feel able to explore her feelings openly with other members of the team and try to be aware of any prejudices she may have (Heywood, 1991).

Information

A clinic may well have a protocol to follow during the selection phase. This should include supplying the couple with an information sheet on DI but it must be stressed that any information sheet should not take the place of discussion but rather be a basis for further discussion. An information sheet can be excellent for the couple to take away with them, to digest and to encourage them to think of implications of the DI from many angles. It is important that no-one commences DI with unrealistic expectations, and information given must include the expected live birth rate for that particular clinic.

The couple should also be given the opportunity to view the excellent video provided by the HFEA, entitled *Donor Insemination – The Next Step?* It can either be viewed in the privacy of their own home, or, if they do not have a video recorder, the nurse should be able to arrange viewing, again in private, within the clinic setting. The video can be invaluable in focusing the couple's thoughts and bringing forth much more two-way discussion.

The information sheet and video should then be supplemented with an appointment, to give the couple the opportunity to discuss many aspects of DI with someone working within the DI programme. In the HFEA video, the three couples involved all intend to tell the child of its conception by DI. This is one of the points most often raised in response to the video.

Telling the child

'Telling the child' is one of the most important decisions for most couples considering DI (Haimes, 1992; Snowden and Snowden, 1993). One of the authors of this chapter has worked in an infertility clinic now for many years and has seen a slow but definite swing towards openness with the child and with the extended family. Couples previously seldom thought that they would definitely tell the child about his or her conception, and some doctors were known to actively discourage the couple from openness and steer them towards keeping it a lifelong secret (Neuberg, 1991). Treatments such as DI were little heard of and seldom understood, and a social stigma was attached to male infertility (see Chapter 2). The advent of the Warnock Report (Warnock 1985) and the setting up of the HFEA may have helped this treatment to become more acceptable.

The HFEA guidelines state that, during counselling, couples should be encouraged to consider telling the child of his or her origins. However, the ultimate decision lies with the couple. The husband of the woman being inseminated will be regarded as the legal father of the child, unless he does not consent to treatment and can prove this. If the woman is unmarried, her male partner will be the legal father of the child. In both cases, clinics should obtain consent from the partners.

Secrecy is very difficult to live with, and if a couple intend to withhold from the child his or her origins, they may feel that they cannot take the risk of telling any of their close family and friends. In my experience, couples who intend telling the child, and who are open with the family, cope better while on treatment. A treatment programme can be stressful in itself, without the added strain of keeping it a secret and trying to make excuses for the times they have clinic appointments.

When discussing with the couple the possibility of telling the child, it is the responsibility of the nurse to encourage the couple to look at the situation from many different angles and to help them focus on the decision that would most benefit the eventual child. It can be helpful to encourage couples individually to draw up a list of the advantages and disadvantages of telling and not telling the child, taking into consideration themselves, the child and the extended family. It is common for the couple to be divided in their decision, and an experienced nurse can help the couple to understand one another's view and, when necessary, to seek independent counselling.

Counselling

The nurse is a constant knowledgeable figure within the clinic setting and can build up a rapport with the couple, enabling them to discuss all aspects of DI as it relates to their lives and their family circle. On the negative side, it can be said that the couple may feel unable to disclose any relationship problems to the nurse, as they feel she has influence over whether they move on to, or remain on, a donor treatment programme. In these situations, it is important that independent counselling is readily available for the couple and that they are aware of the channel to access this service. The nurse should be trained in the skills needed to recognise how and when a couple should move on to independent counselling, and each nurse should be aware of her own limitations.

The amount of time spent in the counselling process prior to starting treatment is, from the authors' experience, greatly affected by two things. First is the reason for DI. If the man's fertility has been proven, and DI is being considered for other reasons, the decision is generally easier. The man who has already had children, followed by a vasectomy, appears more able to accept the concept of DI. This situation is relatively common when a man is in a new relationship; however, on the reverse side of this, his new partner may feel cheated by the fact that he had a vasectomy, and angry and resentful that he 'chose' to be rendered infertile. In the main, however, women are more able to express their feelings verbally, and by doing so, can come to terms with the situation more comfortably, as discussed below.

The second factor influencing the acceptance of DI is how the couple were told the results. Mason (1993) explores this aspect quite deeply. The couple who have been told of their male factor problem insensitively may have a great deal of anger, hurt and disbelief to work through before they can move on to consider the option of donor insemination. If a couple are upset over their handling, they may never return to the clinic to consider their options further.

It is important that counselling be available not only prior to commencing treatment, but also during treatment and when the treatment comes to an end, including both when a pregnancy is achieved and when treatment ends without a pregnancy.

The nurse plays an invaluable role during the whole process; the support that she can show to the couple can help them through some very difficult times. It is not unusual for one to be the driving force in the relationship, which is not necessarily a problem. In many aspects of life, couples are divided, but if their communication is good, decisions are ultimately made and their lives will continue smoothly. Counselling and support are extremely valuable in keeping the communication pathway open.

In an ideal situation, counselling should also be available throughout the years that the child grows up. It would not be unnatural for the family to encounter problems or doubts as the child grows, and there should be a service available for these families. However, in this case, a one-way system would be more appropriate. Few couples would welcome regular contact from the clinic, however well intentioned. This could be regarded as an invasion of their privacy and could be seen as a constant threat. It should, however, be made clear that each couple is welcome to contact the clinic at any future time with any question or problem, however minor it may seem.

Although it is difficult to generalise, women appear more keen on openness than do men (Greil et al, 1988). In general, a woman shares more of life's problems with friends and family (Brannen and Collard, 1982), and as the child would be genetically hers, the fear of rejection is not there. Men, on the other hand, tend not to share their problems and are not quite so used to frank discussion of personal matters (Mason, 1993). It can also still be very difficult for men to disassociate their infertility from virility, which acts as a block. Many may also fear rejection by the child that knows of his or her origins.

The national organisation DI Network welcomes contact from couples considering DI. It offers support and knowledge from couples who have been through the same dilemmas.

Information about donors

In order to answer fully the couple's questions, the nurse must familiarise herself with all aspects of the programme. Apart from practical issues, such as timing of the insemination, the majority of questions asked are about donor recruitment. The answers to these questions are not always the same for each individual clinic. Recruitment procedures can vary from clinic to clinic, but certain factors are governed by the HFEA. Figure 6.2 considers some of the questions related to the donor programme in Aberdeen.

The HFEA Code of Practice (HFEA, 1993) has strict guidelines on the recruitment of semen donors, so that the individual clinic can either recruit for their own use, or buy from another centre, safe in the knowledge that the criteria will have been met. These guidelines cover not only recruitment but also the storage and use of donated sperm. For example, the guidelines recommend that no more than 10 children be born from one donor, but a donor can set a lower limit if he wishes. The British Andrology Society (1993) has also produced guidelines for the screening of donors.

1. *Who are the donors?*
   Most of our donors are students but not medical students. In the main they are at University studying for a degree.

2. *How do you advertise for donors?*
   We advertise in the local student magazine and by posters in the University.

3. *To what extent can you match the donor with the male partner?*
   An attempt is made to match as many characteristics as possible. Race is essential. Eye colour, hair colour and build are also closely matched, and blood group is always taken into account.

4. *Are all donors fertile?*
   Not all donors are known to be fertile when initially recruited, but if fertility is not proven reasonably quickly, then that particular donor is no longer used on the programme.

5. *Is the donor told of pregnancies achieved?*
   No. A donor is not informed of any pregnancies achieved.

6. *Will the donor know who we are?*
   No. A donor gets no information about who his donated samples are used for.

7. *Will I get semen from more than one donor?*
   It is possible that if it takes several cycles of treatment to achieve a pregnancy, that you will receive sperm from more than one donor. However, in any one cycle of treatment, the semen from only one donor will be used.

8. *Is the donor paid?*
   Donors are allowed to be reimbursed for any expenses incurred whilst travelling to the clinic, but no payment is made for the donated sample.

9. *What tests does the donor have?*
   Donors have an extensive medical and physical history check, and also have blood tests to exclude, as far as possible, hepatitis B and C, syphilis and HIV antibodies. Chromosome analysis is also undertaken, as is a serum antibody test for CMV. Urethal swabs for gonorrhoea and chlamydia are also cultured.

10. *Is there a limit to the number of pregnancies a donor can have?*
    Only 10 live births should be achieved by any one donor.

Figure 6.2   Questions often asked about donor insemination.

A donor may consent for his sperm to be used in an attempt to achieve a pregnancy but may not consent to his sperm being used for research purposes.

Thus, the nurse must be conversant with the recruitment, screening and payment methods of her own centre or of the centre from which her clinic buys its semen supply. In some centres, the nurse may also be involved in donor recruitment, but in many, the staff who carry out DI never encounter donors.

Treatment issues

The practical issues surrounding DI can be quite daunting. Many couples will have to travel a great distance to the nearest clinic. Ideally, a couple should be able to choose which clinic they attend, and they should be able to compare methods, success rates and prices. In the larger cities, this might be possible, but for the rest of the UK, the choice is often made purely on the least distance to travel, which can still be many hundreds of miles.

One important factor influencing success rates is the timing of the insemination (Templeton, 1985). It is important that the insemination be carried out at the appropriate timing in the woman's cycle, i.e. at the time of ovulation. There are various methods of pinpointing the right day, and the protocol used by an individual clinic depends on the resources available. An attempt can be made by simply working out the most likely day of ovulation according to her usual cycle. More precise timing can be achieved by hormone testing mid-cycle. About 24–36 hours prior to ovulation, the hormone LH surges, as it finally prepares the egg for release. It is possible to detect this hormone in both blood and urine samples. If a clinic has available a daily laboratory service for serum LH testing, the woman can attend mid-cycle for a daily blood test. Within the authors' clinic, we ask a woman with a 28-day cycle who lives locally to attend daily from day 12 of her cycle, anticipating that the LH surge will happen within the next few days. Normal or basal LH levels are variable, and an LH surge is defined as a rise to more than 2.5 times the median of the previous day's levels.

The women attend the authors' clinic for blood sampling before 9.00 a.m. The blood is tested in the laboratory during the morning, and the women telephone in at around noon for their results. If the LH surge is detected, insemination is carried out that afternoon. If the surge is not detected, they return each morning for repeat blood sampling. However, this clinic covers an extremely wide geographical area, so this method is impractical for many women and the authors encourage the use of commercially bought urine kits manufactured specifically to pick up the LH surge as it is excreted in the urine. These home-testing kits are fairly easy to use, and the woman is able to pinpoint for herself the right time for insemination and phone the clinic to arrange treatment. Again, if a woman has a 28-day cycle, she should start home testing her urine from day 12. Within the authors' clinic, both of these methods achieve similar success rates (Cant et al, 1989).

Not all clinics will be able to offer the ideal of a 7-day service, and, in such cases, insemination would be timed for the working day nearest to ovulation.

Another influencing factor is where the sperm is deposited within the reproductive tract. Clinics will occasionally deposit the sample simply within the vagina or in the posterior fornix. It is more appropriate to deposit the sample of donor semen within the cervical mucus at the external os. For this, a speculum examination is required to visualise the os.

Research on IUI in DI cycles has shown that this is a very effective method of treatment (Byrd et al, 1990; Patton et al, 1992). This, however, is a more involved method of treatment, requiring more resources and more technical skills. IUI involves depositing the semen sample directly into the intrauterine cavity (see Chapter 4). Again, speculum examination is required, and a very fine sterile catheter is threaded through the cervical canal into the uterus and the sample deposited. This method also requires specific laboratory preparation of the semen prior to insemination.

Continuity of care is important to couples attending the clinic, and they tend to be more relaxed when the treatment is to be carried out by someone they know. Unfortunately, some couples can find medical staff intimidating, and they may be less likely to discuss anxieties with them than with a nurse. Also the nurse is almost invariably female, and a woman having a vaginal examination may find it more acceptable for it to be carried out by another woman.

The atmosphere of the clinic is very important. The couple should be able to trust the clinic and feel relatively comfortable in attending it, and they should be able to expect privacy and confidentiality. It is also important that the male partner should not feel excluded from the treatment process. He should be made welcome and, if both wish, be present at the time of insemination. However, if he does not wish to be present, or for practical reasons cannot be present, he should not feel guilty. There are other ways in which he can show his support. For example, he could attend the clinic with his partner but wait in the waiting room while the actual insemination is carried out. Alternatively, his support can be shown by making an effort in other areas of their life, such as having the evening meal ready or going out for a meal together.

In this area, the nurse should be sensitive to interpreting the feelings of the couple. It is true that not all men would wish to be present. It is also true that some women would not wish them to be present; in the authors' experience, some women cannot relax with their partners present. This, in turn, makes the insemination slightly more difficult and painful. Should the woman not wish her partner in the room while the insemination is carried out, she should be supported in her decision. Again, if both can be encouraged to communicate and share their feelings, a mutual compromise should be more easily reached.

Before starting treatment, it is important that each couple should have a treatment plan to follow. Each clinic should have management protocols laid down that are clearly understood by the staff and the couples, showing how many cycles should be carried out before laparoscopy. It should also show whether or not drugs should be employed to induce ovulation.

As discussed in Chapter 4, the highest success rates are achieved in the first four cycles of DI (Effective Health Care, 1992; RCOG, 1992). If pregnancy has not been achieved by this stage, this is perhaps the best time to consider laparoscopy. If laparoscopy findings are normal, the clinic protocol should show how many more cycles of DI should be offered or whether a change in management should be considered. It would be appropriate to consider superovulation with IUI at this stage.

In the eventuality that tubal damage is diagnosed, its extent will determine whether or not it is of value continuing treatment. Should tubal blockage be unilateral, it is feasible, with the use of ultrasound scanning, to determine on which ovary ovulation is occurring, and treatment could continue optimistically.

Pregnancy

With modern accurate HCG tests, pregnancy can now be confirmed very early. In the authors' clinic, pregnancy testing is offered when the woman is 5 days late with her expected period; in some clinic it may be offered earlier.

However, for HFEA registration, pregnancy is diagnosed when, on ultrasound scanning, a fetal heart beat can be visualised. With the use of vaginal ultrasound, this can be ascertained when the expected period is about 14 days late, i.e. at 6 weeks gestation. A scan would only be carried out following a positive pregnancy test.

The risk of miscarriage is no higher than normal following treatment by DI. The pregnancy, once achieved, is at no higher risk of abnormality, miscarriage or premature labour than is any pregnancy achieved through normal intercourse, nor is the risk of multiple pregnancy higher, unless drugs have been used to stimulate superovulation. In this instance, the risk should have been discussed clearly, so that the couple have realistic expectations of the pregnancy, but it is not surprising if they are more tense than would be usual. The couple could have put a major degree of effort, and a large part of their lives, into achieving this pregnancy, so it would not be unusual for their reaction to any antenatal problems to be more pronounced or acute.

It is possible for couples who have achieved a successful pregnancy and birth by DI to go on to enlarge their families. However, it will not always be possible to have the second, or third, child by the same donor, and not all couples would wish the same donor. It is the authors' experience that most couples prefer the same donor for a subsequent pregnancy, but only rarely have they seen a couple choose no further treatment if the same donor is unavailable. The HFEA Code of Practice states that only 10 children should be born by donor insemination to any one donor. However, should any of these 10 families wish to consider a further pregnancy, the HFEA allows that: should there be semen stored, treatment is allowed using the same donor.

Confidentiality

Although the nursing and medical professions are bound at all times by the rules of confidentiality, it must be remembered that the extent of this is not always apparent to patients. Time must be taken to clarify what confidentiality means and to listen to what patients expect. DI carries with it its own set of boundaries surrounding confidentiality, which have been laid down by the HFEA and must be strictly adhered to.

It must be clear, for the couple's peace of mind, who will be informed of or aware of their treatment. Those informed include the HFEA and the nursing and medical staff *within* the licensed clinic. The GP can be informed of their treatment, with the couple's consent. Should the couple register with a new treatment centre, details of their treatment can be forwarded if the second clinic is also covered by a HFEA licence.

CONCLUSION

As this chapter has illustrated, the nurse in this specialist field can expand her role considerably, depending on adequate training and expertise, and this expansion can facilitate opportunities for discussion and sharing feelings with her patients, in addition to providing continuity of care. She should be accountable and responsible for her actions, developing the scope of her professional practice but working within her professional competence (UKCC, 1992 b, c; RCN Fertility Nurses Group, 1993).

References

Adams J, Franks S, Polson D et al (1985) Multifollicular ovaries: clinical and endocrine features and response to pulsatile gonadotrophin releasing hormone. *Lancet*, **ii**: 1375–8.

Adams J, Polson D and Franks S (1986) Prevalence of polycystic ovaries in women with anovulation and idiopathic hirsutism. *British Medical Journal*, **293**: 355–9.

Baird D and Wilcox A (1985) Cigarette smoking associated with delayed conception. *Journal of the American Medical Association*, **290**: 2979–83.

Baram D, Tourtelot E, Muechler E and Huang K (1988) Psychosexual adjustment following unsuccessful in vitro fertilisation. *Journal of Psychosomatic Obstetrics and Gynaecology*, **9**: 181–90.

Barber D (1991) *Nurses Performing Embryo Transfer: Successful IVF Outcome.* Paper presented at the European Society for Human Reproduction & Embryology, Paris, June 1991.

Botting B, Macfarlane A and Price F (eds) (1990) *Three, Four or More.* London: HMSO.

Brannen J and Collard, J (1982) *Marriages in Trouble.* London: Tavistock.

British Andrology Society (1993) British Andrology Society Guidelines for Screening of Semen Donors for Donor Insemination. *Human Reproduction*, **8**(9): 1521–3.

Brook C, Jacobs, H and Stanhope, R (1988) Polycystic ovaries in childhood. *British Medical Journal*, **296**: 878 (editorial).

Byrd W, Bradshaw K, Carr B, Edman C, Odom J and Ackerman G (1990) A prospective randomised study of pregnancy rates following inter-uterine and intracervical insemination using frozen donor sperm. *Fertility and Sterility*, **53**: 521.

Cant S, Bell L, Emslie C, et al (1989) Timing of ovulation for artificial insemination. *Health Bulletin*, **47**(1), January, 9–12.

DoH (1992) *Folic Acid and the Prevention of Neural Tube Defects: Report from an Expert Advisory Group.* London: DoH.

Effective Health Care (1992) *The Management of Subfertility*, Issue 3. Leeds: Leeds University.

Golombok S, Cook R, Bish A and Murray C, (1993) Qualities of parenting in families created by the new reproductive technologies: a brief report of preliminary findings. *Journal of Psychosomatic Obstetrics and Gynaecology*, **14**: 17–22.

Greenfeld D, Diamond M and Decherney A (1988) Grief reactions following in vitro fertilisation treatment. *Journal of Psychosomatic Obstetrics and Gynaecology*, **8**: 169–74.

Greil A, Leitko T and Porter K (1988) Infertility – his and hers. *Gender and Society*, **2**(2): 172–99.

Haimes E (1992) Gamete donation and the social management of genetic origins. In: Stacey M (ed.) *Changing Human Reproduction*, London: Sage.

Hamilton-Fairley D, Kiddy D, Watson H, et al (1991) Low dose gonadotrophin therapy for induction of ovulation in 100 women with polycystic ovary syndrome. *Human Reproduction*, **6**: 1095–9.

Harlass F, Plymate S, Fariss B and Belts R (1984) Weight loss is associated with correction of gonadotrophin and sex steroid abnormalities in the obese anovulatory female. *Fertility and Sterility*, **42**: 649–51.

Heywood A (1991) Immaculate conception. *Nursing Times*, **87**(22): 62–3.

HFEA (1993) *Code of Practice*, 7.9 p35 and annex A.

Hull M (1987) Epidemiology of infertility and polycystic ovarian disease: endocrinological and demographic studies. *Gynaecological Endocrinology*, **1**: 235–45.

Hull M (1990) Indications for assisted conception. *British Medical Bulletin*, **46**(3): 580–95.

Hull M (1993) Implications and Risks of IVF and GIFT To Be Discussed with Couples. Unpublished protocol, University of Bristol.

Hull M, Eddowes H, Fahy U, et al (1992) Expectations of assisted conception for infertility. *British Medical Journal* **304**: 1465–9.

Human Fertilisation and Embryology Act (1990) Schedule 3 para 3 (1) (b) and s 33 (5)-(7) and s 13 (b).

Kiddy D, Hamilton Fairley D, Bush A, et al (1992) Improvement in endocrine and ovarian function during dietary treatment of obese women with polycystic ovary syndrome. *Clinical Endocrinology*, **36**: 105–11.

Levene M, Wild J and Steer P (1992) Higher multiple births and the modern management of infertility in Britain. The British Association of Perinatal Medicine. *British Journal of Obstetrics and Gynaecology*, **99**(7): 607–13.

Neuberg R (1991) *Infertility*. London: Thorsons.

Mason M-C (1993) *Male Infertility: Men Talking*. London: Routledge.

Patton P, Burry K and Thurmond A (1992) Intra-uterine insemination out-performs intracervical insemination in a randomised controlled trial with frozen donor semen. *Fertility and Sterility*, **57**: 559–64.

Polson D, Mason H, Saldahna M and Franks S (1987) Ovulation of a single dominant follicle during treatment with low-dose pulsatile follicle stimulating hormone in women with polycystic ovary syndrome. *Clinical Endocrinology*, **26**: 205–12.

Polson D, Adams J, Wadsworth J and Franks S (1988) Polycystic ovaries – a common finding in normal women. *Lancet*, **i**: 870–2.

RCN Fertility Nurses Group (1993) *Standards of Care for Fertility Nurses*. RCN Standards of Care Project. London: RCN.

RCOG (1992) *Infertility Guidelines for Practice*. London: RCOG Press.

RCOG (1994) RCOG Guidelines: Use of gonadotrophic hormone preparations for ovulation induction London: RCOG.

Rosevear S, Holt D, Lee T et al (1992) Smoking and decreased fertilisation rates in vitro. *Lancet*, **340**: 1195–6.

Schover L (1994) Psychological screening and the success of donor insemination. *Human Reproduction*, **9**(1): 176–8.

Snowden R and Snowden E (1993) *The Gift of a Child*. Exeter: University of Exeter Press.

Stockwell F (1972) *The Unpopular Patient*. London: RCN.

Templeton A (1985) *In vitro Fertilisation and Donor Insemination*, pp. 45–9. London: RCOG.

UKCC (1992a) *Standards for the Administration of Medicines*. London: UKCC.

UKCC (1992b) *Code of Professional Conduct*, 3rd edn. London: UKCC.

UKCC (1992c) *The Scope of Professional Practice*. London: UKCC.

Van der Spuy Z, Steer P, McCusker M et al (1988) Pregnancy outcome in underweight women following spontaneous and induced ovulation. *British Medical Journal*, **296**: 962–5.

Warnock M (1985) *A Question of Life: the Warnock Report on Human Fertilisation and Embryology*. Oxford: Basil Blackwell.

Weaver S, Clifford E, Gordon A et al (1993) A follow-up study of 'successful' IVF/GIFT couples: social–emotional well-being and adjustment to parenthood. *Journal of Psychosomatic Obstetrics and Gynaecology*, **14**: 5–16.

7

Ethical dilemmas

Richard Rowson and Elizabeth Bryan

INTRODUCTION

Nurses are not only professional carers but also friends to patients, participants in discussion about them, formal or informal teachers of other staff, citizens, tax payers and voters. In all of these roles, they may have an interest in the ethical dilemmas that surround the provision of treatments for infertility. Even if they are not directly responsible for treatment decisions or for counselling clients, they will wish to understand the sorts of issue involved and the different ways of thinking about them.

The subject of ethics is as complex as it is interesting. The complexity arises both in the perennial philosophical debates about how we should (or should not) reach our moral judgements and in the startling new options, both for individuals and for society in general, that are offered by the new reproductive technologies.

In this chapter, we look first at the many ways in which judgements can be made and the different perspectives that different people will bring to the task. We shall consider, for example, various views of the moral status of the embryo and fetus and the idea that this may change with its stages of development. We shall also study different views of the basic elements of morality, including individual self-determination, judgement in terms of the consequences and greatest net benefit and appeals to what is 'natural', 'fair' or a 'moral right'. We then go on to look at several major moral issues in the realm of infertility treatment, describing many of the sometimes conflicting 'principles', 'rights', ideals and other considerations that different people will regard as relevant in the context of infertility treatment. We shall see how these create conflicts not only between people but also within any given individual, who may find him or herself having to make some sort of balance, as between rival goods or alternate dangers.

We shall not be attempting, therefore, to produce a single set of coherent moral judgements but rather to display as many as possible of the arguments that can regularly be employed to justify the very many different positions that medical and nursing staff, policy makers, managers and citizens will no doubt continue to adopt.

MORAL POINTS OF VIEW RELEVANT TO FERTILITY NURSING

The moral status of prenatal human life

The moral status that people ascribe to prenatal life varies enormously and crucially affects their views on how it should be treated.

Views of prenatal life as having an unchanging moral status

There is a spectrum of views that sees prenatal life as having an unchanging status from conception to birth.

At one end of this spectrum is the 'conservative' view that prenatal life has the same moral status as that of human adults. Some religious believers think that this moral status arises from the coming into existence at the moment of fertilisation of a soul, which has sacred value. Others think that at fertilisation, a unique genetic entity comes into being and that this uniqueness gives the conceptus its significant value. Whatever the beliefs that give rise to the view, its basic claim is that it is only acceptable to treat prenatal life in a particular way if it is acceptable to treat adults in a relevantly similar way.

Thus, creating embryos and then allowing some to die, whether in fertility techniques or in embryo research, is as morally unacceptable as deliberately creating a situation in which adults are brought together and then left to die. Moreover, just as it is unacceptable to disregard the well-being of a group of adults and use them simply as material for research that will benefit others, so it is unacceptable to treat embryos as living human tissue for non-therapeutic research purposes.

Consequently, in this conservative view, our moral concern should be to enhance the prospects of any embryos that are alive, and we should not bring about situations in which it is not possible, or in which we do not intend, to attempt to do this.

The conservative view on abortion is, basically, that terminating a pregnancy is not permissible if it would be unacceptable to end an adult life in relevantly similar circumstances or for relevantly similar reasons. So, if it is unacceptable to kill one adult in order to prevent him causing damage to the mental, physical or social well-being of another, it is equally unacceptable to terminate a pregnancy in order to prevent it damaging the mental, physical or social well-being of the mother or anyone else.

But what of situations in which continuation of the pregnancy is likely to cause the death of the mother – how would 'conservatives' view this? Their response would again be to draw on the analogy of adults, and here two views are possible. Some hold the view that if one adult were about to kill another, we would be morally entitled to do whatever was necessary to prevent him doing so, and if killing the aggressor were the only way to do this, killing him would be morally acceptable. Others, however, disagree with this and consider that any moral responsibility we have to protect the lives of others does not go so far as to justify killing a person who is about to kill someone else. Thus, on the basis of this analogy, whereas some 'conservatives' think it is morally permissible to carry out an abortion to save the life of the mother, others disagree.

At the other end of the spectrum of the unchanging status of prenatal life is the 'liberal' view that moral status, from conception to birth, is no higher than that of other human tissue or bodily organs.

Most people regard tissue and organs as having a much lower moral status than do human beings and think that they can be treated in whatever way is necessary for the well-being of humans. The 'liberal' view is that, just as we are entitled to enhance someone's quality of life by giving medication to human tissue and organs, by performing invasive surgery on them or by destroying them altogether, so we are entitled to do the same to prenatal life. Thus, abortion at any stage, using embryos for non-therapeutic purposes, and fertility techniques and research that involve creating embryos and deliberately letting them die, are all morally acceptable, providing they are carried out to further human well-being.

A mild version of this liberal view is that the status of prenatal life is sufficiently high for us only to be entitled to interfere with it or destroy it if the effects we are seeking are considerable, such as the prevention of a life of very poor quality or the prevention of harm to people whose lives would be severely adversely affected by a pregnancy going to full term.

A stronger version of the view is that the status of prenatal life is sufficiently low for us to be entitled to interfere with it or destroy it even if the improvement in well-being we seek is relatively trivial. This view seems to be held by people who consider that abortion at any stage is morally acceptable, even if the mother seeks it for such reasons as to prevent disruption to career objectives or holiday plans.

A third view of prenatal life as having unchanging status is known as the 'potentiality' view. This view lies on the spectrum between the conservative and liberal views, since it considers that prenatal life does not have as great a value as adult life, nor as little as human tissue and organs, but has unique value as a potential adult. The value put on its potentiality varies from little more than that of other human tissue, to almost as much as adult life. Depending on this variation, proponents of the potentiality view may regard interference or destruction of prenatal life as being almost as readily justified, as in the liberal view, or almost as difficult to justify, as in the conservative view.

Views of prenatal life as having a changing moral status

As well as the spectrum of opinion that sees prenatal life as having an unchanging moral status, there are views that its status increases as pregnancy continues. According to these views, it becomes increasingly difficult to justify terminating or interfering with prenatal life the more it develops, and there is a view that this moral status continues to grow after birth.

The following changes in development have been put forward as being morally significant, and as justifying ascribing increasing moral status.

Fertilisation.   Some people consider that gametes gain value at fertilisation, since at that point, genetic changes take place, which can be seen as the creation of a new centre of life. In this view, the 'morning after pill' avoids some of the moral objections that other contraceptives – such as the IUCD – attract, since prior to fertilisation, no new centre of life is being destroyed, as none yet exists.

Implantation.   Some people consider that the moral status of the blastocyst increases once implantation occurs, since it then has significantly increased chances of survival.

Embryo 'primitive streak' development.   As the Warnock Report (1984) expresses it, this physiological change is 'the beginning of individual development of the embryo' or the beginning of an organism that could become a particular person. Some people consider that, at this stage, the embryo becomes an organism whose interests are continuous with the interests of a potential individual person, so it begins to acquire the value we attach to a person. Since implantation and primitive streak development take place at approximately the same time – around the 15th day after fertilisation – many people consider that we need much greater moral justification to terminate or interfere with life after this stage than prior to it. These seem to be the considerations that led the Warnock Committee, for example, to recommend that research on embryos should not continue beyond 14 days after fertilisation.

Developments in the nervous system. Some people think that the gradual development of the nervous system is a morally significant change. They consider that, as the fetus develops a greater capacity to experience pain, we have an increasing moral obligation to avoid causing it to suffer.

'Quickening'. Many people feel that once a woman becomes aware of the fetus moving, this initiates or, at least, significantly develops, the mother–offspring relationship. They see the value of the fetus as being increased by virtue of the fact that it is now within such a prized human relationship.

Viability. Becoming physiologically capable of surviving outside the womb is seen by many as a significant change, since the fetus thereby acquires a degree of self-sufficiency and independence of the mother. However, the level of physical development that is necessary for a fetus to be considered 'viable' may vary according to the medical facilities available. In a society in which there are neonatal intensive care facilities, a fetus may be considered viable at an earlier stage than in a society in which there are none.

Birth. Traditionally, of course, birth has been seen as vastly changing the moral status of new life. This is reflected in the vocabulary we use: we 'terminate' a pregnancy but 'kill' a baby. Rather like 'quickening', the process of birth changes the nature of the mother–offspring relationship. Moreover, the baby becomes a social presence and thereby gains social importance in the lives of others. Some people, however, have challenged the vast change in moral importance that we traditionally ascribe to the newborn baby. They have argued that, at birth, the newborn does not itself acquire any morally significant new abilities or physiological attributes. In this view, we should not regard causing suffering or death to a neonate as morally worse than causing suffering or death to a fetus in the final stages of pregnancy.

Mental and personal development. For some people, the moral value and respect due to a human being increases as it develops the mental abilities and individual characteristics of a person. In this view, as a human becomes more aware of herself as an individual, and, as she forms desires and expectations and becomes able to make informed choices, so it becomes increasingly difficult to justify any treatment that interferes with these expectations and decisions. Since moral status grows with the development of these capacities, the moral status of babies and children who have yet to develop them is not equal to that of older humans.

Taking into account some or all of these factors leads many people to consider that the moral status of life increases during pregnancy and, for some, continues to do so after birth.

We now move on to other views that also play a significant part in these debates.

Respect for autonomy

Many people see the obligation to respect individual autonomy – or self-determination – as an essential element in morality. Several lines of argument support this view. One is that the ability to make decisions about their lives, by working out priorities and weighing up the pros and cons of alternative actions, gives people 'human dignity'. In this view, human beings are debased – being treated as 'things' rather than 'persons' – if they are not allowed to exercise this ability. Another argument is the simple one that if· we value our *own* opportunities to be self-determining, we should value them for others. Yet another consideration is the view that people can only be fully responsible for their actions if they do them freely, with no coercion from others. Consequently, if people are not allowed this freedom, they are prevented from taking moral responsibility for their actions.

Since a fetus is not able to make conscious decisions, and so has no autonomy tó be respected, our concern should be to respect the autonomy of others. Some people think this should be done by acceding to all requests for abortion and assisted fertility, whether or not this will involve deliberately creating embryos, some of which will be allowed to die. This is the strong version of the liberal view we have already considered. Others, while agreeing that autonomy should by fully respected, think that the autonomy of the client or patient should not always take precedence over the autonomy of health-care professionals. Professionals may, for example, foresee harmful consequences resulting from complying with a particular request, so consider that they have a moral obligation to refuse it.

Utilitarianism

The view that we have a moral obligation to seek the best consequences is known as consequentialism or utilitarianism, as it judges the value of actions by their usefulness, or utility, in bringing about desirable results.

When we have a decision to make, it often seems that each option before us will bring about a mixture of benefits and harms. From the utilitarian viewpoint, we should, in such situations, compare the benefits and harms of each option and choose the one we think will give the greatest net benefit. This means considering what economists call the 'opportunity costs' of each option. Whenever we have limited resources at our disposal, we have to recognise that, in bringing benefits to some patients, we lose the opportunity to bring benefits to others. Awareness of these lost opportunities should be part of our consideration in large-scale decisions (such as the priority to be given to providing assisted fertility services or to meeting other health-care needs) and in small-scale decisions (such as. whether or not to give more attention to one patient than another).

Our moral duty then, according to utilitarianism, is to choose the course of action that we, at the time of making our decision, are convinced will bring the greatest benefit, taking into account the likely outcome for everyone we are able to affect by our actions.

Many utilitarians consider that all moral judgements – such as those on the acceptability of alternative fertility techniques or the treatment of particular patients – should be made solely on assessment of the likely benefits and harm of each option. They consider that there is no obligation to consider other factors, such as the moral status of life. So, while they would include in their assessment any pain and pleasure caused to pre- and postnatal life, they would not see that life, whether pre- or postnatal, as having moral status in itself.

Appeal to nature

The idea that nature gives a guide as to what should and should not be done is very popular. Actions seen as 'unnatural', or as 'going against' or 'interfering with' nature, are often seen as wrong.

Since even the simplest treatments in health care, such as bathing a wound with saline solution, interfere, to some degree, with the course of nature, it is difficult to claim seriously that *all* interference with nature is wrong. Indeed, nature itself could be seen as indicating the opposite. For as intelligence is part of human nature, is it not natural for people to use their intelligence to interfere with nature in order to create more favourable outcomes for themselves? If this is agreed, the most we may want to claim is that interference of a certain sort, or beyond a certain level, is wrong.

But can 'facts of nature' tell us where to draw the line between acceptable and unacceptable types and levels of interference? Antibiotics may involve greater biochemical interference with nature than does hormonal treatment for assisted fertility, yet some people who consider the latter unacceptable interference are happy to accept the former. Similarly, skin grafting may involve far more complex surgical and medical intervention than in vitro fertilisation, yet people who accept the former may reject the latter. It seems, then, that it is often not the *degree* to which nature is interfered with, but the *purpose* of the interference, to which many people object.

In fact, the purpose and type of interference that is considered acceptable varies enormously from culture to culture and person to person, and there seem to be no facts of nature, as such, that dictate a single view on which types of interference are acceptable. Indeed, it is not the simple fact that nature is interfered with that makes people reject an activity as wrong but the fact that it is interfered with in ways that they do not, *for some other reason*, like, perhaps, because they are not used to it or because it does not fit in with their cultural standpoint. Claims that particular processes are wrong simply because they interfere with nature can, therefore, be deceptive.

Fairness

Many people feel strongly that we should treat each other fairly. One way of explaining 'fairness' is to say that it means treating everyone alike, unless there is a relevant difference between them that justifies or requires us to treat them differently. In this view we should, for example, treat all women alike by making assisted fertility services available to all, unless we find that there are differences between them that are relevant to the provision of these services. Any such difference may justify, or require, us to withhold services from some patients.

But what differences should be regarded as relevant? Someone who holds the utilitarian view might argue that it would be morally wrong to make assisted fertility available to women who are unlikely to provide children with a reasonable quality of life. We may agree with this but disagree on which women fulfil these conditions. Should we consider women above a certain age, or lesbian women or women in mixed race relationships as being unlikely to provide adequately for their children? Our answer will depend on the sort of provision we regard as necessary for children – material wealth, a household that conforms to some social norm or adults *in loco parentis* who have particular qualities of character. However, it could be asked further, who are we to make this judgement? Should we not simply respect the autonomy of the women who make the request?

Thus, we see that fairness, while being a powerful moral ideal, is one that some people think should, at times, give way to other moral considerations, such as the obligation to seek the best consequences or to respect autonomy. Moreover, it is an ideal that is capable of being interpreted and applied in accordance with many different criteria, depending on what other moral, social and religious attitudes a person has.

Appeal to rights

Much discussion of moral issues is expressed in terms of 'rights' – people talk of the 'rights of the unborn child' and 'every woman's right'. 'Rights' can be legal or moral. The former are based on the law of the land, whereas the latter are based on moral viewpoints, and it is these we are concerned with.

If someone is considered to have a right to something, he is regarded as having a claim or entitlement to it, and the rest of us have an obligation either to help him to achieve it or, at least, not to deprive him of it. Thus, if every women has a right to abortion on demand, the gynaecologist has an obligation to perform it, and the rest of us have an obligation not to interfere.

The language used in talking about moral rights sounds like factual statements rather than expressions of moral opinions. So, 'Jane has a right to decide this for herself' seems to be identifying a fact about Jane, rather like identifying any other facts about her, such as 'Jane has green eyes'. Consequently, a moral disagreement expressed in terms of rights seems to be an argument over a factual matter: 'Jane has this right'; 'No, she does not'. As long as the protagonists continue to think only in terms of rights, their argument is unlikely to progress beyond a series of assertions and counterassertions.

However, were they to explore the reasons for their claims, they might increase their understanding of one another's point of view. The person who claims that Jane has a right to make up her own mind may, for instance, have based her view on the need to respect people's autonomy if their decision is well informed. Similarly, the person who claims that Jane does not have this right may think that Jane's decision will not be well informed, since someone of her age cannot understand the issues, or she may think that any decision made by Jane is unlikely to bring about the best consequences for all concerned. Only if their discussion identifies such reasons for their views can proponents of the two approaches assess the justification for their claims about rights.

When claims about rights are investigated, they generally turn out to be based on one or more of the moral views we have already looked at. So, for example, claims that 'all women have a right to x' can be seen as derived from the principle of fairness, that 'patients have a right to choose' from the view that autonomy should be respected, and that 'everyone has a right to health care' from a combination of the views that health care for everyone will result in the best consequences and that everyone should be treated alike. Claims of 'natural rights' may be derived from the view that the facts of nature give a basis for making moral judgements.

Moral Dilemmas

We have now concluded our review of the main moral points of view relevant to issues in fertility nursing. For most people, however, dilemmas are inevitable, because they find themselves seeing some values in most of the basic moral points of view that we have described. They may put much weight on 'the sanctity of life' but also care a great deal about equal treatment, good social consequences, the autonomy of the individual and 'the woman's right to choose'.

If moral philosophers could find a single all-embracing basis for moral judgement, this would prevent any argument and confusion, but as each one will start from such different standpoints, this is not possible. However, this variety of views and perspectives is valuable in enabling health professionals to see a difficult case from all angles and hence increase their sensitivity to both the potential costs and the benefits of any particular treatment or, indeed, its refusal.

We could now list all the most important moral issues arising from infertility treatment and spell out the different judgements that would be made over each one from the various moral points of view that we have described. This would however take several chapters and still not help those who have no single set of moral beliefs. Instead, it might be more helpful to look at several major issues in turn and sketch some of the dilemmas that may arise with each one.

There are of course some treatments for infertility, such as surgical unblocking of a damaged fallopian tube or antibiotics for an infection, that would give rise to no serious moral dilemmas, except perhaps for those minorities who are opposed in principle to medical intervention of any kind. In other cases, the problems may be resolved by the use of psychosexual counselling, requiring no medical intervention at all.

WHO SHOULD DECIDE?

A first major issue for medical professionals, as for the public at large, is simply 'Who should decide?' If someone who is, for example, single, unmarried or emotionally disturbed or who already has four children asks for an assisted conception or DI, who has the right to say yes or no to her original request?

There are at least four possible sources of authority to consider. One must be the would-be parent and her partner, if any. We have already discussed the claims of their autonomy, but have additionally said that the conscience of the infertility specialist must also be respected. Medical and nursing staff are, therefore, a second source of authority. Moreover, doctors or nurses may not themselves object to performing the particular procedure but will be bound by any contrary decision from the local ethics committee. The profession may sometimes have national ethical guidance, as was the case with the Interim Licensing Authority before the passage of the Human Fertilisation and Embryology Act 1990.

Government policy, and law in particular, is a third source of decision-making, and the Human Fertilisation and Embryology Act (see Chapter 8), for example, declares that infertility clinics practising IVF must be licensed, regulated and monitored.

Laws may be morally right or wrong (as in Nazi Germany, where the destruction of unwanted people was permitted), so the fourth source of moral authority, namely the popular vote of a healthy democracy, can take on special importance. Ultimately, the voter should have some role in deciding what procedures should be allowed and what health-care priorities are to be pursued.

All four levels are concerned with human opinion, and at all four, there may be strong religious or philosophical influences; some of these call on what are said to be 'absolute' principles.

OPINIONS ON ASSISTED CONCEPTION

IVF involves fertilisation outside the body; GIFT also requires the withdrawal of the egg from the body, even though fertilisation eventually occurs within the fallopian tubes. Both methods give rise to complex moral issues, and some religious authorities – and individuals – have objections of absolute principle to both of them.

Although various views on assisted conception have been expressed within Judaism, traditional importance is given to 'the sanctity of the marriage bond' and 'the Jewish concept of an intimate personal partnership with God in the generation of life' (Jacobovits, 1975). So, while techniques that enable a married couple to fulfil their sacred duty to procreate may be viewed favourably, they are likely to be disapproved of if they can be construed as adultery. Consequently, IVF may be accepted provided the gametes are those of husband and wife, but using the gametes of a donor may be unacceptable. Moreover, processes involving the destruction of fertilised eggs may be seen as devaluing human life and the use of surrogate mothers as debasing a woman by using her as an incubator.

In the Vatican's view, scientific treatment of infertility, as such, is acceptable, but substitution of the laboratory dish for parental acts of love is thought to be an evil. The benefits to the otherwise childless are not believed to be adequate to excuse departure from what is seen as a profound principle. Historically, this Vatican teaching goes back to the 1887 Decree of the Holy Office (Denziger and Schoenmetzer, 1967), condemning the artificial insemination of women, but, in recent years, many individual Catholics, including some priests, have taken a different view.

The Vatican is not alone in saying that children should be generated by acts of love, but it has less support in insisting so absolutely that children should not (as others see it) be generated from unusual, but still loving, action assisted by technology. The Catholic Church's objection to IVF is not, therefore, the same as its objection to abortion, although the destruction of fertilised eggs in IVF is another of its objections. Whether the same objection is raised against GIFT is less clear, because the Vatican appears to have been silent on the subject.

A similar absolutist case is put by people of other denominations and religions who see IVF and equivalent manipulations as 'meddling with human souls', whether by 'killing' (rejecting) some embryos or 'manufacturing' (implanting) them. Generally speaking, however, religious bodies have been cautious in stating dogmatic ethical views. They have rightly warned of dangers but have avoided being too specific about particular procedures until their implications become more clear.

Some agnostics or atheists also see the procedures as an example of gross interferences with the processes of 'Mother Nature' or the workings of 'Fate', which we discussed earlier.

Many people are troubled by some of these doubts, feeling that so profound an intervention at the very outset of life shows recklessness, if not arrogance, on the part of those responsible.

A BRAVE NEW WORLD?

Some people fear that humans could slide from procreation without coition to a Brave New World run by eugenicists, controlled, in turn, by tyrants choosing what sorts of people they want to breed. We are already able, technically, to select ova and sperm from preselected donors, select again among the various embryos created in vitro and transpose the 'products of conception' to suitable surrogate mothers. It is, therefore, no longer fanciful to imagine ruthless rulers striving to impose their own racist, ethnic, religious or other ideas, nor is it impossible to imagine a regime using gender selection deliberately to reduce the number of females in order to restrain population growth. Not everyone would find that easy to argue against, whatever sense of outrage they might initially have.

Many authorities would argue that popular feeling, democratic institutions and professional standards will be strong enough to resist such extreme abuse, but two other fears for the future should also be mentioned. One is of the increasing 'medicalisation' of natural processes, which not only puts more power in the hands of doctors – and often governments – but also encourages a sense of powerlessness. The other is fear about the alleged 'commodification' of reproduction, whereby the child could become just another commodity to be purchased. Some fear that we are on the threshold of 'designer sperm' and 'designer ova' being selected and manipulated to produce the perfect, customised baby, as if selected from a catalogue.

What are the limits? Rarely have medical professionals and citizens in general had to weigh up so many potential dangers against such real potential benefits. How can we decide which procedures or treatments are morally acceptable and which are not? Who is entitled to what treatment and at whose expense? What degree of interference in physical (and psychological) processes is tolerable and what is not? And what, perhaps most importantly of all, of the resulting children? Might they be the prime sufferers of our medical enthusiasms?

Most of the ethical dilemmas seem inescapably to involve a choice between evils. Almost every technical solution can bring its own problems. Ways have been found to enable a parent to avoid having a boy in order to circumvent the danger of a sex-linked genetic disease. Does this open the door to people insisting on having boys for merely social or cultural reasons? Is this the beginning of a 'slippery slope' from medically justified choices to choices for reasons of social preference or even just selfish convenience? On grounds of client autonomy and individual choice, sex selection may seem acceptable, but what of the possible encouragement of male domination, macho values or population imbalance? Some feminists, among others, are the more worried because of what they see as the apparent domination of males, and of typically masculine perceptions, in gynaecology and its related areas (Pfeffer, 1993).

So many of the arguments used against the various forms of assisted conception are based on the idea of a 'slippery slope' (whether towards Brave New World tyrannies, Frankensteinian excesses, eugenic selection or 'commodification') that some points about this particular style of argument should be made. It has to be recognised, firstly, that there can, in principle, be something to this fear. There is little doubt that there are political dictators, entrepreneurs, reckless scientists or demanding consumers who could try to go too far down the slippery slope. Restraints are essential to civilised society, and their gradual erosion can be serious. Nevertheless, slippery slopes work both ways. If we are to curtail research or a patient's rights to a strong voice in her or his treatment, where are we going to stop? Are governments (or doctors) to control everything? Are not our pluralistic societies healthier for having few absolute rules and for dealing with *actual* rather than *potential* difficulties as they arise? Is it not better, in general, to learn as we go rather than to construct logically plausible, but often unrealistic, fantasies about where an activity *might* eventually lead? Storage of embryos *could* gradually lead to their black market trading, but so could kidney transplantation have led to the murder of people for the sake of their kidneys. DI could have led to widespread genetic incest, and so on. The truth is that a multiplicity of restraints – part personal, part professional, part legal – have kept any such tendencies at bay. Possibilities do not always become actualities: we need to be conscious of them but need not be entirely ruled by them.

WHO SHOULD BE TREATED?

In recent years, there have been passionate debates about which kinds of patient should qualify for infertility treatment, whether private or public, and who should receive it free of charge from the State health service. Most of these debates recognise a dilemma between acceding to a client's autonomy and acting in accord with the professional assessment of long-term benefits. When a doctor says 'no', he or she may be accused of playing God. When the answer is 'yes', the doctor may be charged with irresponsibility or extravagance. Different doctors, policy makers, voters – and clients – will take different positions.

Some of the basic issues seem to be these:

- Should doctors be prepared to give infertility treatment to everyone, or whom should they refuse?
- Who should be entitled to free infertility treatments?
- In a crowded world, should anyone be given infertility treatment anyway?

Some procedures are simply illegal. In the UK, the HFEA Code of Practice (1993) stipulates that no more than three embryos can be transferred in IVF treatment, in order to avoid high multiple births. Similarly, doctors may not deliberately select the sex of embryos to be transferred for any but strictly medical reasons. Some doctors will, either as individuals or on the instruction of their hospital's ethical committee, refuse to carry out some procedures, such as IVF, on a surrogate mother.

Perhaps the most testing questions arise where the doctor has a mixture of medical, ethical and social hesitations in relation to particular procedures or sorts of client, mainly as a result of utilitarian considerations. As discussed in Chapter 2, few doctors would be prepared to assist conception in women in their late 50s. They would not think it fair to the resulting children or perhaps sufficiently safe for the mother. Many would hesitate to treat a woman over 45; most would stop by 50, even when the woman was paying for private treatment. Nor would doctors wish to proceed where there is likely to be a serious genetic malformation or where either partner was an alcoholic, a user of hard drugs, a prostitute, a suspected child abuser or HIV positive.

In considering whether to proceed with assisted conception, most doctors will have the likely prospects of the child (or children) produced at the centre of their thinking. The welfare of the child is also a key element of the HFEA's outlook and its guidance to licensed centres. In this context, the medical staff may wonder, for example, whether the couple's motives may be suspect or their partnership appear to be unstable. Some people would say these are not matters for medical staff to judge, but both could plainly affect the prospects of the would-be child.

Moral questions inevitably arise with single people who want a child. Few clinics would collaborate with a single man who wanted to procreate, say with the help of a surrogate mother. Some doctors would, however, help a single woman where the motivation was good and reasonable domestic security was assured.

Over one-quarter of today's families are brought up by single parents, often very well, and some would point out that single women make better parents than unhappy couples. This more utilitarian approach leads, therefore, to the conclusion opposite to that of high principle.

HIGH MULTIPLE BIRTHS: TWO SPECIAL MORAL DILEMMAS

Ovarian stimulating drugs, with or without IVF and GIFT, produce an unusually high incidence of triplets or more, unless careful precautions are taken. The number of triplets born in the UK, for example, nearly trebled between 1983 and 1993 (OPCS, 1993). In many countries, there are now limits, sometimes legal ones, on the number of embryos or eggs that can be transferred (Gunning and English, 1993). The use of drugs on their own is, however, more difficult to control, as these can be prescribed by any registered medical practitioner, whether or not he or she has had training in the treatment of the infertile.

Triplets, quadruplets and larger deliveries can inflict heavy strains on the children themselves, on the parents, on neonatal care units and their nurses and, indeed, on the health and social services at large (Botting et al, 1990). A triplet (or higher) pregnancy can be hazardous, and mid-trimester abortions are especially painful to couples for whom it is their first and long awaited pregnancy. As these mid-trimester abortions are not recorded in the perinatal mortality figures, the extent of this bereavement is greatly underestimated.

High multiple birth babies tend to be born very small and early, with a high risk of neonatal complications and long-term learning difficulties, if not disability or death (Bryan, 1992). The perinatal mortality is about 10 times that of singletons, and survivors may block cots in the neonatal intensive care units for many months. It is also very difficult for the parents, practically, financially and psychologically, to relate to and care for three or more babies at the same time. The National Triplet Study found that the help received by these families was often inadequate and that professionals underestimated their needs. Social services sometimes stepped in only when a crisis had occurred (Price, 1990).

There are many reasons, therefore, why triplet and higher multiple pregnancies should be discouraged. Many feel that health workers have a moral obligation to limit the risks. Although those practising IVF and other forms of assisted conception show such restraints, more careful monitoring of ovulation induction is urgently needed.

The second moral dilemma is much more difficult, and health professionals continue to be deeply divided over it (Bryan et al, 1991; Evans et al, 1991). An embryo reduction in a higher multiple pregnancy is now quite widely practised in the UK and more often elsewhere (Price, 1994). Pregnancies as large as nonoplets have been reduced during the first trimester to two (or sometimes three) embryos. This reduction gives a far better chance of the couple ending up with the healthy baby they originally sought rather than, as so often happens, a tragic saga of babies born dead, weak or dying.

The dilemmas are clear and focus on the moral status of prenatal life, on the one hand, and assessments of benefits, on the other. In this sense, the basic moral conflict here would be between those adhering to an absolute principle, such as that barring any 'killing' (assuming the 'conservative' view that prenatal life is equivalent to adult human life), and those who, on a roughly utilitarian basis, seek to weigh 'disbenefits' against benefits. There is little doubt that some potentially healthy embryos are killed in this procedure, and there is some small danger of precipitating a total miscarriage in what may be the couple's only pregnancy. However, the chances of ending up with one or two healthy babies are also increased (Evans et al, 1993).

There is also inevitable dispute over what number of fetuses justifies reduction, and down to what number. Many UK obstetricians refuse to perform reductions on triplet pregnancies. Such a refusal, when it happens, can present a further moral dilemma for a couple who feel overwhelmed by the prospect of three, probably frail, babies; they must then decide whether to continue or to terminate the whole pregnancy. If the couple decide on a full termination, the doctor who refused to perform the reduction is almost bound to feel the more distressed.

Some medical staff refuse to undertake an embryo reduction not on absolutist grounds but out of concern about the possible long-term psychological impacts of embryo reduction on both the parents and the children (Bryan 1994). Little is yet known about these, because the procedures are still fairly new. Various problems could arise. In the first place, a couple may be emotionally torn when they celebrate safe arrivals, while still grieving the would-be babies they have not only lost but have themselves decided to lose. If a survivor is disabled, some parents may, rightly or wrongly, feel even more distressed. Parents may also be concerned about what, if anything, they should later tell the surviving children about the siblings they lost before they were born. Moreover, some fear that lasting psychic damage could be done to the survivors following their sudden intrauterine bereavement (Lewis and Bryan, 1988).

However, many experts dismiss these particular fears, and only long-term follow-up studies will determine whether or not there are real grounds for anxiety. Somewhat similar dilemmas arise in the area of DI, egg donation and surrogacy, in all of which the child could feel that something unnatural, or worse, had been done. This is partly why the Human Fertilisation and Embryology Act insists on the provision of counselling and confidentiality.

There is also widespread, if not universal, agreement that some of the opposition to the new methods of assisted conception is due to their unfamiliarity. Surprise can become shock, even disgust. The so-called 'yuk' factor can affect anyone. Yet, over the years, we have become well used to all sorts of procedures, from blood transfusions to organ transplants, that would have upset many when they were first performed. Nevertheless, interventions in the reproductive process take us to new levels, as would any permitted genetic manipulation of egg, sperm or embryo. The most recent rumblings of public disgust have been over the possibility of using ovarian tissue from the cadavers of adults or from aborted fetuses because of the shortage of donated eggs, as discussed in Chapter 2.

CONCLUSION

As with so many other issues we have discussed, both the medical and nursing professions, and society at large, may have to go through an involved learning process before settled conclusions are reached. It is, however, clearly necessary to continue weighing the various real or potential objections against the moral positives of treatment, not least the joy of the infertile when they achieve a family.

References

Botting B J, Macfarlane A J, Price F V (1990) *Three, Four and More. A Study of Triplet and Higher Order Births*. London: HMSO.

Bryan E M (1992) Higher order births. II. Pregnancy and delivery. In: Bryan E M (ed.) *Twins and Higher Multiple Births. A Guide to their Nature and Nurture*, pp. 192–200. Sevenoaks: Edward Arnold.

Bryan E M (1994) Problems surrounding selective fetocide. In: Abramsky L and Chappel J (eds) *The Human Side of Prenatal Diagnosis*. pp. 149–56. Oxford: Blackwell.

Bryan E M, Higgins R and Harvey D (1991) Ethical dilemmas. In: Harvey D and Bryan E M (eds) *The Stress of Multiple Births*, pp. 35–40. London: Multiple Births Foundation.

Denziger H and Schoenmetzer A (1967) '*Enchiridion Symbolorum*'. Rome: Herder.

Evans M I, Drugan A, Bottoms S F, Rodeck C A, Hansmann M and Fletcher J C (1991) Attitudes on the ethics of abortion, sex selection, and selective pregnancy termination among health care professionals, ethicists, and clergy likely to encounter such situations. *American Journal of Obstetrics and Gynaecology*, **164**: 1092–9.

Evans M I, Dommergues M, Wapner R J et al (1993) Efficacy of transabdominal multifetal pregnancy reduction: collaborative experience among the world's largest centers. *Obstetrics and Gynecology*, **82**: 61–6.

Gunning J and English V (1993) *In Vitro Fertilisation*. Aldershot: Dartmouth.

HFEA (1993) *Code of Practice*. London: HFEA.

Jacobovits I (1975) *Jewish Medical Ethics*. New York: Bloch.

Lewis E and Bryan E M (1988) Management of perinatal loss of a twin. *British Medical Journal*, **297**: 1321–3.

OPCS (1993) OPCS Series FMI. London: HMSO.

Pfeffer N (1993) *The Stork and the Syringe: A Political History of Reproductive Medicine*, pp. 30–47. Oxford: Polity Press.

Price F V (1990) Who helps? In: Botting B J, Macfarlane A J and Price F V. (eds) *Three, Four and More. A Study of Triplet and Higher Order Births* pp. 131–52. London: HMSO.

Price F V (1994) Tailoring multiparity: the dilemmas surrounding death by selective reduction of pregnancy. In: Lee R and Morgan M (eds) *Death Rites: Law and Ethics at the End of Life*, pp. 175–95. London: Routledge.

Warnock M (1984) *Report of the Committee of Enquiry into Human Fertilisation and Embryology*. Cmnd 9313. London: HMSO.

Further Reading

Almond B and Hill D (eds) (1991) *Applied Philosophy: Morals and Metaphysics in Contemporary Debate*. London: Routledge.

Beauchamp T L and Childress J F (1989) *Principles of Biomedical Ethics*, 3rd edn. New York: Oxford University Press.

Chadwick R (ed.) (1990) *Ethics, Reproduction and Genetic Control*. London: Routledge.

Dyson A and Harris J (eds) (1990) *Experiments on Embryos*. London: Routledge.

Harris J (1985) *The Value of Life*. London: Routledge.

Hursthouse R (1987) *Beginning Lives*. Oxford: Blackwell.

Morgan D and Lee R G (1991) *Human Fertilisation and Embryology Act 1990*. London: Blackstone.

Overall C (1987) *Ethics and Human Reproduction: A Feminist Analysis*. London: Allen and Unwin.

Rowson R H (1990) *Introduction to Ethics for Nurses*. London: Scutari Press.

8

The role of the Human Fertilisation and Embryology Authority

Veronica English

BACKGROUND

The first child resulting from IVF was born in 1978. While it was seen as a good thing that hope could now be brought to thousands of infertile couples, and that scientists would be able to understand the earliest stages of human life, there was also public concern that these new medical and scientific technologies could be used for other ends, which might overstep the boundaries of ethical acceptability.

As a result of this public concern, the government in 1982 set up a Committee of Inquiry. This Committee was chaired by Mary, now Baroness, Warnock. The prime function of the Warnock Committee was to consider what policies and safeguards should be adopted for infertility treatment and embryo research. The Committee published its findings 2 years later, in 1984. The Warnock Report (Warnock, 1984) was debated extensively in Parliament and in the public arena. One of the main recommendations of the report was that a statutory body should be set up to license and monitor embryo research and any infertility treatment involving the fertilisation of eggs outside the body or the use of donated sperm or eggs.

While the government began preparing and framing its proposals for legislation, the RCOG and the Medical Research Council (MRC) established the Voluntary Licensing Authority (later renamed the Interim Licensing Authority) which, as the name suggests, operated a voluntary system of regulation of clinics providing IVF treatment and embryo research (Gunning and English, 1993). The Government's White Paper – its proposals for legislation – appeared in 1987 (DHSS, 1987), and debates were held in both Houses of Parliament in the following year. The Human Fertilisation and Embryology Bill was introduced in 1989 and became an Act of Parliament in November 1990 (HMSO, 1990).

THE HUMAN FERTILISATION AND EMBRYOLOGY ACT 1990

Following the recommendations of the Warnock Report, the Act set up an independent statutory body called the Human Fertilisation and Embryology Authority (HFEA) to regulate the field of infertility and embryo research. Certain activities were made illegal under any circumstances, namely:

- to introduce an animal embryo into a woman's body;
- to introduce animal eggs or sperm into a woman's body;
- to introduce a human embryo into any animal;
- to replace a nucleus of a cell of an embryo with a nucleus taken from a cell of any person, embryo or subsequent development of an embryo.

Certain activities may only be carried out under licence from the HFEA. These include:

- the creation or use of an embryo outside the body, whether for treatment or research;
- the use, in treatment, of donated human sperm or eggs;
- the storage of human eggs, sperm or embryos.

Undertaking any of these activities without a licence is a criminal offence, punishable by imprisonment, a fine or both.

The criteria for licensing under the Act reflect those aspects of the new reproductive technologies about which there had been most concern. These are the fertilisation of eggs outside the body, the donation of sperm, eggs or embryos and the storage of sperm, eggs or embryos. Other infertility treatments fall outside the licensing process and are not regulated by the HFEA. For example, artificial insemination with husbands' or partners' sperm, ovulation induction and techniques such as GIFT, in which no donation is involved, do not require a licence. When the Act was debated in Parliament, there were attempts to include GIFT in the licensing process, because of concerns about multiple births and because both sperm and eggs are handled outside the body, although fertilisation takes place in the fallopian tubes. A regulation-making power was included in the legislation, so that the HFEA's licensing powers could be extended in the future should Parliament consider this necessary. The HFEA may also give guidance to clinics on non-licensable activities, and paragraph 7.9 of the HFEA's Code of Practice (HFEA, 1993) states that 'No more than three eggs or embryos should be placed in a woman in any one cycle regardless of the procedure used'. The HFEA is currently undertaking a survey of all hospital consultants, to establish the extent of GIFT treatment in non-licensed centres.

The HFEA has 21 members from diverse walks of life. It is a requirement of the Act that the chairman and deputy chairman and at least half of the membership are not involved in medical and scientific practice and that both men and women are represented. Members are appointed by the Secretary of State for Health, on the basis of their personal experience and abilities and not as representatives of any particular group or organisation.

FUNCTIONS OF THE HFEA

The HFEA has a number of statutory obligations: it has to operate a licensing system, collect information about and maintain a register of all licensed treatments, issue a Code of Practice giving guidance to centres and provide information for licensed centres, those seeking treatment and the wider community.

The Code of Practice

The Code of Practice forms the backbone of the HFEA's work, and, together with the Human Fertilisation and Embryology Act, can be seen as the 'rule book' for infertility clinics. It seeks to protect and balance the interests of infertile people, donors and the children resulting from licensed treatment. In framing the Code of Practice, the HFEA was guided by the requirements of the Act and by:

- the respect that is due to human life at all stages in its development;
- the right of people who are or may be infertile to the proper consideration of their request for treatment;
- a concern for the welfare of children, which cannot always be adequately protected by concern for the interests of the adults involved;
- a recognition of the benefits, both to individuals and to society, that can flow from the responsible pursuit of medical and scientific knowledge.

The aim of the Code of Practice is to promote the best possible professional and ethical practice, without being unnecessarily restrictive.

The Code includes guidance for centres on staffing, facilities, counselling, information and standards of practice. Everyone involved with providing licensed treatments should be familiar with the Code of Practice.

The Code of Practice distinguishes between those areas that are governed by the Act, which *must* be complied with, and those that specified by the HFEA, which *should* be complied with. Centres are expected to abide by the Code of Practice unless they have very good reasons not to; in these cases, details of why the Code was not followed should be included in the patient's notes for inspection by the HFEA. Some sections of the Code leave room for discretion on the part of the team involved in the treatment, while others, such as that on the maximum number of embryos to be replaced, do not.

The 'Person Responsible', designated on the licence application, has legal responsibility for all activities within the centre. He or she is responsible for ensuring, for example, that the staff appointed have the appropriate training and experience, that proper procedures are in place and that the guidance given in the Code of Practice is adhered to. The Code of Practice, in addition to giving guidance on the standard of staffing and facilities expected, also gives information about assessing clients, donors and the welfare of the child (see below), and gives guidance on specific matters. For example, an upper age limit of 35 years is set for female donors and 55 for male donors, and detailed information is given about the tests that are to be carried out to minimise the chance of infection. The HFEA also sets a limit of 10 live births from a single donor, which centres are expected to adhere to, except in exceptional circumstances, such as when a particular donor is required for a full sibling to an existing donor child. In these circumstances, the HFEA must be notified that the limit of 10 has been exceeded. If the donor has specified a limit, this must never be exceeded.

Considerable emphasis is placed on counselling and information in both the Act and the Code of Practice. It is a legal requirement that everyone seeking treatment or considering donation is offered counselling and is given sufficient information to enable them to make an informed decision. The Code of Practice defines three different types of counselling: information counselling, support counselling and therapeutic counselling. In addition to professional counsellors, the HFEA recognises the value of the counselling role of infertility nurses, who often have a closer relationship with the patient than do any of the other staff. Many centres send their nurses on counselling courses, which is a move that the HFEA encourages.

The Code of Practice will also include guidance relating to surrogacy. Section 30 of the Human Fertilisation and Embryology Act will bring into being parental orders, which will allow the transfer of legal parental responsibility to the commissioning parents when a child is born to a surrogate mother. At the time of writing, the government is finalising the regulations, and the HFEA Code of Practice will be revised to include guidance to licensed centres when these take effect.

The Code of Practice also gives guidance to those centres seeking a licence to carry out research involving human embryos. The research must be considered by the HFEA to be necessary or desirable for one of the following purposes:

- to promote advances in the treatment of infertility;
- to increase knowledge about the causes of congenital disease;
- to increase knowledge about the causes of miscarriage;
- to develop more effective techniques of contraception;
- to develop methods for detecting the presence of gene or chromosome abnormalities in embryos before implantation.

Every research project must have been considered and approved by a properly constituted ethics committee before being submitted to the HFEA.

Some centres have ethics committees to consider clinical issues as well as research. In many cases, these committees are used to consider the details of particularly difficult cases and to give advice to the clinical staff at the unit on how to proceed. These committees have a wide-ranging membership, including some scientific and medical staff, and also a considerable lay input, to reflect the views of the general public. As the committees are usually made up of people who live locally, they are also able to take account of the local population and their specific needs. Although centres are not required by the HFEA to have an ethics committee to advise on clinical practice, many centres welcome the opportunity to discuss difficult cases with an independent multidisciplinary group.

In addition to the Code of Practice, the HFEA issues Directions on various issues, such as payment to donors, import and export of gametes and embryos and records to be kept. It is a condition of all licences issued that these Directions are adhered to. In order to help centres to keep track of the guidance given, the HFEA provides all licensed centres with a Manual For Centres, which contains all of the guidance and Directions issued.

The Licensing Function

The HFEA's primary role is to inspect and license centres undertaking work covered by the Human Fertilisation and Embryology Act. Each centre and every research project involving the use of human embryos must be separately licensed. When an application for a licence is received, an inspection of the clinic is arranged. The inspection team usually consists of four people, one of whom may be a member of the HFEA, and may include a clinician, a scientist, a counsellor and a member of HFEA staff.

During the inspection, compliance with the Act and the Code of Practice is checked. The facilities are inspected, and the staff are asked about their experience and training and the procedures being used at the centre.

Part of the inspection includes considering the centre's compliance with the sections of the Act relating to counselling and the welfare of the child; the Act states that everyone considering treatment or donation must be offered counselling. The Authority discusses with the counsellor the uptake of counselling, the way in which counselling is presented and any difficulties that have arisen.

The Act also states that before offering treatment to anyone, the centre must take account of the welfare of any child who may be born as a result of the treatment ('including that child's need for a father') and the welfare of any other child who may be affected. The Code of Practice gives guidance on how to translate this ideal into practice, while stressing that all people seeking treatment are entitled to a fair and unprejudiced assessment of their situation and needs. This means that no group of women is automatically excluded from treatment, but, for instance, where the child will be legally fatherless, for example when a single woman is seeking treatment, the centre must pay particular attention to the prospective mother's ability to meet the child's needs throughout his or her childhood. Where appropriate, the centre may also consider whether or not there is anyone else within the woman's family or friends who would be willing to share the responsibility for meeting those needs and for bringing up and caring for the child. For all potential patients, the centre must consider factors such as their commitment to having and bringing up a child, the age and medical and social history of those concerned and any risks of harm to the child, either from inherited disorders, problems during pregnancy, neglect or abuse. This may include seeking information from the patient's GP or other professionals. Enquiries are made at the inspection to determine what systems the centre has in place to fulfil this obligation and how successful these systems have been.

Following the inspection, the team prepares a report to be submitted to a Licence Committee, which is made up of five members of the HFEA. The Licence Committee will decide whether or not to grant a licence and whether or not any specific conditions should be attached to the licence. These conditions will normally relate to breaches of the Code of Practice, where aspects of a centre's practice must be improved within a certain time scale. Compliance with the conditions is monitored both between inspections by HFEA staff and formally at inspections by the inspection team. If the Licence Committee has concerns about a particular centre, or if there are a large number of conditions, a licence may be issued for a short period, with a subsequent inspection. Annual inspections are carried out routinely, but the HFEA may inspect any centre at any time, with or without giving prior notification. If a centre is not given a licence or the licence is removed, that centre cannot legally carry out any licensable activities.

Before the decision of a Licence Committee takes effect, the applicant has the opportunity to make representations to the Committee. If, after representations, the Licence Committee confirms its decision, the applicant has the right to appeal to the full HFEA. If the applicant is still unhappy with the decision and considers that there are grounds on a point of law, a further appeal may be lodged with the High Court.

Information

The HFEA is obliged to keep a detailed register of:

- the treatment of individual patients;
- the use made of all sperm or eggs provided by donors;
- all outcomes of licensed treatments.

The register has a dual purpose. Firstly, it provides a way of monitoring the work and success rates of centres. Secondly, the Act permits anyone over the age of 18 to have access to information about their genetic background. The aim of this is to prevent related individuals from marrying and to allow children born from donation to have some information about their origins. The Act allows for regulations to be made specifying what information may be given. Such regulations have not yet been formulated. The government's attitude is that there should be a period of time for further consultation before such far-reaching changes are implemented. The regulations could allow the name of the donor to be given, but the Act expressly prohibits the identification of donors to be applied retrospectively; this information would only be revealed for those donating after the regulations have been made. As it stands, some think that children should indeed have full rights to information about their genetic history, while others have argued that the disclosure of the donor's identity would greatly inhibit people's willingness to donate (see Chapter 2).

In order to gain information about the motivations and attitudes of donors, a survey was commissioned by the HFEA in 1993. Questionnaires were completed by 144 potential sperm donors and a control group of 136 male students who had never donated sperm. A combination of a desire to help others and the payment offered influenced their decision to donate, although 62% said that they would not have donated had they not been paid. For those who had not considered donation, the major factor appeared to be lack of motivation rather than serious concerns about the donation itself. Some donors and non-donors expressed concerns about how they might feel about possible offspring in the future and how their current or future partner might view this. Only 8% of the donors believed that identifying information about the donor should be given to the child, and almost two-thirds said they would not donate sperm if the law allowed identifying information to be given to the offspring when they reached 18 years of age.

The study also considered the attitudes of 135 female students towards egg donation. Whereas over 90% were aware of the possibility of donating eggs, only 10% had considered doing so, almost all of whom were motivated by a desire to help others. The women appeared to be more concerned than the men about the existence of offspring that they would never know.

While the evidence of this survey suggests that disclosing the identity of donors could threaten the supply of donor sperm, the child's needs must also be considered. Experience from adoption suggests that some children have a psychological need to know their genetic origins in order to establish their personal identity. A balance needs to be reached between the interests of all those concerned.

The information provided by this study about the motivation of donors will inform debate on whether donors should be paid or whether, as with blood donation, the act should be purely altruistic. The Act itself says that no payment may be made for gametes or embryos, except in accordance with Directions. In 1991, the HFEA issued a Direction that maintained the *status quo* but that was to be reviewed within 2 or 3 years. Cash payments of up to £15 could be paid for each donation, with no limit on the other benefits in the form of treatment services that would be provided. In this context, 'treatment services' related to free IVF treatment or sterilisation. This practice of offering free treatment in return for egg donation attracted considerable media interest, with concerns being expressed that women who could not afford private treatment were being exploited and pressurised into donation. The HFEA has now begun a full review of the payments and benefits that can be offered in return for donation.

In addition to providing information about donors, the register of information allows the HFEA to monitor the success rates of individual clinics. As part of the licensing process, the HFEA ensures that each centre quotes its own success rates, in terms of the number of live births, and that the information given is accurate. There have been calls for the HFEA to publicise each centre's success rates, from the register, to give patients accurate information, in order to help them to choose a clinic. While the HFEA is keen to provide as much information as possible to help patients, it is strongly of the opinion that misleading information is worse than no information at all. A centre's success rates depends on a number of factors, one of the most important being the type of patient treated. To give out raw data in terms of the number of patients treated and the number of live births would not compare like with like and would not necessarily help patients to find the best clinic for them. The HFEA is, therefore, looking at various ways in which the data could be presented so that they genuinely assist patients in making this choice. However, success rates are not the only factor in choosing a clinic, and the HFEA also advises potential patients to consider practical issues, such as costs, the length of the waiting list, the travelling involved and the range of services offered by the clinic. The HFEA provides a leaflet for patients, *Treatment Clinic: Questions To Ask*, that covers these issues, and a list of licensed centres.

As part of its information-giving function, the HFEA also provides leaflets on: *In Vitro Fertilisation, Egg Donation*, and *Sperm and Egg Donors and the Law*. The HFEA also has a leaflet, *The Role of the HFEA*, that explains the Human Fertilisation and Embryology Act and the HFEA. In addition to these general leaflets, each clinic is required to have its own information leaflets, giving details about treatment at that particular clinic. These are checked during inspections to ensure that they are easy to understand and do not contain any information that could be misleading.

In its attempt to ensure that patients have as much information as possible available to them before making decisions, the Authority has also produced two videos: *IVF: The Next Step?* and *DI: The Next Step?* These videos, which are specifically aimed at those considering treatment, give information about the treatments themselves, counselling, the HFEA and the information register and also contain interviews with past patients talking about their own experiences and feelings. The videos are available at licensed centres to be lent to patients to watch at home in their own time. They do not contain all of the information that patients will need, but, rather, they are intended to raise more questions for patients to discuss with their clinic.

Policy Function

The HFEA recognises that there is a wide range of views on most of the matters it deals with. The members provide a balance of views but by no means a full range of knowledge and opinion. In reaching its decisions, the HFEA has two overriding priorities. These are that the interests of all those involved – including the public – are recognised by properly informed analysis of the issues, and that both people seeking treatment and donors should receive the highest possible standards of service. The HFEA considers it important to consult, by public debate if appropriate. It sets out to anticipate future possibilities that raise important social and ethical issues and to encourage informed debate.

The HFEA has carried out two public consultation exercises, one on sex selection and one on donated ovarian tissue. In January 1993, a consultation document was published that sought views on the use of sex selection techniques for social and medical reasons, using both sperm-sorting techniques and embryo biopsy. Over 2000 documents were sent out on request, and around 200 responses were received. The HFEA's conclusion was that sex selection for social reasons, i.e. because the parents preferred a girl or a boy or wanted to choose the birth order, was not acceptable in licensed centres. This view was supported by over two-thirds of those who replied. In principle, the use of sex selection techniques for medical reasons, where there was a severe sex-linked genetic abnormality, was considered to be acceptable, providing the scientifically tested embryo biopsy method was used.

The HFEA's second public consultation was covered extensively by the media, and the response from the public far exceeded the HFEA's expectations. In total, 25 000 copies of the consultation document were sent out, and around 10 000 responses were received. This consultation sought the public's views on the possible future use of ovarian tissue from live adult donors, from cadavers and from aborted fetuses, in both research and infertility treatment. While these possibilities are some time away, the HFEA wished to stimulate a wide-ranging public debate and begin to consider some of the broad ethical issues before it began receiving requests for licensing. In July 1994, the HFEA reached the conclusion that, in principle, it had no objection to the use of ovarian tissue from live adult donors, dead women or fetuses for research, providing the appropriate consent had been given. However, each project that required the fertilisation of eggs outside the body would need to be scrutinised and licensed by the HFEA. For infertility treatment, the HFEA had no objection to the use of ovarian tissue from live adult donors. In principle, the HFEA did not object to the use of ovarian tissue from cadavers for treatment, but it would not allow this until more detailed information was available on the possible psychological effects on the child, and on the parents, of using eggs from a dead woman. The HFEA also wished to give more consideration to issues of consent before allowing this to proceed. On the use in treatment of ovarian tissue from aborted fetuses, the HFEA decided that this was totally unacceptable and would not be permitted.

Another issue on which there has been considerable media interest is the age of women receiving treatment. This was stimulated by a report that a 59-year-old British woman had given birth to twins after treatment in Italy with a donor egg. Although the HFEA sets an upper age limit of 35 for egg donors, there is no upper age limit for those receiving treatment. The HFEA takes the view that there is no age below which it is always acceptable to treat and above which it is always wrong. The guidance given to centres is that each case should be considered on its merits, but, in every case, the centre must take account of the welfare of the child, the parents' ability to meet the child's needs throughout his or her childhood and the age and medical history of those concerned. The decision of whether or not to treat rests, in all cases, with the staff at the centre under the responsibility of the Person Responsible, although the centre must be prepared to justify its decision to the HFEA if requested. The HFEA monitors the age of those receiving treatment through the information register. If a centre were repeatedly treating older women, or if the HFEA were concerned about the age of anyone receiving treatment, the centre would be asked to explain why it had decided to treat in those particular cases and to show how it had followed the guidelines set down in the Code of Practice. The number of women of 50 and over in Britain receiving licensed infertility treatment is very small. Between 1991 and 1993, only 25 women (0.06%) out of the 45 000 receiving treatment were aged 50 or over.

As new ethical issues arise, the HFEA's role is to consider all aspects of them in detail and to provide guidance to centres on how to proceed. In some cases, the HFEA is asked to comment on the decisions made by clinics about treatment. In such cases, enquiries are made with the centre to establish the facts, and the HFEA then decides whether it wishes to comment, whether any further guidance is required and whether any action needs to be taken against the clinic itself, such as adding conditions to its licence. In one particular case, the media asked for comment about a black woman and her mixed race partner who had been treated with an egg from a white donor. The case had been linked with a case in Italy in which a black woman chose to have an egg from a white donor so that the child would not suffer from racial discrimination. When the HFEA heard the facts of the case from the clinic concerned, it became clear that the two cases were completely different. In the British case, the woman had been on a waiting list for a number of years, but there were no black donors available. After counselling, she decided to use a white donor as her only chance of having a child. The HFEA concluded that the centre had followed the guidelines in the Code of Practice and had acted appropriately in the circumstances. However, the HFEA made it clear that it would not condone the choice of a donor from a different ethnic background for purely social reasons. Such policy decisions are notified to centres in regular letters from the Chairman, in the HFEA's Annual Reports and in revisions of the Code of Practice.

Some issues are brought to the HFEA's attention through both formal and informal discussions with those working in the field. This liaison with centres enables the HFEA to give full consideration to the issues before it begins to receive applications for licensing. This was the case with donated ovarian tissue and also with cloning. Cloning by nuclear substitution is forbidden under the Act, but cloning by splitting embryos is not. It was brought to the HFEA's attention that cloning by embryo splitting, to create identical twins, could improve the success of IVF in cases in which only one egg fertilised. The HFEA gave detailed consideration to the social and ethical implications and concluded that it would not license the use of cloning by splitting embryos for treatment or for research directed towards treatment.

CONCLUSION

As one issue is resolved, there are invariably others to replace it. In addition to new issues, all of the HFEA's policies are regularly reviewed to take account of developments and changes in public opinion. The HFEA will continue to liaise with those in centres and in the wider field to ensure that ethical considerations are not overtaken by scientific developments.

References

Gunning J and English V (1993) *Human In Vitro Fertilisation*. Aldershot: Dartmouth.

HFEA (1993) *Code of Practice*. London: HFEA.

DHSS (1987) *Human Fertilisation and Embryology: A Framework for Legislation*. Cmnd 259. London: HMSO.

HMSO (1990) *Human Fertilisation and Embryology Act 1990*. London: HMSO.

Warnock M (1984) *Report of the Committee of Inquiry into Human Fertilisation and Embryology*. Cmnd 9314. London: HMSO.

9

Counselling

Margaret Inglis and Jennifer Clifford

INTRODUCTION

When a couple (or individual) have a problem conceiving and seek medical help, they will have particular psychological needs, whether or not treatment is successful; these should be recognised and supported by all members of the caring team (Inglis and Denton, 1992). The nurse, as a member of this team, will have a pivotal role. She is the person with whom the patient has most contact; she may often be perceived as more available and approachable than other members, with knowledge ranging from the technical and medical aspects of the treatment to the emotional and psychological stress it causes. As a mediator for the couple between these two dimensions, she is, therefore, crucial in the provision of a continuum of care.

This mediating function is already reflected in the number of nurses taking a counselling role in the fertility treatment setting. An RCN Survey among the FNG (RCN Fertility Nurses Group, 1990) revealed that over half the clinics surveyed were using nurses as counsellors. Many nurses commented that they did not feel they had the skills to deal with the degree of distress and anxiety they encountered; the acquisition of counselling skills would, therefore, seem to be essential.

The speed of progress in reproductive medicine has meant that techniques are introduced and treatments become available ahead of society's capacity to understand and process the current and long-term emotional, psychological and social implications of their use. IVF, GIFT, ZIFT, micromanipulation, sperm and eggs donation, surrogacy, post-menopausal treatment and the use of fetal material have all raised profound concerns (Rosenthal, 1992; McWhinnie, 1992). The couple are in the front line in this debate, caught between their desire for a child and their own and society's questions about the methods they might need to consider.

The nurse may come across patients with a fertility problem in many different settings and not just the licensed clinic. These settings could be the surgery of a general practice, the gynaecology clinic, an outpatients department or a family planning clinic. The care of the couple must extend beyond simply the management of organic disorder, which has been the medical model of care. These patients are people in far more emotional than physical pain; they need time, patience and help to deal with diagnosis and the possibilities and implications of treatment. The nurse can combine the medical, the psychological and the social in the care she offers.

In this chapter, we shall look at the special psychological needs of the infertile couple and outline some of the research that has elucidated these, the HFEA's statutory requirements for counselling (Human Fertilisation and Embryology Act, 1990), some definitions of counselling and the spectrum of psychological care that clarifies the contributions from different members of the team, and how counselling skills and the use of trained counsellors would offer more comprehensive care. Finally, the results of some recent research are shown, which demonstrate how much and what sort of counselling couples actually use (Pengelly et al, 1995).

The couple will be viewed as the patient throughout this chapter, because, in most cases a couple will be involved; even if the male partner is not present, he is very much part of the dynamic. Whatever the cause of infertility, the woman will usually be the focus of treatment. The male partner can feel marginalised and without a role and may well act this out by removing himself from the situation (see Chapter 1). Sometimes, one partner will ask for counselling on his or her own; this may often concern the strain on the relationship or anxieties about the partner. Some clinics treat single women, which will require appropriate acknowledgement and sensitive and tactful care.

UNDERSTANDING THE SPECIAL NEEDS OF THE INFERTILE COUPLE

'Because the fundamental purpose of parenthood is the promotion of life and the continuation of the species, procreation has an archetypal significance for the individual and society' (Clulow and Mattinson, 1988: 129).

For most couples, the diagnosis of infertility comes out of the blue; it undermines assumptions held for as long as they can remember – that they will grow up and have children (Cook, 1987). They are forced to face the fact that this may never happen. They will miss out the adult developmental stage of parenting, they will not be grandparents, and they will feel separated from friends and family in a significant and meaningful part of their lives, namely the raising of a family.

The impact of involuntary childlessness can affect the sense of identity both as individual and as couple (Hirsch and Hirsch, 1989). The pressures of these deeply painful issues can tear away at marital, sexual, social and career relationships. Fertility problems can increase marital conflict and decrease sexual self-esteem, satisfaction and frequency of intercourse (Andrews et al, 1992).

There can be religious and cultural pressures that exacerbate the stress, maybe pushing people to persist with treatment after they might have given up had they felt free to do so, or forbidding the use of the treatment that would have been the most likely to succeed. Extremely sensitive handling of these areas of difficulty and conflict is necessary.

The couple may begin to feel that they are losing control of their lives. They are having to hand themselves over to science to achieve what others do so easily; they may feel that Fate or God has dealt them a terrible blow and that the reassuring rhythm of generation following generation has been cruelly disrupted. They might experience a kind of existential disorientation. What happens now? Where do we go from here? How do we deal or even think about this now that the unthinkable has happened? What's the point of anything?

This bewilderment can result in a dependency on those seen as being able to act effectively when they cannot, namely the treatment team. The nurse may feel she is being seen in a quasiparental or even magical way: 'She can make wishes come true'. This is particularly so when the nurse is actually administering the procedures, as in ovulation stimulation, scanning, embryo transfer and DI.

In this situation, the couple is extremely vulnerable to exploitation (Harrison, 1991). Another, possibly newer, treatment can seem like the inevitable next step, and the couple move inexorably on to the assisted conception treadmill. 'Doing something' can feel better than waiting, taking stock and possibly experiencing the pain. A good unit will provide the opportunity for reflection with the nurse, counsellor or consultant, which would give the option of calling a halt.

THE CRISIS OF INFERTILITY

The 'crisis of infertility', as it is sometimes called, is a bereavement, and the couple will experience many feelings similar to those who have lost a loved one through death; this has often led to counselling on the bereavement model being offered, without recognition of the many other conflicting feelings that might be present. Continuing hope may well be felt very strongly, and this may be represented in fantasy by 'the child in waiting'; 'I know just what he looks like.' There has not been a death. There may well be a terrible loss, but, crucially, there has not been a life, so society does not recognise this loss, and there is no focus for the grief (Houghton and

Houghton, 1987). Because many couples are reluctant to identify themselves as infertile, particularly if the male partner has the problem, this grief will be particularly private (Hunt and Meerabeau, 1993). The inability to conceive is felt to be shameful and something to be kept secret. The couple will feel increasingly isolated and not reach the support they need. Communicating with each other becomes more difficult, and very powerful feelings of guilt, shame, envy, hatred and misery alienate one from the other. At this stage, specialist counselling could prove helpful in assisting the couple to 'meet' one other emotionally once more.

THE COUPLE AS A COPING MECHANISM

The relationship of the couple has been found to be one of the main sources of support at all stages of investigations, treatment and afterwards, whatever the outcome (Pengelly et al, 1995; Callan and Hennessy 1989). The 'roller-coaster' of emotions that they endure is particularly stressful; there is often a rapid succession of very powerful feelings, veering from euphoric optimism (when a couple are shown their embryos) to bitter despair (when a woman has a period or miscarries). It should be remembered here that the sight of their embryos might well be the closest a couple get to having a baby.

On a psychodynamic level, the couple may well find a gender-based division of labour to help them achieve some kind of psychic stability. This may be protective not only of the partner but also of the self. Pengelly et al (1995) found that men were liable to become more anxious than women about experiencing overwhelming emotion and allowed women to carry and express these for them. Women were more anxious about finding solutions and dealing with practical matters and delegated these to their partners. This psychological division of labour functioned well enough to afford mutual support. Each unconsciously delegated those tasks that caused them the most anxiety and consciously tried to sustain the other in carrying their delepated tasks out.

Sometimes a couple do not achieve this sort of psychological arrangement; there could be unconscious ambivalence about becoming a parent, particularly if one partner is already 'the child' and the other 'the parent' in the relationship, or if there have been unhappy childhood experiences of being parented. Protracted investigations will, anyway, put pressure on the best of relationships, and sometimes the earlier goal-oriented, positive, united, coping defence breaks down. To help the couple to deal with the loss and despair following repeated failures, to reach the decision to stop what may well have become almost a way of living, could require specialist counselling. The nurse may have to adjust her own approach from the optimistic to the more reflective. It is difficult for couples in this situation to ask for help, especially when there has been no prior contact with the counsellor (Dennerstein and Morse, 1985; Hunt and Meerabeau, 1993).

If the appropriate recognition is not given, the couple will often creep away and hide their grief, and the team unconsciously collude with this disappearance, because of their inability to deal with their own feelings of failure. It can prove too upsetting, anyway, for the couple to return to the place that is a painful reminder of so much unfulfilled hope and searing disappointment. This does not mean that their care should abruptly stop, but counselling in a different place could be offered and encouraged. The offer of a combined session with clinician or nurse and counsellor can effect a successful transition at this stage. Here, the couple can express their grief and be helped to understand that they have done all *they* could to achieve a pregnancy, from which many are able to drive some comfort; they may also be able to consider that now might be the time to look at other creative ways of living, either by parenting in other ways, for example adoption, or by coming to terms with childlessness (Paulson and Sauer, 1991). If couples can survive the infertility experience with self-confidence and self-esteem, this should be regarded as a successful outcome.

The man and woman with a fertility problem need space and time to express emotions, a place and person to enable them to process and think and find words, and to have feelings named, acknowledged and recognised as not being neurotic. This is where the use of counselling skills and awareness of specialist counselling criteria are crucial.

COUNSELLING PROVISION

The HFEA has laid down clear guidelines on counselling; it does, however, only deal with licensed clinics. The special needs, though, apply to anyone, wherever they seek treatment, and there should be counselling provision in unlicensed clinics and other centres where infertile couples seek help.

A brief résumé is given here, but for anyone involved in infertility treatment, the HFEA Code of Practice is essential reading (HFEA, 1992). This states that everybody seeking licensed treatment, i.e IVF or the use of donor gametes, **must** be given 'a suitable opportunity to receive proper counselling about the implications of taking the proposed steps'. Counselling should be clearly distinguished from information-giving, provisional advice from a clinician or assessment for suitability for treatment. Nobody is obliged to accept counselling, but it is generally recognised as being helpful.

Three distinct kinds of counselling are detailed (see Chapter 8):

1. *Implications counselling*: this aims to enable the person concerned to understand the implications of the proposed course of action for

himself or herself, for his or her family and for any children born as a result of treatment.

2. *Support counselling*: this aims to give emotional support at times of particular stress, for example when there is a failure to achieve a pregnancy.

3. *Therapeutic counselling*: this aims to help people to cope with the consequences of infertility and treatment and to resolve the problems that these may cause. It includes helping people to adjust their expectations and to accept their situation.

Implications counselling must be made available to everyone, as must the provision of support and therapeutic counselling, when it is deemed appropriate. Counselling should be viewed as a normal part of the care offered, not exceptional or an optional extra for those felt to be 'not coping'. Specialist counselling should be available, if need be away from the unit. Uptake of counselling will be considerably affected by whether it is presented positively, or negatively as a last resort. A self-referral is always the best; this will be facilitated by clear written information and a positive verbal offer. This information will most often be presented by the nurse at first interview and should be reoffered at different stages of investigations and treatment. Adequate time and the proper environment should be available for 'an atmosphere conducive to discussion'. The opportunity to be counselled individually or as a couple should be offered; group sessions may also be provided but are not considered adequate on their own. It should be clear that counselling is available at any stage, particularly when a person has decided to go ahead with treatment, especially with donated gametes, after both oral and written information have been given. There is often some overlap between information-giving and implications counselling.

DEFINITIONS OF COUNSELLING

The British Infertility Counselling Association in its leaflet (1990) defines general counselling thus: 'Counselling is a process through which individuals and couples are given an opportunity to explore themselves – their thoughts, feelings and beliefs, in order to come to a greater understanding of their present situation, and to discover ways of living more satisfactorily and effectively. Given this opportunity, they will often change their perspectives, become less stressed and so be in a better position to make more informed decisions for the future.'

The counsellor 'should demonstrate a capacity for offering support, non-judgmental acceptance and unconditional respect within a confidential relationship'. Counselling 'should assist the patient to learn and grow from the past; to live in the present and to be better equipped to deal with the future'.

THE CONTINUUM OF PSYCHOLOGICAL CARE

The different aspects of emotional and psychological care interconnect and overlap in the infertility treatment setting. All members of the team will contribute in varying degrees. The nurse's role actually encompasses many of these areas; she will be closely involved with the physical aspects of the procedures and will need to understand how infantilising it can be to have to hand over one's body to medical personnel to regulate bodily functions. This is particularly the case when sexual organs are involved. The nurse will then treat and inform with tact and discretion.

Nurses will be largely responsible for information-giving, which, although it is distinguished from counselling, can so easily overlap with implications counselling. The British Association for Counselling makes the important distinction between the use of counselling skills and counselling, namely the intention of the user. The nurse, for example, might well be using counselling skills by listening and reflecting with patients when she is giving them information, but she will still be perceived as a nurse in a nursing role.

In stressful situations, information given is often not remembered. Ambivalence, high anxiety levels, stress and sheer incomprehension can lead to misunderstanding, frustration and confusion. Information should be given with patience and care, allowing time for facts to be understood, questions to be formulated and answered, and feelings to be expressed, acknowledged and contained. This will help to allay some of the anxiety and assist the patient in making informed consent.

The complexity of some procedures now offered in licensed clinics is daunting, and couples will vary enormously in their level of knowledge and their ability to receive it. Some patients know (and let it be known) that they have as much knowledge as any professional. If the nurse can see this as a coping mechanism, an attempt to wrest back a bit of adult power and autonomy, it is more easily managed. The nurse will usually be the person to whom people will turn for clarification, reiteration and reassurance about the information from any source. The nurse will, inevitably, need to reflect on the ethical, legal, social and moral issues involved for herself and for her patients.

IMPLICATIONS COUNSELLING

The implications of any particular process will inevitably come into information-giving; the couple may have strong feelings about a suggested course of treatment, and these need to be acknowledged and any issues raised and clarified. The nurse will need to hold and contain the anxieties during this exchange, be able to recognise her own feelings and differentiate her own anxiety from the patient's. She should avoid being judgemental or dismissive of hopes and fears but should outline realistic expectations without being overly reassuring. This is not an easy task and requires particular sensitivity and maturity.

The implications of infertility treatment are long-lasting and profound, and the task of dealing with the more philosophical, social and moral aspects may require the skills of the trained infertility counsellor; for example, have this couple really thought about what it means or could mean when they have told their family and friends that they are using donor gametes but are not planning to tell their child? The nurse may not have the time or availability to wrestle with such dilemmas. If the couple seem to be having particular problems, the nurse would see this as a reason for referral to the specialist counsellor.

INDICATIONS FOR REFERRAL TO THE SPECIALIST COUNSELLOR

Indications for referral include:

- when the amount of time allocated for support frequently overruns;
- when the individual or couple have had a previous history of needing psychological help, or there are current concerns about their psychological stability;
- a history of protracted investigations, treatments and evidence of depression;
- couples contemplating receiving donated gametes;
- couples contemplating surrogacy;
- the presence of marital or sexual problems, for example if there seems to be a marked discrepancy in one partner's desire for any proposed treatment or even a child;
- issues about the patients' own parenting and childhood that feel unresolved and problematic;
- issues surrounding unresolved loss or failure; for example, if the couple are using donor gametes, have they dealt with the loss of their own biological child?
- when the nurse feels in any way out of her depth or overwhelmed by the feelings in the session;
- inexplicable worries; the experienced nurse will pick up important unconscious signals.

While the nurse may well feel that specialist counselling is badly needed, it has to be offered to the patients without pressure on them to comply. They need to be informed that they may be charged for the counselling and that they need not accept the referral. Reissuing the offer at a later stage might prove useful, as the couple's needs and perceptions change, but this must ultimately be their decision.

The specialist counsellor will be someone with an intensive and dedicated training who will offer counselling sessions in a place preferably apart from the bustle of a treatment centre, in comfort, in privacy and without interruption. It is a time for the couple to use as they wish. Here they can look in greater length and depth at what the infertility experience has meant for each of them, what it is doing to them, why they are responding in this particular way and what issues or implications are specially fraught for them – maybe their difficulties with the unit, each other or family and friends. It is particularly important to help patients to cope with the decision to end treatment.

In some cases, the couple or individual may need or choose to have more prolonged therapy, probably because their situation has forced them to attend to unresolved issues in their lives. The counsellor may be able to offer this personally, but if not, the unit should have available someone competent to work with such patients.

The pace of development has meant that nurses are at the moment, doing much of the counselling, but it is hoped that a working party will report soon for the HFEA on the training needs of counsellors and that nurses who wish to take on a fuller counselling role will have clearer pathways delineated for them. It does, however, seem that nurse and counsellor can and do complement one another's work very satisfactorily in some settings.

RESEARCH INTO THE USE OF COUNSELLING

Research has recently been completed by the author and others (Pengelly et al, 1995) which has tried to assess the actual demand for counselling, as opposed to the perceived need.

In this study, the offer of counselling with the specialist counsellor was made in writing and verbally to individuals and couples contemplating IVF. Twenty-nine couples accepted the offer to be interviewed, and 62% (18 couples) accepted one or more sessions of counselling.

The requirements for counselling seemed to split into three main groups, determined by the number of sessions requested and the nature of the problems presented. Thirty three per cent of couples requested only one session and used this to discuss topics concerning their treatment. Much of this would have come under the umbrella term of implications counselling. Particularly frequent topics were:

- elucidation of success and failure rates;
- the uncertainty of outcome;
- the invasiveness of the procedures;
- the side-effects of the drugs;
- the possibility of abnormality;
- the chances of multiple pregnancy.

There were also concerns about scarce resources and interaction with the medical system; issues of stigma, secrecy, implications for other family members and the welfare of the child; and how to cope with the demands of treatment and investigations on career, general well-being and sexual and marital relationships. Women, particularly, felt concern that their fertility problem should be an experience that was shared with their partner. This group mainly used their one session for the extra time and neutral space it afforded to examine and process information they had already been given, to reflect with the counsellor on the implications of the treatment choices they had, if any. They were looking for help in finding coping skills, how best to marshal their emotional resources and keep the right balance of optimism and realism. Their stated coping mechanism was to maintain a positive outlook, with a psychological division of labour, the woman, for the most part, expressing the feeling and the man providing the support. At this stage, these coping strategies appeared to be effective.

The second group (17%) took up two or three sessions of counselling. This seemed to indicate the need for more support. The women needed acknowledgement from their partner of the demands that the programme made on them and more overt reassurance about the sharing of responsibility of having a baby by assisted conception techniques. Generally, couples from these two groups did not want to explore or analyse their feelings very deeply and were not psychologically available for in-depth counselling. Maintaining a positive attitude was their way of coping, and although negative feelings were acknowledged, any kind of exploration was felt not to be helpful at this time.

For the third group of 10%, these coping mechanisms had ceased to function. All of this group had been involved in protracted investigations and treatment, sometimes up to 7 years' duration. All the usual ways of coping seem to have been eroded with time, and there was an increasing sense of hopelessness; communication had become difficult, painful and limited. Raphael-Leff (1991) found in her clinical experience that 'the repeated trauma of prolonged failure to conceive aroused self doubts and eroded the couples' sexual and emotional resources ... and poses a threat to each partner's personal and general identity and to their mutual future legacy'. This reinforces the importance of efficient organisation and good implications counselling.

During the sessions, these couples came to understand their own unmet needs, so long suppressed by the supremacy of their need for a baby. They began to establish some common ground and share the mutual feelings of isolation and failure. These were often linked to unresolved feelings of loss and abandonment around their own parenting and early development. Hirsch and Hirsch (1989) also reported that dissatisfaction with the relationship because of poor communication had improved greatly with counselling. Fear of a future without children or whether the relationship would survive could be voiced, even if not extensively addressed. Emotional resources were rediscovered and revitalised, and this enabled the couple to retrieve some of their own autonomy, rather than remain dependent on the counsellor.

This study shows that half the group to whom specialist counselling was offered as a *routine* part of care will accept at least one session. They were mostly asking for extra time and dedicated space to process information and reflect on options with a sympathetic and knowledgeable third party.

TRAINING IN COUNSELLING

The advances in reproductive technology have increased the demands on the nurse, particularly in the area of psychological and social awareness. There needs to be a fit between the needs and demands of the couple and the training pathway to provide for their requirements. If the nurse acquires counselling skills, she will greatly enhance her ability to provide this psychological support and cope more effectively with any implications counselling she might be required to do. This is an expansion of the nurse's role, rather than a new one. Should she wish to have a full counselling role, she will need to undertake the required training and abide by a recognised code of ethics and practice; regular supervision is also required. The specialist counselling role is quite separate from the nursing role but complementary to it.

CONCLUSION

People who suffer from infertility are a normal group who experience abnormal stress (Edelman, 1990). These couples may have to re-examine their relationships and life expectations and question their motives in their search for a child, in a way than people with children are never required to do. This exercise may demand great strength and endurance by the couple if they are not to resort to secrecy, keeping a low profile and becoming part of an invisible group who do not get the resources and support they need, whether they become parents or remain childless.

Medical technology has offered hope, and, in some cases, the couple will have a baby. Many, however, will have endured much distress during all their investigations and treatment, with no baby at the end. Even the birth of a baby (or babies) can present its own problems, which are particularly difficult to articulate when the couple feel they should only be happy and grateful. A child that has been so yearned for may have been the symbol of something missing in the relationship and present the parents with unexpected difficulties, with jealousy and feelings of abandonment. If couples are to make informed choices and be prepared for all that lies ahead in terms of fertility treatment, they need to have adequate time and space to process and reflect. They need to have access to support and counselling before, during and after treatment.

If treatment fails, with the couple at their lowest ebb and most in need, they are often least likely or equipped to ask for counselling. Couples can and do come to terms with being childless and find other ways of exploring their parenting capacities and living creatively. For many, however, the pain of infertility is never quite assuaged, and there is always a sense of loss.

The nurse who can listen sensitively and ascertain where the couple are, wait and reflect with them and acknowledge but not rush in with some solution to allay her own anxieties, will enable the couple to find in her or in the specialist counselling, but ultimately in themselves, the resource they need at this time:

> If you really want to help somebody, first of all you must find him where he is and start there. This is the secret of caring. If you cannot do that it is only an illusion, if you think you can help another human being. Helping somebody implies your understanding more than he does, but first of all you must understand what he understands. If you cannot do that, your understanding will be of no avail. All true caring starts with humiliation. The helper must be humble in his attitude towards the person he wants to help. He must understand that helping is not dominating, but serving. Caring implies patience as well as acceptance of not being right and of not understanding what the other person understands. (Kierkegaard, 1859)

References

Andrews F M, Abbey A and Halman L J (1992) Is the fertility problem different? The dynamics of stress in fertile and infertile couples. *Fertility and Sterility*, **57**(6): 1247–53.

British Infertility Counselling Association (1990) *Counselling: Guidelines for Practice*. London: BICA.

Callan V J and Hennessy J F (1989) Strategies for coping with infertility. *British Journal of Medical Psychology*, **632**: 343–54.

Clulow C and Mattinson J (1988) *Marriage: Inside Out*. London: Penguin.

Cook E P (1987) Characteristics of the biopsychosocial crisis of infertility. Journal of Counselling and Development **65**: 465–70.

Dennerstein L and Morse C (1985) Psychological functioning in IVF. *Clinical Obstetrics and Gynaecology*, **56**: 316–22.

Edelman J (1990) Emotional aspects of IVF procedures: A Review. *Journal of Reproductive and Infant Psychology* **8**: 161–73.

Harrison R F (1991) Aims and objectives in the infertility clinic: the practical issues. *International Journal of Infertility*, **36**(4): 204–5.

HFEA (1992) *Code of Practice*, part 6, pp. 28–33. London: HFEA.

Hirsch A M and Hirsch S M (1989) The effects of infertility on marriage and self concept. *Journal of Obstetric, Gynaecological and Neonatal Nursing*, **18**(1): 13–20.

Houghton D and Houghton P (1987) *Coping with Childlessness*. London: George Allen and Unwin.

Human Fertilisation and Embryology Act (1990) schedule 3, para 3(1)(a) London: HMSO.

Hunt M and Meerabeau E (1993) Purging the emotions: the lack of emotional expression in subfertility and the care of the dying. *International Journal of Nursing Studies*, **30**(2): 112–23.

Inglis M and Denton J (1992) Infertility nurses and counselling. In: Templeton A A and Drife J O (eds), *Infertility*. Berlin: Springer–Verlag.

Kierkegaard S (1859) Cited in Davis H and Fallowfield L (eds) (1991) *Counselling and Communication in Health Care*. Chichester: Wiley.

McWhinnie A M (1992) Creating children: the medical and social dilemmas of assisted reproduction. *Early Child Development and Care*, **81**: 39–54.

Paulson R J and Sauer M V (1991) Counselling the infertile couple: When enough is enough. *Obstetrics and Gynaecology*, **78**: 462–64.

Pengelly P, Inglis M and Cudmore L (1995) Infertility: Couples' experiences and the use of counselling in treatment centres. *Journal of Psychodynamic Counselling*, October.

Raphael–Leff J (1991) *Psychological Processes of Childbearing*. London: Chapman & Hall.

RCN Fertility Nurses Group (1990) *Report of a Professional Survey*. London: RCN.

Rosenthal M B (1992) Infertility: psychotherapeutic issues. *New Directions for Mental Health Services*, **55**: 61–71.

10

Support groups

Liz Latarche, Liz Meerabeau and John Dickson

INTRODUCTION

In this chapter, we will discuss the factors to be taken into account in setting up and running a support group for people with fertility problems and reflect upon the experience of one of the authors (Liz Latarche) of running one such group, in Norwich.

Much of the literature on support groups is about self-help groups, which Richardson (1984: p. 1) defines as 'groups of people who feel they have a common problem, typically concerned with a medical, social or behavioural condition, and have joined together in order to do something about it'. Self-help groups, as their name implies, do not have professional involvement in running them. However, many of the issues discussed in relation to self-help groups are also relevant to support groups run by professionals, such as nurses.

There has been a great increase in the number and variety of self-help groups in both Britain and the USA since the early 1970s (Tracy and Gussow, 1976; Robinson and Henry, 1977). One reason for this growth may be the increasing education of patients and clients. Silverman (1980) states that groups can provide information on how to cope with problems, practical help and a feeling of being cared about. Richardson (1984) states that they may, in addition, have a pressure group function, campaigning for improved services. Rosenberg (1984) sees the essential features of a self-help group as being the sharing of a problem with others experiencing the same stress, the stigma attached to the problem, public 'confession' of the problem, shared language and a shared level of expertise.

There are two self-help organisations for the involuntarily childless – Child and ISSUE – to which many support groups are affiliated, and the nurse planning to set up a support group in her own organisation will probably want to find out first whether or not there is already an affiliated group in the locality. For people with a fertility problem, social support may be the most important benefit of joining a group, since, as indicated in Chapter 1, the infertile couple may feel unable to gain support from talking to friends and family. For the professional, Brown (1992) gives the following advantages and disadvantages of groupwork. Advantages are that a group can be a source of mutual support; attitudes, feelings and behaviour can be changed by the process of role modelling; every member is a potential helper; and a group may be more economical of time than is one-to-one working. Disadvantages include the fact that a group is complex to plan and needs resources, and the nurse setting up a group needs, therefore, to obtain managerial support. The individual will receive less exclusive attention than in one-to-one work, and confidentiality is harder to maintain. Llewelyn and Haslett (1986) also point out that, in certain circumstances, a group can be non-therapeutic; the example they give is a case study of a group for people with depression, where the group emphasised solidarity, which hampered individuals making progress with their own symptoms.

GROUP MEMBERSHIP

The idea of forming a group may come from one or more patients who will become members; it is important, at this stage, to gauge the need for the group and to ensure that there will be sufficient support for it to be worth while. Bertcher and Maple (1977) consider that a group is most successful when members are homogeneous on descriptive attributes (such as gender and race), but heterogeneous on behavioural attributes. This may be difficult to take into account if the group has open, changing membership and the convener does not know from one session to the next who will be attending, but it is important to be aware of the discomfort that a group member may experience if, for example, he or she is the only black person in the group, and that other group members should resist the tendency to ask that person to be a spokesperson for their culture. A man may also feel uncomfortable in a group that consists mainly of women, and this will need consideration in view of the tendency for men to be more reluctant than women to join groups or talk about their personal problems (Thornes and Collard, 1979; Greil et al, 1988). The leader will also need to be sensitive to the needs of single people who attend a group of which the members are mainly couples.

Some couples or individuals may seek frequent intensive participation, while others prefer more limited involvement. A couple may join because of their own personal problem and leave when this is resolved; this may be a positive move and indicate success in treatment or coming to terms with infertility. If the group is open, disadvantages include precariousness and lack of continuity, although the group also may be more flexible and open to change. Couples who are currently undergoing infertility treatment are likely to be in the majority, although those who have been successful in their treatment or who have come to terms with their childlessness may also continue to need the support of a group. The group dynamics of this situation may need careful handling by the group leader, since the needs of these individuals may differ, and there are likely to be tensions; some infertile couples find pregnant women, or those who have been successful in treatment, difficult to accept. However, the experience of the Norwich group was that they helped to balance the group and could be seen as an incentive to continue with treatment. They can also help the couple to focus on pregnancy, birth and the early years of parenting, which are often neglected when they can only think about the next treatment cycle. It may not be appropriate for the boundaries of membership to be too restrictive; in the Norwich group, several mothers and daughters wished to attend, especially on evenings when speakers had been arranged. There was clearly a great deal of understanding and empathy between mother and daughter and the need to support one other.

The group will also need to consider whether professional workers can become members or whether a supporter role is more appropriate. Inviting a knowledgeable professional to give a talk will not only provide the group with information, but also create the opportunity for building good relationships, which can be crucial to the success of the group.

SETTING UP THE GROUP

This stage should not be underestimated; it requires time, creative energy, good communication skills and clear thinking. It is important to identify the overall aims of the group and the balance that will be achieved between information-sharing and discussions about feelings. Llewelyn and Haslett (1986), in a study of groups for widows, depressives and asthma sufferers, found that different groups found different factors helpful. The asthma group was the most highly rated and provided both guidance from guest professional speakers and the opportunity to learn from other members; Llewelyn and Haslett comment that neither of these opportunities is available in routine medical care. The first meeting of the Norwich group illustrated this balance. One of the consultants gave a talk, after which one of the patients spoke about her need to meet people who had had the same experience. When she had finished, her husband unexpectedly stood up and shared his feelings about the heartache and sadness he felt when it was 'day 1 again' and his wife had her period. All the men in the room nodded in recognition and spontaneously began to move into smaller groups and strike up their own conversations, which went on for the rest of the evening.

A suitable venue, reflected, for example, in the character of the room and how welcoming, comfortable and accessible it is, will make a great difference to the success of the group. Seating is important, and a lecture-room layout should be avoided. The use of a room in the infertility unit has the advantage of being in a place already known to the members and likely to be free, but some may find it difficult to relax there, especially if their treatment has not been successful. If the nurse is the group leader, there may also be issues about holding the group on her 'territory', which may increase any tendency for the group to become dependent upon her and may prevent it finding its own identity. Alternative venues may include church or community halls, an upstairs room in a pub (although this will not be appropriate for certain religious groups) or even members' own homes. Car parking is a factor to consider, and it is helpful if the meeting place is geographically central to the catchment area of the unit. Safety may also be an issue to consider, particularly since meetings are often held in the evening. It can be difficult to make a decision about a venue when potential numbers cannot be accurately estimated; at the first meeting of the Norwich group in 1989, about 20 people were expected, but 52 turned up. It is useful, if possible, to have a venue that is adaptable and can accommodate a reasonable number, without feeling daunting if only a few attend. It is also advisable to check the fire regulations for the number the venue can accommodate. The availability of refreshments is important to consider, since the chance to break from the formal setting allows members to divide into smaller groups and to develop friendships and explore common interests.

PUBLICITY

Publicity is likely to be an ongoing issue in a group that has a changing membership. Various media, such as the press and local radio stations, can be used. It may be helpful to have a 'human interest' angle, but this needs handling with care, particularly if the journalist is not known to the group. Concentration on the story of one individual may be invasive of his or her privacy and sensationalised, and pseudonyms may be advisable. It may also divert attention from giving a clear identity to the group. Local radio stations can be invaluable, both for catching the interest of the general public and for giving advice via phone-ins. The former may be enhanced by linking the item to an event such as National Infertility Awareness Day, which in 1994 was held on 21 June. Written information has the advantage that the individual can keep it to consider months later; local free papers can be helpful as they are often looking for copy and their aim is to advertise local news and initiatives.

Posters, cards or leaflets in clinics, surgeries and family planning clinics are another route for recruitment. It is important to discuss this with the staff concerned, since they can be helpful in drawing potential members' attention to the group. They may, on the other hand, be dubious about whether or not a group will increase their patients' anxiety or assertiveness in asking for particular treatments (Kelleher, 1991), which will need discussing.

FUND-RAISING AND CAMPAIGNING

Funds can be raised from various sources. A subscription or joining fee may be appropriate, plus a charge for refreshments. Fund-raising events, such as a raffle or a sponsored run, help to raise the necessary finances and also increase public awareness of the group; they may also help group dynamics by providing an aim and an enjoyable activity. Factors that will need to be considered are whether there is a risk of losing money on any activity and whether or not permission is needed, for example from a local authority.

Campaigning has become more common, with National Infertility Week in 1993 and National Infertility Awareness Day in 1994. Both were used as opportunities to lobby Parliament.

COMMUNICATION AND GROUP DYNAMICS

In much groupwork (e.g. Brown, 1992), it is useful to have a contract, in which the aims, individual goals and expectations, group values and ground rules are agreed. This is less easy when the group membership changes frequently, but it is still important to consider.

Group leadership requires a balance between the task and group maintenance skills (Bertcher, 1993). Truax and Carkhuff (1967) identify the important attributes of the leader as being empathy, genuineness and non-possessive warmth. If a nurse is leading the group, she may feel that her existing interpersonal skills are sufficient, but it is helpful to acquire further skills or at least to explore how her existing skills are transferable, for example by discussion with an appropriately trained social worker. In social work, it is quite common for a group to have co-leaders (Brown, 1992), which could be considered for an infertility support group, although it is, of course, more expensive in staff time. Block and Llewelyn (1987), in a small study of various self-help groups with non-professional leaders, found that leaders who had had some group leadership training tended to dominate the group less, although member satisfaction was similar in both types of group. Training can also help the leader to handle situations such as members getting 'stuck' in certain roles, such as the silent one or the disruptive one. The leader will also need to consider to what extent she wishes to share her own feelings.

Tuckman's (1965) work on the stages groups go through is widely used;

these are 'forming', in which members learn how to be members of that particular group, 'storming', in which the group is still fragile and there is conflict and jostling for position, 'norming', in which the group's culture is established, and 'performing', in which the group becomes largely self-sufficient. Brown (1992) considers that, to a certain extent these stages are passed through at each group meeting, which may particularly be the case when there is a changing membership. Simple techniques, such as starting the group off in pairs (not the pair they came as), can be useful for learning the other's name and introducing them to the group, since many people find that plunging straight into group introductions can be threatening. To encourage new members to feel part of an established group, it is useful to give one group member the remit of welcoming new members and introducing them to others in the group who will be helpful and sympathetic and encourage them towards more active participation in the group. If this role is taken by the nurse, it is important that, once introductions are made, she steps back and allow members of the group the space and time to develop their own relationships in the way they see fit. Encouraging members to share transport to and from the meeting may be another way of increasing communication. Apart from the demoralisation that can occur in the group if membership is not sustained, it can also be embarrassing if an external speaker has been invited and it can lead to financial difficulties if subscription numbers are reduced.

Once the group is established, talks from guest speakers are effective for promoting group discussion and exchanging knowledge and experiences. An interesting and varied programme for the group is essential and could include sessions on alternative medicine, such as reflexology and aromatherapy. The experience of the Norwich group was illuminating. The reflexology evening, in which the speaker had the men in the group sitting on tables with their partners massaging their feet, demonstrated that couples need to be reminded of the art of touch. The aromatherapy speaker gave a brief history of the therapy, then explained the use of essential oils and demonstrated the art of simple massage. A range of oils was available at the end of the meeting for couples to massage each other within the privacy of their own homes; it was interesting that the women chose relaxing and stress-reducing oils, whereas the men chose aphrodisiacs! The feedback from the evening was that it had brought back some spontaneity and enjoyment into their sex lives, which infertility treatment can so often destroy.

Communication in the form of a newsletter can also have an important function in allowing members to express their feelings, either openly or anonymously; the newsletter can also carry accounts of the meetings and can be useful for maintaining contact with 'lapsed' members. Telephone contact can give support to couples who wish to remain anonymous or who live far from the clinic.

CONFIDENTIALITY

As previously discussed, it is good practice for the group to establish ground rules, one of which should concern confidentiality. Within a group setting, one tends to share personal experiences or information, and the risk of breaching confidentiality is always present. It is helpful to tell members who are thinking of attending the group that the others attending will have had similar treatment and will, therefore, respect their need for confidentiality. The Norwich group noticed early in its development that two groups were forming and that those who were receiving donor gametes expressed a greater need for confidentiality, since they had not told their family and friends. This issue is also discussed in Chapters 1 and 6.

GROUP ORGANISATION

It is important for the group to develop a structure that is organised but informal enough for all its members; this structure will need to encompass ways of reaching decisions on how the group should be run. Some groups may elect a committee, including a chairperson, secretary and treasurer, and have an AGM. Publicity officer is also a useful role, and it is worth considering how this can be linked to liaison with other organisations and professionals. A contact person for information on forthcoming events and speakers is also useful.

ENDING

As writers such as Brown (1992) point out, some groups may have a finite lifespan, while in others, there may be personality clashes that contribute to its ending. Ending, or 'mourning', is the last stage identified by Tuckman (1965), and, like the other stages, needs careful handling. Even if the end of the group is planned rather than unplanned, members often want to postpone it, and there may be unfinished business. It can be helpful to end with a ritual such as a party, to help members say goodbye to each other, although, hopefully, some will have struck up relationships with each other and will continue to meet as friends.

References

Bertcher H (1993) *Group Participation: Techniques for Leaders and Members*. Newbury Park, CA: Sage.
Bertcher H and Maple F (1977) *Creating Groups*. London: Sage.
Block E and Llewelyn S (1987) Leadership skills and helpful factors in self help groups. *British Journal of Guidance and Counselling*, **15**(3): 257–70.

Brown A (1992) *Groupwork*, 3rd edn. Aldershot: Ashgate.

Greil A, Leitko T and Porter K (1988) Infertility: his and hers. *Gender and Society*, **2**(2): 172–99.

Kelleher D (1991) Patients learning from each other: self-help groups for people with diabetes. *Journal of the Royal Society of Medicine*, **84**: 595–7.

Llewelyn S and Haslett A (1986) Factors perceived as helpful by the members of self-help groups: an exploratory study. *British Journal of Guidance and Counselling*, **14**(3): 252–62.

Richardson A (1984) *Working in Self Help Groups: A Guide for Local Professionals*. London: Bedford Square Press NCVO.

Robinson D and Henry S (1977) *Self-help and Health: Mutual Aid for Modern Problems*. London: Martin Robertson.

Rosenberg P (1984) Support groups: a special therapeutic entity. *Small Group Behaviour*, **15**(2): 173–86.

Silverman P (1980) *Mutual Help Groups: Organisation and Development*. London: Sage.

Thornes B and Collard J (1979) *Who Divorces?* London: Routledge and Kegan Paul.

Tracy G and Gussow Z (1976) Self-help groups: a grass roots response to a need for services. *Journal of Applied Behavioral Science*, **12**(3): 381–96.

Truax C and Carkhuff R (1967) *Towards Effective Counselling and Psychotherapy: Training and Practice*. Chicago: Aldine.

Tuckman B (1965) Developmental sequence in small groups. *Psychological Bulletin*, **63**(6): 384–99.

11

Infertility and adoption today

Alan Burnell

INTRODUCTION

Although the practice of adoption has a long history in the UK, it was only legally recognised in England and Wales in 1926, when the first Adoption Act was passed, and in Scotland in 1930. The annual number of adoptions in England and Wales rose steadily from under 3000 in 1927 to a peak of over 21 000 in 1946; the figures then declined and stabilised to 13 000 each year during the 1950s. In 1960, the number increased once more, reaching peaks in 1968 of over 24 000 and in 1974 of over 22 000. These high numbers reflected the increase of divorce, made easier by the Divorce Law Reform Act of 1969, and the growth of step-parent adoptions. Over the past few years, the number of adoption orders being registered has declined rapidly, owing to a lack of available babies and the discouragement of step-parent applications. During the 1980s, about 10 000 orders a year were granted.

To appreciate the reasons for these changes, it is important to understand the multiple functions that adoption serves and how the purpose of this legal procedure reflects social conditions and attitudes. The Adoption Act of 1926, like most major pieces of social legislation, fulfilled a number of objectives. The desire to help secure the position of the many illegitimate children who had been born during the First World War and its aftermath provided a significant impetus to its passage. The first Adoption Act formalised the legal status between adopted children and their new parents, endowed adopters with both rights and duties towards their new children and irreversibly severed links between children and their natural parents. This was thought to represent the interests of children, natural parents and adopters. It also enabled natural mothers to secure the status of children born illegitimately, or of a previous marriage, together

189

with their new husbands. Less frequently, the adoptive parents would be the natural father and his new wife (Bullard et al, 1991).

From 1926, adoption societies mainly served the interests of childless couples who were unrelated to the adopted children, providing them with white healthy babies, the illegitimate children of unmarried mothers. The close links of adoption societies with religious bodies illustrated the strong moral welfare aims of 'rescue' directed at the child and mother clients (Churchill, 1979).

FLUCTUATIONS IN NUMBERS

Fluctuations in the overall numbers of adoptions, and in the ratio of parental to non-parental applications, reflected important changes in the law, in medical knowledge and in social attitudes (Thoburn et al, 1986; Social Services Inspectorate, 1993). The passage of the Abortion Act in 1967 led not only to a decline in the number of illegitimate births, but also to a consequent reduction in babies being placed for adoption. At about the same time, the increasing availability of contraception, in particular the oral contraceptive pill, meant that fewer unwanted babies were born. In the last 20 years, the stigma attached to unmarried mothers and illegitimate children has decreased, and there has been an improvement in the financial and supportive services available to single parents. Unmarried mothers consequently become more likely to keep their children rather than place them for adoption. During the last 2 or 3 years, however, financial pressures and medical doubts about the long-term effects of the oral contraceptive pill have led to a slight increase in the number of babies requiring adoption.

Nevertheless, the net effect of medical and social changes since 1926 has been an overall reduction in the number of babies needing placement. However, the number of couples wishing to adopt infants has always remained high, well in excess of the number of children available. In the late 1960s, the waiting lists of adoption societies grew rapidly. The societies responded by becoming more rigid in their requirements concerning the age, religion, health and residence of prospective adopters. Such restrictions, while reflecting the view of adoption workers about the social and psychological qualities required by adopters, had special power in a field in which the supply could not meet the demand.

Thus, in the late 1960s, at a time when it was estimated that there were up to 10 couples applying to adopt every child available, adoption society workers were in a position of great power to pick and choose from many applicants who contacted them. Triseliotis (1970), in his survey of Scottish agencies, found results broadly similar to those of Goodacre (1966), who looked at practice in England, and reported that initial eligibility criteria varied enormously from agency to agency, representing 'the views, principles, personal beliefs and prejudices of individual workers or committees'. Triseliotis also examined the ways in which the agencies assessed applicants, concluding that the 'selection of adoptive couples was mainly decided on the basis of factual and environmental information, and only exceptionally on the assessment of the emotional, personal and psychological suitability of the applicants'. This was despite assertions in professional training and literature that maturity, marital stability, attitudes toward fertility, heredity, environment and motivations should all be assessed as part of the process of determining the selection of parents. The overall trend of these assessment practices was that, as Holman (1978) in the UK and Schorr (1975) in the USA describe, adoption agencies served as vehicles for redistributing to respectable middle-class families the children of those who had deviated from convention.

CHANGING APPROACHES TO 'MATCHING'

A further historic component of the practice of adoption that should be noted was that of 'matching', in which workers attempted to ensure that adoptive parents received children with, as far as possible, a family history similar to their own with regard to factors such as race and physical appearance, personality and intelligence, class and religious background. This matching practice inevitably encouraged the idea of secrecy; the more the child resembled the adopters, the more tempting it was to conceal his or her origins. However, as acceptance of the existence of two sets of parents and less conventional family models (largely caused by divorce and remarriage) became increasingly common, attitudes towards adoption and difference in families became correspondingly more open. Therefore, during the 1970s, the idea of matching, with its overtones of deceit, fell into disrepute. Agencies began to expect a high degree of tolerance as far as the wishes and capabilities of prospective adopters were concerned. Applicants who were not open to the suggestion of a baby from a very broad range of racial, social and cultural backgrounds were liable to be rejected, on the grounds that if they were seeking a close replacement for the baby they might have had, they would not be able to cope with the reality of bringing up someone else's child and the task of explaining about adoption (Thoburn et al, 1986; Social Services Inspectorate, 1993).

INNOVATIONS IN PRACTICE

The decline in the number of babies available for adoption put pressure on the agencies to change. An especially influential enterprise was initiated in 1965 by the International Social Service of Great Britain, an agency that already supervised children brought from overseas to this country for adoption; the British Adoption Project's (BAP) aim was to demonstrate that black and mixed parentage infants born in the UK could be successfully placed for adoption. The children involved in the project were young; two-thirds were under 6 months old at placement, so that they did not differ in age from the majority of children adopted by non-relatives at that time. However, the racial difference from their mainly white adopters was highly significant as far as future developments were concerned. Most BAP adopters had, of necessity, to approach adoption not from the standpoint of seeking in the adopted child a biological expression of themselves, but from the position of openness and acceptance of difference. The success in terms of recruiting adopters of the BAP led to the founding of the Adoption Resource Exchange (ARE) in 1968, initially to coordinate adoption agencies' homefinding efforts for black children, but 4 years later its coverage was extended to include all children with special needs. The ARE was deliberately created in order to continue to build upon the innovative experience of the BAP. The placement of older children for adoption led to a greater awareness of the necessity of keeping the past alive for the child and to the development of related techniques, such as life story books. It also became increasingly common for adoptive parents to be prepared for the reality of adopting a particular child. However, the position regarding the preparation of adopters of babies remained relatively static. In order to select from a large group of hopeful couples, social workers had to narrow the limits of acceptability for consideration, by imposing absolute requirements regarding factors such as age and duration of marriage.

During the assessment procedures, frequently and revealingly referred to by all concerned as 'vetting', the most pervasive expectation, and the least tangible and easy to define, became the ability to satisfy the social worker about 'motivation'. However, the definition of acceptable motivation was at best rather nebulous and at worst contradictory. Social workers, whose training regarding the analysis of such complex issues varied a great deal, could easily make conflicting interpretations. The wish to change a baby's first name, for instance, could be regarded as a healthy sign of bonding or an alarming and insensitive denial of the existence of the family of origin. As Thoburn states in her review of the literature (Social Services Inspectorate, 1993), much of the research is 'consistently inconsistent'.

THE CURRENT SYSTEM AND THE ADOPTION LAW REVIEW

Today the picture is that over half of all adoptions are step-parent adoptions (DoH and others, 1993). Only about 1 in 20 prospective applicants who want a baby are successful, not because the others are unsuitable, but because fewer babies are available. This has made the processes of applying for adoption an increasingly competitive business, and agencies have responded to the demand by setting age limits and having other implicit or explicit criteria for suitability. Increasingly, couples have looked to adopt children from other countries. Intercountry adoption, as it is called, has produced considerable heated professional, political and popular debate (Social Services Inspectorate, 1993). However, the reality is that it has been on the increase. Predominantly infertile couples have increasingly looked to obtain children from, for example, India, Sri Lanka and Eastern European and Latin American countries. Such children are typically in the care of an orphanage and are not usually babies by the time the legal and practical steps that need to be taken in order to adopt have been finalised.

ADOPTION TODAY AND THE ADOPTION LAW REVIEW

Because of these changing patterns of adoption, the government instigated a review of adoption law and practice (DoH and Welsh Office, 1992). The White Paper is now published (DoH and others, 1993), and the law is likely to change in the near future.

Several major changes are likely to ensue:

1. Arbitrary age and other criteria are likely to be removed, with adoption assessments being made based on 'common sense' and objective and explicit criteria.

2. Contact with families of origin and 'openness' in adoption will be considered to be much more important, and the secrecy surrounding adoption will be reduced.

3. Step-parents are likely to be encouraged to use alternatives to adoption. A 'parental responsibility order' is being proposed.

4. Those couples (and the emphasis is still on married couples) who wish to adopt from other countries will have to apply in the same way to an adoption agency, to be 'approved', before their papers will be passed to another 'sending' country, where they will be matched to a child.

HOW DO PEOPLE BECOME ADOPTION PARENTS?

The majority of couples who wish to adopt babies have had or are undergoing fertility treatment (Social Services Inspectorate, 1993). The average age at which women have their first child has currently increased to

27 years of age. One consequence of this is that fertility problems often do not become an issue until, for many couples, they are in their late 20s or older (Houghton and Houghton, 1984). Once infertility treatment is embarked upon, couples find themselves in their late 30s or early 40s before they consider adoption. They have then found that many agencies will not consider them, as one or both are over 40 years old. (Forty has been, for some agencies, the arbitrary age limit for accepting couples.)

The normal procedure is for a couple to approach a voluntary or statutory adoption agency near to where they live, to become adoptive parents. Agencies may or may not offer an information-giving interview, depending on whether or not they currently require adoptive parents. Many local authorities still recruit couples and put them on a 'waiting list'. The voluntary adoption agencies tend to prefer to respond to people who show an interest in particular children. The British Agencies for Adoption and Fostering publish a *Be My Parent* book, which has pictures and profiles of children needing new families; these tend to be older children and children with special needs. The work of finding families for such children has become the specialisation of voluntary adoption agencies, such as Barnardos and Parents for Children.

Local authorities' practice varies enormously, but they still tend to deal with baby adoptions, as these are regarded as being relatively straightforward. They may also deal with the placement for fostering and adoption of children who have been removed from their family of origin because of neglect or abuse. The difference in philosophy and practice between agencies makes it confusing for prospective adoptive parents to get a clear picture of what to do and what children they may be able to adopt. The Parent to Parent Information on Adoption Service is a national self-help organisation run by adoptive parents that provides a great deal of helpful information to prospective parents and runs support and information groups.

Having gathered information and been accepted by an agency, an often frustrating period of, typically, up to a year of preparation and assessment begins for the couple. In some agencies, this is carried out by one social worker from the Fostering and Adoption Team, completing an assessment form covering such aspects as family background, occupations, attitudes and marital relationships. Other agencies have group preparation and assessment procedures, in which a group of prospective adopters together learn about what adoption means today, meet other adoptive parents and are also assessed as couples. The philosophy behind this approach is that couples remove themselves from the programme if they feel adoption is not what they expected or want.

Once the preparation and assessment procedure are completed, all couples who wish to proceed go to the next stage, i.e. acceptance by the agency's adoption panel. The panel has legal, medical and adoption experts, as well as laymembers with an interest and involvement in adoption. The common procedure is the Form F assessment, which the adoption or family finding social worker completes and discusses with the panel. A recent innovation by some progressive agencies is that the prospective adopters also attend the panel to answer questions.

If accepted, and if the couple have not been recruited for a specific child that they or the agency have identified, the matching procedure will begin, in which a child will be discussed with the couple to see whether or not they feel that they may be the right couple for the child. If it is a baby or a very young child, several couples may be considered in tandem, and, sadly, the process then may appear to the prospective parents as a competition. From the agency's perspective, they are selecting the family that they feel will meet the needs of the child and may also accord with the wishes of the birth parent, usually the mother.

Again, practice varies enormously between agencies. However, the preferences of birth parents are, by law, to be considered and respected, especially regarding race, religion and culture. Once again, the more progressive agencies allow birth parents a large say in the selection procedure and encourage the couple who are chosen to meet with the birth parent. Although such meetings are often difficult for both parties, they are generally perceived as positive for parents and, subsequently, for the child. It reduces the level of fantasy they each may have about the other and engenders a degree of cooperation, consent and choice.

Once the selection process, however mutual, has been completed and a child (or children in some cases in which siblings are involved) have been matched, the 'match' has to be approved by the panel. If that is agreed, an introduction of 'new parents' and child or baby is effected, usually at the foster home. Depending on the age of the child, this process may take weeks or months, or even longer if the child is older. Once settled in their new family (for a legal minimum of 3 months), prospective adoptive parents can then apply to their County Court to adopt.

A further assessment will then take place. The Court will appoint an independent reporting officer (or guardian *ad litem* if the adoption is contested), to make a report for the Court. The report provides the Court with information about all parties to an adoption and makes a recommendation on whether adoption is in the child's best interest. It is now typical for this whole process to take a minimum of 1 year and more often 2 or 3.

Infertility treatment and adoption assessment

Again, there are differing perspectives on the relationship between infertility treatment and adoption assessments. The more traditional approach was to expect couples to have ceased infertility treatment and 'come to terms with their infertility' before proceeding to adoption and the assessment process; the period of time considered appropriate was often 1–2 years. However, the older age at which couples begin to start a family has meant that couples have often only just begun infertility treatment before they have to consider adoption. This can put them in a double bind, because if they proceed with treatment, they may then be 'too old to adopt'. In recognition of this, many agencies now only expect couples to have ceased treatment, although some request that during the assessment/ matching/introduction period, the couple use contraception to avoid pregnancy during placement. Interviews by researchers of such couples has revealed that, increasingly, with the rapid advance of modern medical technology, couples do not give up the hope or the wish to conceive their own child or the belief that treatment may one day be effective for them (Meerabeau, 1989). This leads couples often to feel that they need to deceive the adoption agency on their contraception practice and intentions regarding infertility practice.

It has been argued that the assessment process becomes distorted as couples are aware that it is competitive and that they have to convince the social worker and the adoption panel of their suitability. As a consequence, prospective couples feel unable to be open and honest about their actions, intentions and genuine preferences for a child. With the shortage of babies for adoption, couples feel under intense pressure to be considered at all and to accept the child they are offered, i.e. older children and siblings.

One response to this conflict and tension between the desire to conceive and the desire to adopt is for couples to be offered pre-adoption counselling. Here, they can talk in confidence with a counsellor, who is independent of both the treatment and adoption assessment processes, about how they genuinely feel and the dilemmas that infertility presents. The author's experience is that without access to such counselling, uncontaminated by the fear that further treatment may be refused or their adoption application declined, adoptive parents can be catapulted through an arduous and distressing process. From the decision to make a family, to the recognition that fertility may be an issue, to fertility treatment, and then to an adoption assessment process, little attention is given to the impact of the process on the couple as a couple and as individuals. There is pressure to hide feelings and to remain positive and optimistic. Without a chance to explore and share their feelings, couples can be left vulnerable, and the consequences can be felt long after the adoption is formally completed.

Infertility and the lifecycle

The traditional view of baby adoption was that adoption was something that all parties grew away from. The birth mother would 'forget' and start a new life. The adopters would take the child as their own, as adoption would be something that happened in the past. As a result of the authors' experience over the past 8 years and of that of other researchers, not only in the UK but also in America, Australia and New Zealand (Social Services Inspectorate, 1993), we have now revised our view of the impact of adoption on the lives of all parties involved. We now have a clear picture of the significance that adoption has for all parties throughout their lifecycle. For adoptive parents, adoption is no longer seen as a cure for or solution to infertility. Infertility can remain an issue for the parents, both individually and as a couple, which continues to affect the process of adoption.

If a couple have had no opportunity during the fertility treatment and assessment for adoption process to talk through their feelings about infertility, it can interfere with their ability to form a positive attachment to the child they have adopted. In the author's experience of postadoption counselling, infertility has to be perceived as a loss. As such, parents, both as a couple and individually, have to mourn that loss. The stages of grief resolution are shock, anger, depression and integration and acceptance (Shapiro, 1988). This is not a fixed or smooth sequential pattern of stages of feelings. With infertility, shock and denial are clear to see in couples who fail to accept that they are either infertile or are untreatable. Anger can manifest itself as anger at the treatment process or with each other. Depression may not, in our experience, manifest itself until after the adoption and the child is placed. It is often only when parents has been caring for a toddler who is not their own for some time that they find themselves feeling depressed – 'postadoption blues'. The parents have to relinquish their image, often unconscious, of their ideal child. In the postadoption counselling process, helping parents to acknowledge and recognise their ideal child, for example a blue-eyed, blonde-haired baby girl, and acknowledge that the child they have adopted is not that child, is a very important step towards enabling them to integrate and accept the loss that infertility brings. Many writers on adoption now recognise that successful adoption is about recognising the acceptance of difference (Kirk and McDaniel, 1983). For some couples who may have experienced the early death of a baby or multiple miscarriages, this process of grief reaction can be complicated. The parents can have unconscious expectations of the adopted child being a replacement for babies who have died, so the grief reaction can trigger previous losses and bereavements, often unacknowledged when they were experienced. Many adoptive parents whom the author has counselled can clearly describe their ideal child in detail and often link it to a baby that died or fetus that was lost. In this way, infertility, however caused or manifested, can complicate the bonding process.

The next lifecycle task for adoptive parents is explaining adoption to their adoptive children. Today, full and open discussion of the child's family of origin, and sometimes contact, is not uncommon. This is a difficult area for adoptive parents. It can often trigger again a reminder of their infertility, possibly brought into harsh relief by contrast with the fertility of the birth parents. Despite the adoptive parents' positive statements about the child's family of origin as encouraged by adoption workers, parents can feel anger and resentment inside at the casual or callous way, as they may perceive it, in which their adopted child was treated. It is part of the role of a postadoption counsellor to help adoptive parents to be aware of and express the conflicting feelings they feel towards the birth parents, and how infertility and the sadness it brings does not go away completely. If this is not dealt with, it can hinder a balanced exploration and explaining of adoption to the child.

In middle childhood, children who are adopted often experience distress over their adoption. As they develop a more grown-up understanding of their circumstances, they experience a period of what is called 'adaptive grieving', when they, like their adoptive parents, realise that for them, despite the gains, adoption involves losses that need to be acknowledged and mourned. If adoptive parents find this issue painful and are denying it, it is difficult for children to express their grief, and they often deny and repress it. This only submerges the issue until adolescence.

At adolescence the child's energy, sexuality and fertility can come as a painful reminder of the parents' infertility. Parents the author has seen who see their teenagers as presenting with problems have often not expressed their painful feelings that adolescence resurrects for them. Even the birth of an adopted child's children, once they are adult, can further remind the adoptive parents that 'grandparenthood', though joyous, can be tinged with sadness as their children experience the pregnancy and birth they were denied.

Infertility, gender and culture

The lifecycle stages outlined, and the recurrence of infertility as a factor, are further complicated by issues of culture and gender. How the couple between them manage the issue of responsibility is important. Intellectually, most couples will not attribute blame; but counselling couples reveals an acute awareness of who is responsible and the emotional reaction that each partner has to this. Men's and women's reactions to their own and their partner's fertility are issues to be addressed, and cultural attitudes to fertility have a significant bearing on this. An important question that couples consider and articulate in counselling is whether or not they should stay together as a couple. Is the partnership robbing one of them of the possibility of parenthood? One further question this raises for postadoption counselling is that of whose adoption is this: his, hers or theirs? Helping partners, and subsequently parents, to be open about this is often one of the harder issues to explore.

Conclusion

In this chapter, the current policy on adoption has been reviewed, with particular reference to its effect on infertile couples. It can be concluded that the loss involved in infertility needs to be acknowledged and counselling offered, if adoption is to be successful. Realistic information on the adoption process needs to be given, and it should be possible for the couple to pursue both treatment and adoption simultaneously. Above all, it should be acknowledged that adoption is not a solution to infertility but an alternative pathway to parenthood.

References

Bullard E, Malos E and Parker R (1991) *Custodianship: Caring for Other People's Children*. London: HMSO.

Churchill S (1979) *No Child is Unadoptable*. Beverly Hills, CA: Sage.

DoH and Welsh Office (1992) *Review of Adoption Law*. London: HMSO.

DoH, Welsh Office, Home Office and Lord Chancellor's Department (1993) *Adoption: The Future*. London: HMSO.

Goodacre I (1966) *Adoption Policy and Practice*. London: George Allen and Unwin.

Holman R (1978) A class analysis of adoption reveals a disturbing picture. *Community Care*, **13**: 210.

Houghton P and Houghton D (1984) *Coping with Childlessness*. London: George Allen and Unwin.

Kirk H and McDaniel S (1983) Adoption policy in Great Britain and North America. *Journal of Social Policy*, **13** (1): 75–84.

Meerabeau E (1989) *Parents in Waiting: The Experience of Subfertile Couples*. Unpublished PhD thesis, University of London.

Schorr A (1975) *Children and Decent People*. London: George Allen and Unwin.

Shapiro C (1988) *Infertility and Pregnancy Loss: A Guide for Helping Professionals*. San Francisco: Jossey Bass.

Social Services Inspectorate (1993) *Research Which Has a Bearing on Adoption or Alternatives to Adoption*. London: DOH.

Thoburn J, Murdoch A and O'Brien A (1986) *Permanence in Child Care*. Oxford: Basil Blackwell.

Triseliotis J (1970) *Evaluation of Adoption Policy and Practice*. Edinburgh: Department of Social Administration, University of Edinburgh.

Useful addresses and organisations

British Agencies for Adoption and Fostering
11 Southwark Street, London   SE1 1RQ
Tel: 0171–407 8800

British Infertility Counselling Association
35 Whiston House, Bingham Court
Richmond Grove, London   N1 2DH
Tel: 0171–354 8927

British Medical Ultrasound Society
36 Portland Place, London   W1N 3DG

CHILD
Charter House, 43 St Leonards Road, Bexhill on Sea
East Sussex TN40 1JA
Tel: (01424) 732361 Fax: (01424) 731858

DI Network
PO Box 265, Sheffield   S3 7YX

Family Planning Association
27–35 Mortimer Street, London   W1N 7RJ
Tel: 0171–631 0555

Human Fertilisation and Embryology Authority
Paxton House, 30 Artillery Lane, London   E1 7LS
Tel: 0171–377 5077

ISSUE (The National Fertility Association)
509 Aldridge Road, Great Barr, Birmingham   B44 8NA
Tel: 0121–344 4414

Multiple Births Foundation
Queen Charlotte's and Chelsea Hospital, London   W6 0XG
Tel: 0181–740 3519

NEEDS (National Egg and Embryo Donation Society)
The Regional IVF Unit, St Mary's Hospital, Whitworth Park,
Manchester   M3 0JH
Tel: 0161–276 6000

Parent to Parent Information on Adoption Services
Lower Boddington, Daventry, Northamptonshire   NN11 6YB
Tel: (01327) 60295

Post Adoption Centre
5 Torriano Mews
Torriano Ave
London   NW5 2RZ
Tel: 0171–284 0555

PROGRESS
27–35 Mortimer Street, London   W1N 7RD
Tel: 0171–436 4528

Royal College of Nursing
20 Cavendish Square, London   W1M 0AB
Tel: 0171–409 3333

**United Kingdom Central Council for Nursing, Midwifery and
Health Visiting**
23 Portland Place, London   W1N 3AF
Tel: 0171–637 7181

DI NETWORK

DI Network is a group of parents with children conceived by donor
insemination (DI) and those contemplating or undergoing treatment.
The aims of the Network are:

- to provide support to existing parents, to the children themselves and
  to those contemplating or undergoing treatment;

- to increase public awareness and acceptance of DI.

For parents with children conceived by DI, a major issue is whether or not to tell their children, other family members, or friends. DI Network was founded in 1993 by a group of parents whose decision was to tell their children about their origins and who have come together to support each other.

CHILD – NATIONAL SELF-HELP SUPPORT ORGANISATION FOR PEOPLE SUFFERING FROM INFERTILITY

Child is a national support group and a registered charity for those suffering from infertility. Its members comprise mostly those who are undergoing or have previously undergone infertility treatment. Some have natural children but are suffering from secondary infertility; others have adopted children or are hoping to adopt. Many GPs, specialists, nurses, infertility counsellors and social workers, along with other sister organisations who have a related and supportive interest, are also members.

Apart from two part-time employees, the remainder of the work is covered by volunteers from all over the country. The day-to-day administration of the charity is covered by a National Committee, made up from members of Child.

Child offers advice, information, support and especially a caring, understanding, listening ear through a 24-hour telephone answering service; helplines on most types of infertility and treatment, which are manned by members of Child who have been through a certain type of infertility or treatment and are happy to exchange experience and information with others; quarterly newsletter **ChildChat**; over 35 factsheets on infertility subjects; medical advisers to whom members can write for advice; general meetings; regional groups and main contacts nationwide.

All enquiries will be helped as much as possible and have access to Child's services, such as the factsheets, which are also available to non-members. Annual membership fees are £15 per year.

Child also produces a booklet entitled *Choosing A Clinic*, which gives advice on how to decide where to go for the more advanced forms of treatment, such as IVF, and lists the clinics where this and other forms of treatment are available. Child also has several other publications on infertility available for purchase.

ISSUE (THE NATIONAL FERTILITY ASSOCIATION)

ISSUE is the UK's largest and oldest independent support group for people with fertility problems; it exists to provide continuing help for people experiencing difficulty in having children, including:

- **comprehensive literature**, including factsheets, medical and counselling updates and a quarterly magazine, ISSUE;
- **up-to-the-minute information** about fertility diagnosis and treatment and the many non-treatment alternatives open to the individual;
- **personal support**, through its experienced head office team of experts and counsellors, regional Contacts and 'Helpful Members' network.

Coping strategies are very personal, but many recipients have felt that the support they receive from ISSUE and its Contacts and Helpful Members has enabled them to rebuild their lives – simply by providing a strong foundation of support, a shoulder to cry on or an answer to a specific question. ISSUE provides a growing range of coping and counselling support services.

Adoption and intercountry adoption remain one of the alternatives for many childless couples, and, while ISSUE is not an adoption agency, many people appreciate the support it can offer during what is usually a long and difficult process. It tries to keep up to date with adoption both in the UK and overseas.

By parliamentary and public lobbying, the association continues to campaign vigorously for improved fertility services, raising professional awareness and creating greater understanding among the general public.

ISSUE Support Line is a unique telephone counselling service, which puts people in direct and confidential contact with an experienced infertility advisor, who has the time and expertise to help each caller with his or her medical, legal, psychological or relationship problem on an individual basis.

Information is the backbone of ISSUE's service. Members can tap in to a substantial reference library of data and information, including factsheets covering every aspect of infertility (including costs and success rates, for the following):

- DI (donor insemination);
- IVF (invitro fertilisation);
- ICSI (intra-cytoplasmic sperm injection);
- MESA (micro-epididymal sperm aspiration);
- male/female infertility tests.

The minimum annual fee to be on the mailing list is £15.

Glossary

ACT Assisted conception techniques.

Adnexa Adjacent structures. The uterine adnexa are the ovaries and fallopian tubes.

Amenorrhoea The absence of periods for more than 6 months. This may be primary, if they have never occurred, or secondary.

Anovulation Absence of ovulation.

Ascites Fluid in the peritoneal cavity, causing abdominal swelling. If severe, it will interfere with breathing, and drainage (paracentesis) will be necessary.

Asthenospermia The condition in which sperm have poor motility.

Azoospermia Absence of sperm in the ejaculate.

Chlamydia trachomatis A member of a genus of virus-like bacteria, some of which are sexually transmitted. It can cause trachoma (a serious eye infection), conjunctivitis and non-gonococcal urethritis.

Clomiphene citrate A synthetic, non-steroidal compound used to induce ovulation.

Coitus interruptus Removal of the penis from the vagina before ejaculation; an unreliable form of contraception.

Corpus luteum The yellow body that forms in the ovary after the follicle has released the egg and that secretes progesterone.

Cytomegalovirus A virus that is often symptomless in adults but can cause severe damage, including brain damage, to the unborn child.

Diathermy The passage of high-frequency electric current, used, for example, to stop bleeding during surgery.

DI Donor insemination, previously known as AID (artificial insemination by donor).

DIPI Direct intraperitoneal insemination, in which a prepared sperm suspension is injected into the peritoneal cavity through the posterior vaginal fornix.

Ectopic pregnancy A pregnancy not taking place in the uterus, which generally occurs in the fallopian tube; the growing embryo causes it to rupture, requiring emergency abdominal surgery.

Endometriosis The presence of patches of uterine lining in other parts of the body, such as the abdominal cavity. The condition is often painful and can cause fertility problems.

Epididymitis Inflammation of the epidydimis, the small body on top of the testis that consists of tubules leading to the vas deferens.

Fimbrioplasty Surgery on the fimbriae, or frond-like ends of the fallopian tube.

FSH Follicle stimulating hormone, secreted by the anterior pituitary; it stimulates the ovary to develop the ovarian follicle.

Galactorrhoea Abnormal secretion of milk, caused by a raised level of prolactin in the blood (hyperprolactinaemia). This may be due to a benign tumour (prolactinoma) of the pituitary.

GIFT Gamete intrafallopian transfer, in which both egg and sperm are transferred to the fallopian tube under general anaesthetic.

Gonadotrophin A hormone that stimulates the ovary or testis (e.g. FSH).

Human chorionic gonadotrophin A gonadotrophin produced by the placenta, resembling luteinising hormone in action; its presence in early pregnancy forms the basis of most pregnancy tests. It is used pharmacologically to induce ovulation.

Hydrosalpinx Distension of the fallopian tube by fluid, usually owing to blockage of the fimbriated end.

Hypercoagulability Increased potential of the blood or plasma to clot.

Hypogonadotrophic hypogonadism A condition in which the pituitary does not secrete sufficient gonadotrophins to stimulate the gonads.

Hypospadias A congenital malformation of the male urethra, in which the urinary meatus is on the underside of the penis.

Hypothalamus A structure located above the midbrain, which, among other functions, produces hormones that act on the anterior pituitary.

Hypothyroidism Reduced levels of one or both thyroid hormones.

Hypovolaemia Reduced blood volume.

Hysterosalpingography Examination of the uterine cavity and fallopian tubes under X-ray, using a radio-opaque fluid introduced through the cervix; distension of the cervix can make the examination painful.

Idiopathic Of unknown origin.

Incidence In epidemiology, the number of new cases arising over a given period of time.

Infertility Lack of conception following regular unprotected intercourse for 1 year (the problems with this seemingly simple definition are discussed in Chapter 3). Infertility can be primary (in which no conceptions have ever been achieved) or secondary.

Intrauterine insemination Injection of a prepared semen sample into the uterine cavity.

IUCD The intrauterine contraceptive device.

IVF In vitro fertilisation of the ovum by sperm in a petri dish. Also known as IVF–ET (–embryo transfer).

Laparoscopy Endoscopic examination of the abdominal organs under general anaesthetic; the abdomen is first distended with gas, which may cause referred pain afterwards.

Luteinising hormone A hormone produced by the pituitary that stimulates the final maturation of the ovum.

Luteinised unruptured follicle syndrome   Condition in which the ovarian follicle does not release the egg, despite ovulatory blood levels of progesterone.

Luteal phase   The second half of the menstrual cycle, after ovulation has occurred and the corpus iuteum has formed.

Micromanipulation   Procedures devised to help the sperm penetrate the outer covering (zona pellucida) of the egg.

Mycoplasma hominis   An organism found occasionally in the mouth and frequently in the genital tract. It is often harmless but may cause salpingitis.

Neisseria gonorrhoeae   A bacterium (diplococcus) that causes gonorrhea; also called gonococcus.

Nulliparous   Adjective referring to a woman who has not borne a child.

Oestradiol   An oestrogen secreted by the ovarian follicle, responsible for some of the changes that take place in the uterus before menstruation.

Ovarian hyperstimulation syndrome   A complication of the induction of ovulation, in which there is excessive stimulation of the ovaries, causing them to enlarge, with cyst formation. In severe forms, there are fluid shifts from the circulation into the abdominal cavity, and it may be life-threatening.

Oligomenorrhoea   Infrequent periods; a cycle length usually exceeding 40 days.

Oligozoospermia   Reduced sperm count. The lower limit of the normal sperm count is defined as 20 million spermatozoa per millilitre.

Oliguria   An abnormally low production of urine.

Oocyte   An immature ovum.

Orchitis   Inflammation of the testis.

Polycystic ovary syndrome   Condition in which the ovaries are filled with many cysts, which leads to menstrual irregularities, obesity, acne, greasy skin and excess hair.

PCT   Postcoital test, in which the woman has intercourse at the time of ovulation and a small sample of the cervical mucus is then examined for motile sperm.

PID   Pelvic inflammatory disease; infection of the uterus, fallopian tubes and ovaries.

Pituitary adenoma   A benign tumour composed of glandular tissue.

Pleural effusion   An outpouring of fluid into the pleural space.

Pouch of Douglas   A deep pouch formed by a fold of peritoneum from the front surface of the rectum onto the posterior fornix of the uterus; it contains coils of ileum and sigmoid colon.

Prevalence   In epidemiology, the number of cases existing at a particular point in time.

Prostaglandins   A group of widely distributed substances with a wide range of activities, originally discovered in semen; they are potent stimulators of muscle contraction and dilate blood vessels.

Puerperal sepsis   Infection of the genital tract occurring within 21 days of childbirth or abortion.

Retrograde ejaculation   Ejaculation of semen into the bladder as a result of defective muscle control.

Salpingitis   Inflammation of the fallopian tube.

Salpingolysis   An operation to remove adhesions from the fallopian tubes.

Septum   A dividing wall.

Spermatogenesis   The formation and development of spermatozoa.

Sterility   Not a term that is widely used. Sometimes used to refer to problems that have no remedy (although, with the growth of assisted techniques, fewer problems are irremediable).

Subfertility   Reduced fertility.

Surrogacy   Process by which a fertile woman has a child (often with sperm, and sometimes ovum, donation) and surrenders it at birth.

Teratozoospermia   The condition of poorly structured sperm.

Thromboembolism   A thrombus (clot) that forms on a vessel wall, becomes detached and blocks another blood vessel.

Thyrotropin releasing hormone   Hormone regulating the secretion of thyrotropic hormone which is produced by the hypothalamus.

Thyroid stimulating hormone   (thyrotropic hormone) Hormone that regulates the growth, development and secretory activity of the thyroid. It is produced by the anterior pituitary.

Tubal anastomosis   Surgery to re-establish the continuity of the fallopian tube.

Turner's syndrome   Absence of one of the X chromosomes, leading to multiple abnormalities, including lack of development of the ovaries.

Vaginal fornix   The arch between the vaginal wall and the cervix.

Vaginismus   Muscular spasm of the vagina, causing painful intercourse (dyspareunia).

Varicocele   Varicosity of the veins of the testicle.

Zygote intrafalllopian transfer   Technique in which the fertilised egg (zygote) is laparoscopically transferred to the fallopian tube.

Index